the ancestors

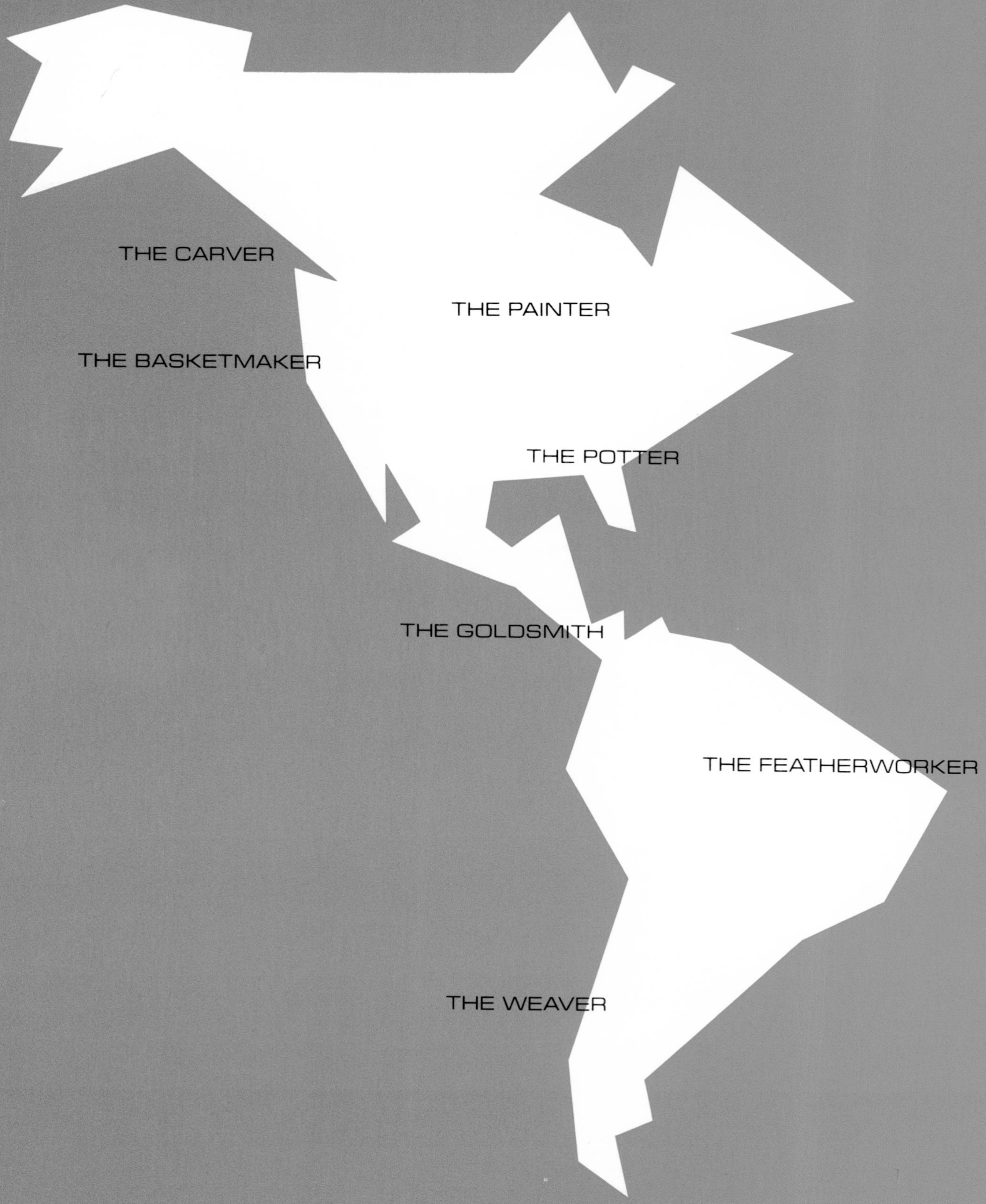

THE CARVER

THE PAINTER

THE BASKETMAKER

THE POTTER

THE GOLDSMITH

THE FEATHERWORKER

THE WEAVER

the ancest⊙rs

NATIVE ARTISANS OF THE AMERICAS

EDITED BY
ANNA CURTENIUS ROOSEVELT
JAMES G. E. SMITH

MUSEUM OF THE AMERICAN INDIAN

Library of Congress catalog card no. 79-89536

ISBN 0-934490-00-7

Typeset by Light Printing Co., Inc.

Printed in U.S.A.
by Light Printing Co. Inc., New York, N.Y.

Designed by Don Werner

Maps and line drawings by Tom Martin

CONTENTS

More than a thousand years ago a band of hunters in what is now the state of Nevada sought to entice wild ducks within killing range through the use of a number of ingeniously fashioned decoys. These remarkably realistic representations survive today, long after their makers and users disappeared. They lay in the arid dust of Lovelock Cave for centuries until they were retrieved by a Museum of the American Indian archaeological expedition in 1924.

The decoys possess a reed armature, covered with duck skin and feathers. Several are exceptionally well-preserved, revealing the expert craftsmanship that produced them. The skill of the ancient artisans who made the decoys is worthy of note. That these fragile objects should have defied decay for so long, despite their organic nature, is even more notable. But there is yet another fact which is of still greater interest. The museum possesses two or three virtually identical decoys that were secured from living Paiute Indians in the early years of this century. They had made them and they were using them in complete ignorance of the fact that their ancestors had done the same things a millennium and more ago. Bereft of manuals on duck decoy manufacture and use, generations of craftsmen and hunters of the Great Basin nevertheless persevered in a tradition that waned only in the face of the irrepressible onslaught of Western civilization. A tradition passed from elder to younger by word of mouth for fifty generations. A tradition of learning. A tradition of artisanship.

The rich diversity and creative genius of Native American artisans is revealed in the product of this genius that has survived. Artifacts made of bone, shell, hide, hair, claws, fibers, wood, precious metals, stone, clay, grass, leaves, quills, carapaces, gourds, feathers, pigments, roots, hooves, horns, coral, and ivory. Artifacts of astounding beauty—intricate, delicate things to adorn. Products of great utility to facilitate work. Products of symbolic significance. Things of the gods, of fertility, of belief and faith. Weapons, costumes, tools, images of deities, jewelry, containers, habitations, watercraft, musical instruments—all the product of man's hand, without which his survival would have been impossible.

Man *did* survive in the New World, spreading from his point of ingress out of Asia over the Bering Strait in the Pleistocene throughout the hemisphere from Arctic to Antarctic. His ability to adapt to his environment, his inventiveness, his tendency to develop skills and to teach them to others is what made his survival possible. He had no complicated machines. But he possessed the loom, he understood metal casting, he knew how to fire clay, he tanned hides, felted wool, abraided, incised, carved, plaited, twined, painted, polished, and engraved.

These ancient artisans created wonderful designs, pleasing to the eye. Their creativity was often inspired by spiritual beliefs. They worked within stylistic traditions that impressed a hallmark on their work just as evident as those from other times and places with which we are very likely more familiar. Their traditions were culture-bound, localized, unique to people and place. And they were often refined to a peak of excellence. When the craftsmen disappear, their craft survives only in the product of their hand. The value of their work is a function of both its excellence and its rarity.

It is doubtful that many, if any, duck decoys are made today by Indian craftsmen in Nevada or Utah. The Lovelock Cave specimens are likely the only remnants of their type and age extant. Their value to science and art is difficult to estimate, but it is great beyond a doubt. They form a part of a great assemblage of other works of man—the product of New World artisans. The collections of the Museum of the American Indian include nearly a million individual items. From this great and abundant resource approximately 400 artifacts have been selected because they are representative of seven important crafts, because of their excellent quality, and because they represent collection strengths.

These artifacts and the artisans who made them are featured in the pages that follow, just as they were featured in the exhibition with which this catalogue is associated.

The Ancestors: Native Artisans of the Americas, an exhibition of the Museum of the American Indian, presented at the U. S. Custom House in New York City, August 1–October 31, 1979, received major support from the National Endowment for the Humanities. It was designed to honor the artisans of old, the persistence of their talent and craft, and those contemporary artisans who carry on the traditions of Native American creativity. There is no greater intrinsic value than the capability of human creations to persevere through time and to be greeted by generations of men and women, even from other cultures, in appreciative terms. We are all beneficiaries of the ancestors.

Roland W. Force, Director
Museum of the American Indian–Heye Foundation

Native American artisans are the subject of this catalogue, which was prepared for an exhibit presented by the Museum of the American Indian. The basic purpose of the exhibit is to explore the interrelationships of crafts with the cultural systems of which they are a part. This approach treats human cultures holistically, explaining their characteristics in terms of the interaction of their parts with each other and with the physical and social environment. According to this point of view, the study of a society will illuminate aspects of a system of craft production, and, conversely, study of a craft will shed light on the social system.

The exhibit focuses on seven different categories of Native American artisan: the painter, the featherworker, the carver, the goldsmith, the basketmaker, the weaver, and the potter. To represent each category, a specific, outstanding, regional craft has been chosen, selected for maximum geographic, temporal, and cultural diversity. The regional artisans featured in the exhibit are: the Sioux painter of the Great Plains, the Karajá featherworker of Brazil, the Haida carver of the Northwest Coast, the Coclé goldsmith of ancient Panama, the Pomoan basketmaker of northern California, the pre-Columbian potter of the Southeast, and the Araucanian weaver of Chile.

In the treatment of each artisan, certain basic themes are followed that establish the relationship of the craft system to other parts of the cultural system. The presentation includes: the technology of the craft, including the materials and techniques of manufacture; the nature of style and significance of substyles; the iconography, or use of symbols and their meanings; the organization of the craft, including the training of artisans and the division of labor; the social and political functions of the artisan and the artifact; the ritual function of the artifact; the economic and ecological relations of the craft, including the supply of materials and tools and the distribution and utilitarian function of the artifact; and the history of the craft, its part in traditional art and technology, and the role of culture contact. By bringing together comparable information about the social context of a number of different Native American crafts, the exhibit may contribute to a better understanding of the similarities and differences in the nature and development of craft systems. The information presented in the exhibit cannot be considered an adequate sample on which to base generalizations about craft systems, but it does reveal some relationships of interest for future research.

The Painter

The Indian societies of the U.S. Great Plains have produced some of the finest pictorial and decorative painters in the world, and the Sioux are quintessential in the regional tradition. Sioux life and art might be considered a product of the contact of the Indians with Europeans, since the bison hunting and gathering economy of the Plains was made possible by the adoption of a foreign domestic animal, the horse. Sioux painting is primarily an unspecialized occupation, part of the regular activities of both men and women. The individualistic iconography of Sioux ritual painting reflects the egalitarian social organization of this hunting-gathering society and the important religious role of men. The images painted by men on hide and muslin usually depict the dreams and war exploits of particular men. On the other hand, the secular decorative painting of the women shows a much more standardized and stylized iconography. This division of labor in painting is a function of the pervasive sexual division of labor in Sioux life. The Sioux painters reacted creatively even in the face of genocide and uncontrollable acculturation, as can be seen in the striking Ghost Dance paraphernalia. Resilient even in the face of great difficulties, contemporary Sioux artists still carry on the excellent tradition of painting today.

The Featherworker

The North American Indians are known for their featherwork, but some of the most beautiful feather ornaments are made by the Indians of the Amazon Basin in South America. In the village society of the Karajá in Brazil, whose economy is based on fishing and slash-and-burn agriculture, the men have developed the art of feather decoration to a high level of excellence. All men make feather ornaments, but some are more highly regarded in the community than others. Among the Karajá, feather ornaments have an important function in everyday personal decoration and as indicators of age-grade status. They are also an integral part of ritual adornment, used to decorate the masks and accouterments of the ceremonial dances in which the Karajá enact their myths. Because of their important roles in both secular and ritual ornamentation, feathers have a high exchange value and are an important article of trade. The coming of the European has threatened traditional Karajá life, and with it the art of featherwork. The cultural changes following upon the entry of the Indians into the wage labor market have lead to the loss of traditional forms of adornment, and the extinction of many birds threatens the supply of feathers. Nonetheless, the surge of tourist interest in beautiful featherwork could be leading to a florescence of the craft.

The Carver

The bold and stylized carvings of the Haida of the Pacific Northwest have long been admired by anthropologists, art historians, and collectors. Haida art was supported by an economy of aquatic and terrestrial hunting and collecting. The artifacts of the carver's art were essential to many Haida activities, from the service of food to burial ceremonies. In Haida society, people were ranked with reference to each other by subtle degrees of family relationship. Nevertheless, a person could gain prestige through the holding of potlatches, the famous exchange feasts of the Northwest Coast Indians. Many of the Haida carvings were actually made for use in potlatch ceremonies. In the rich iconography of the carvings, both real and mythological animals are used in a complex symbolism of rank and lineage. The carver, who was trained by apprenticeship to a relative, was a high-status individual in the system of ranking, often holding the position of chief. Cultural contact with Europeans had a complex effect on Haida life and art, inspiring a florescence early in the historic period through the development of a cash market but nearly causing the destruction of the craft later on, due to a rampant epidemic disease and cultural change.

The Goldsmith

The craft of metallurgy was highly developed in some of the ancient chiefdoms and states of Latin America, and the Colombia–Panama–Costa Rica sphere was an important center of innovation during the last thousand years before the conquest of the New World by Europeans. The Coclé goldsmiths of the chiefdoms of central Pacific Panama made extraordinary technical and aesthetic achievements despite the simplicity of the tools available to them. The goldsmiths, apparently high-ranking specialists, were assisted by slaves and commoners, who mined the alluvial gold and manned the blowpipe bellows. Coclé gold artifacts and styles had a wide geographic distribution beyond central Panama, due to trade, raiding, or travel of master smiths. The iconography of the Coclé goldwork reflects a rich mythology of animals and animal-human creatures, possibly related to ritual validation of the culture's ecological adaptation of fishing, maize cultivation, and hunting and to reinforcement of the hierarchical system of social stratification. The large amount of gold ornaments in the hands of Panamanian elites attracted great interest from the Spanish invaders, and the Indian populations succumbed to the pillage and enslavement that the Spanish brought in their quest for gold.

The Basketmaker

The Pomoan-speaking Indians of northern California have produced some of the finest basketwork in the world. Baskets, made mainly by women, were important in every phase of their life, from the preparation and storage of food, the washing of babies and pubescent girls, to the giving of gifts at weddings and funerals. The primary structures of Pomo baskets show a high development of complex techniques of coiling and twining. For decoration, the basketmakers developed unique ways of incorporating feather, shell, and stone into the weaves of the baskets. Not surprisingly, early American art collectors were entranced by the baskets of the Pomoans, and the expansion of a cash market for basketry brought a florescence of the art, illustrated by the collection of baskets by Mary and William Benson and their correspondence with their patron, Grace Nicholson. The introduction of the steel awl and the interest of collectors in fine detail and speedy manufacture brought a reduction in the size of baskets and development of great virtuosity in technique. At the same time, whole categories of utilitarian baskets ceased to be made, in favor of the types preferred by collectors.

The Weaver

The Araucanian weavers of central Chile are little known, despite the extraordinary quality and design of their textiles. Textiles had multifarious functions in Araucanian life and were used for belts, men's ponchos, women's dresses and shawls, and sleeping blankets, as well as horse trappings and items of trade. The social uses of the textiles today are not well understood, but there are hints in the literature that they formerly played an important part in the expression of individual differences in wealth and status. Like Karajá featherwork and much of Sioux painting, Araucanian weaving is an unspecialized occupation. It has been customary for every woman to weave fabrics for her family, although some women are considered masters of the craft and attract girls from other families as informal apprentices. As in the case of the Haida carver and the Pomo basketmaker, the Araucanian weaver has come under the pressure of commercial demand for her products, and apparently the traditional way of life is being eroded through the policies of the present Chilean regime, and the future of the Araucanian peoples is uncertain.

The Potter

Among the many excellent regional traditions of pottery making that developed in the Western Hemisphere before Columbus, the pottery of the prehistoric cultures of the Southeastern United States is outstanding but not very well known. The collections of C. B. Moore, presented in the exhibit, document the tradition, which spans the last thousand years before the arrival of the Europeans. This pottery shows what high aesthetic achievements are possible with a relatively simple ceramic technology. With only coiling, the paddle-and-anvil technique, low temperature firing, stamping, prefire cutouts, incision, modeling, and biochrome painting, the Southeastern potters made delicate and subtle masterpieces. The making of ceramics as a form of art reached its greatest development in the special funerary pottery that was buried in earthen mounds. This pottery's iconography illustrates a religion concerned with the animal world and a system of social stratification bolstered by war and exclusive sumptuary privileges. The making of pottery may have been a specialized occupation, and some of it was traded long distances. Although the early forays of the Europeans into this territory were brief, the impact of epidemic diseases on the native populations was devastating, and the regional tradition of pottery making flagged. Nonetheless, indigenous pottery making still continues in the overall region among Indians, such as the Catawba.

The Organization of Work

The idea for a comparative craft exhibit came from Roland Force, the director of the museum, who encouraged and expedited the work throughout the six-month term of the project. The co-directors of the project, Anna Roosevelt, curator of South and Middle American Archaeology, and James G. E. Smith, curator of North American Ethnology, decided upon the functional and historical theoretical approach. The seven sections of the exhibit were chosen by the museum's curators and curatorial assistants, each person taking responsibility for one section: Gary Galante—Sioux painting; David Fawcett—Karajá featherwork; James Smith—Haida carving; Anna Roosevelt—Coclé goldwork; Brenda Holland, with Sally McLendon of Hunter College of the City University of New York—Pomo basketry; Gina Laczko—Araucanian weaving; and Katherine Kimball—Southeastern pottery. The exhibit curators chose the artifacts, prepared the scripts for the exhibit, and wrote the articles for the catalogue.

The curators were helped in their work by a number of consultants, without whom the project could not have been done. The consultants were: John C. Ewers and Thomas Biolsi for Sioux ethnology; Gertrude Dole and Christopher Taverner for Karajá ethnology; John Farrand for Amazonian ornithology; Edmund Carpenter and George MacDonald for Haida ethnology; Richard Cooke for central Panamanian archaeology; Robert Sonin for technology of Coclé goldwork and Southeastern pottery; André Emmerich for Coclé goldwork style and iconography; Sally McLendon for Pomo ethnology; Ann Rowe for Araucanian weaving; James B. Griffin for Southeastern archaeology. In general, the consultants provided bibliographic references and generously shared unpublished information. They also read and commented on the catalogue articles. Any errors of fact or interpretation, however, are solely the fault of the authors.

The assistant director of the museum, George Eager, and Anna Roosevelt coordinated the exhibit, and she and Jim Smith edited the catalogue. The catalogue was edited by Nancy Barton and proofread by Elaine Romano. Don Werner, the staff designer, designed and organized the catalogue, and Tom Martin, the curator of exhibits, prepared the maps and line drawings. They also designed the exhibition and took part in the choice of artifacts for the exhibit and illustrations for the catalogue. David, Leah, and Ben Wasserman, of Light Printing Company, Inc. produced, typeset, and printed the catalogue. LeMar Terry designed the lighting for the exhibit. The museum's photographer, Carmelo Guadagno, photographed the artifacts and printed most of the photographs for the catalogue. The Smithsonian Institution and the Peabody Museum of Archaeology and Ethnology, Harvard University, were gracious enough to permit publication of some of their photographs. Adelaide de Menil generously lent a number of her photographs of Northwest Coast scenes for the exhibit. Phyllis Dillon, the conservator of the museum, was in charge of the conservation aspects of the project, and Lynette G. Miller, registrar, took care of shipping. Ken Savary, with the help of David Fawcett, created and executed the audio-visual display. The ethnographic film program for the exhibit was created by Elizabeth Weatherford and Milbry Polk of the New York Visual Anthropology Center in conjunction with George Eager and

David Fawcett. The craft and dance festival was organized by Brenda Holland and run by Shari Segel. Connie Baum and Jacqueline Civello of the museum's administrative staff had the task of typing most of the copy for the catalogue and for the exhibit, and Carol Shookoff retyped two of the catalogue articles. The installation was built by the museum's preparation department, under the direction of Thomas Donovan, and related graphics were executed by Peter Lindt of Design Letters, Edelman Associates, Todays Displays, and Arista Flag Company. The artifacts were installed by Don Werner and Tom Martin with the help of a team of curatorial assistants: David Butler, Lisa Callendar, Gary Galante, Susan Guarascio, Fran Harris, Mary Jane Lenz, and Laurie Tomik.

Funding

The exhibit and catalogue, *The Ancestors: Native Artisans of the Americas*, was made possible by major funding from the National Endowment for the Humanities and contributions from: The New York State Council on the Arts, Atlantic Richfield Foundation, Phillips Petroleum Foundation, Citibank, N. A., The J. M. Kaplan Fund, The Custom House Institute, and others.

The museum's development officer, Elizabeth Beim, with the help of George Eager, and the curators of the exhibit, secured the funding necessary for the exhibit. Jacqueline Reisert, Theresa Riley, and Joy Schwep typed the various proposals for funds, and Charlotte Frick, Ellen Jamieson, and Karen White helped in the final preparation of the proposals.

These and all the people who worked hard and enthusiastically on the exhibit and catalogue deserve heartfelt thanks.

Anna Curtenius Roosevelt
Curator of South and Middle American Archaeology
James G. E. Smith
Curator of North American Ethnology

COLOR PLATES

Color plate 1. Painted muslin tipi cover, Sioux, probably South Dakota. Height:478.7 cm. No. 1. This detail of a tipi cover shows a painting of war exploits: in the midst of pitched battle with Crows, one Sioux runs off a fine herd of horses.

Color plate 2. *A*, painted canvas shield, with feather and horsehair decoration, used in the Buffalo Society Dances, Sioux, Standing Rock Reservation, North Dakota, collected by Frances Densmore. Diameter:51.4 cm. No. 24; *B, Wicasas* shirt of painted hide, decorated with human hair, Oglala Sioux, South Dakota. Length:138.4 cm. Width: 91.4 cm. No. 9. The shirt is painted in cobalt blue and chrome yellow, with a forked, zigzag design in mercury vermillion, representing lightning. It is trimmed with human hair scalplocks. The clusters of flicker feathers on either shoulder contain personal medicine objects. Major John G. Bourke collected the shirt from Little Big Man. It is said to have belonged to Crazy Horse, the famous leader and shirt wearer among the Oglala Sioux.

(Unless otherwise specified, the letters identifying artifacts in the illustrations read from left to right and from top to bottom.)

Color plate 3. Two Karajá headdresses for ceremonial use by males. *A*, nimbus headdress constructed with the rare red tail-feathers of macaws. Height:59 cm. Width:93 cm. No. 6. *B*, head fan worn by boys at puberty. Diameter 130 cm. No. 2. This ornament, made of feathers tied to flexible cotton cord, is stored in a compact form and is unfolded for use only on special occasions.

Color plate 4. *Aruanā* dance outfit, Karajá. Height:67 cm. Width (at neck):30 cm. No. 1. The mask, shoulder cape, and skirt represent fish spirits and are worn by Karajá men in ceremonial dances. The mask, an *ijasó* type, represents an *aruanā* fish and is identified by the feather mosaic on the cylinder over the head.

Color plate 5. *A,* chief's ceremonial headdress, made of carved and painted wood with haliotis-shell inlay, sea-lion bristles, ermine, and cloth, and decorated with two Eagle crests and a Frog, Haida, Kasean, Prince of Wales Island, Alaska, U.S.A. Height:21 cm. Width:17 cm. No. 16; *B,* frontlet of ceremonial headdress, carved and painted in the likeness of a human face, Haida, Skidegate, Queen Charlotte Islands, British Columbia, Canada. Height:19.2 cm. Width:15.2 cm. No. 18. Headdresses of this type were worn by clan or town chiefs on ceremonial occasions, such as potlatches, making peace treaties, or welcoming distinguished guests. Eagle or swan's down was scattered from the crown of the headdress as the chief danced before the guests, the most sincere form of indicating peaceful intent and of honoring them.

Color plate 6. *A*, carved and painted chief's rattle, made of wood and bearing the dorsal fin representing the Killer Whale crest, Haida, Queen Charlotte Islands, British Columbia, Canada. Height:14 cm. Length:28 cm. Width:16 cm. No. 13; *B*, shaman's rattle of wood, painted and carved to represent a human face. Haida, Prince of Wales Island, Alaska, U.S.A. Length:26 cm. Diameter:13.5 cm. No. 3; *C*, elaborately carved and painted rattle bearing the Raven crest, Haida, Skidegate, Queen Charlotte Islands, British Columbia, Canada. Height:12 cm. Length:40 cm. Width:18 cm. No. 14.

Color plate 7. Four Araucanian ponchos, Chile. *A, macuñ trarican.*
Length:124 cm. Width:143 cm. No. 2; *B, macuñ* with *trarican* and
nimin bands. Length: 134 cm. Width:159 cm. No. 1; *C, macuñ
huirican.* Length:132.5 cm. Width:144 cm. No. 5; *D, macuñ.*
Length:112 cm. Width:153.5 cm. No. 7. The wicker basket (no. 46) on
the right holds skeins on naturally-dyed yarns (nos. 34–43).

Color plate 8. *A*, necklace of embossed gold pendants in the shape of carved shell pendants (restrung), Parita, Herrera Province, Panama. Length of pendants:5.8 cm. Weight:91 grams. No. 15. *B*, embossed and clinched gold ear spools, Coclé Province, Panama. Diameter:3.6 cm. Weight:13 grams. No. 22.

Color plate 9. *A*, large cast gold nose clip representing two profile crocodiles, Parita, Herrera Province, Panama. Length:10.5 cm. Weight:52 grams. No. 44. *B*, embossed gold disc representing the Crocodile God wearing antlers, Coclé Province, Panama. Diameter:11 cm. Weight:28.5 grams. No. 48. *C*, cast gold pendant representing a pair of Bat Gods, Parita, Herrera Province, Panama. Height:4.5 cm. Width:9 cm. Weight:85.5 grams. No. 28.

Color plate 10. Pomoan baskets
Top row
A, no. 9
B, no. 28
C, no. 21
D, no. 46
Bottom row
E, no. 25
F, no. 47
G, no. 21
H, no 40
I, no. 29
See artifact listing
for details on each basket.

Color plate 11. *A*, red-slipped effigy vessel representing a turkey buzzard, with lattice-work decoration, Florida. **Height:**22.2 cm. **Diameter:**15.9 cm. No. 25. Effigy vessels of this sort might have served as temple or charnel-house guardians; *B*, jar with relief decoration, Florida. **Height:**9 cm. **Diameter:** 13 cm. No. 20. Showing a true mastery of technique and design, this vessel is an example of Weeden Island craftsmanship at its best; *C*, bowl with five-pointed flaring rim, Florida. **Height:**6 cm. **Diameter:**19 cm. The "kill" hole is clearly visible in this bowl. The incised and punctate decoration seems to represent an open right hand and thus suggests the influence of the Southern Cult; *D*, owl effigy, Florida. **Height:**5.5 cm. **Diameter:**8 cm. No. 31. One of the many Weeden Island representations of the owl, this pottery fragment originally served as the handle of a vessel.

Color plate 12. *A*, large urn with stamped decoration and a "kill" hole knocked in the bottom, Georgia. Height: 42 cm. Diameter: 36 cm. No. 7; *B*, jar with intricate, overall design incised on its shoulders, Florida. Height: 19 cm. Diameter: 16.5 cm. No. 12. This piece may be transitional between the Santa Rosa–Swift Creek and Weeden Island periods; *C*, incised jar with rectangular rim flange, found on the western side of a mound in Florida. Height: 14.6 cm. Diameter: 15.2 cm. No. 21; *D*, stamped rim sherd, found by the Heye-Hodge-Pepper expedition at Nacoochee Mound, Florida. Length: 17.8 cm. Width: 8.3 cm. No. 6.

the Painter

THE SIOUX OF THE GREAT PLAINS

GARY GALANTE

In the nineteenth century, the Sioux occupied an area north of the Platte River, from the Missouri River to the Big Horn Mountains, including sections of what are now Montana, Wyoming, Nebraska, South Dakota, and North Dakota. They depended upon the buffalo for food, clothing, and shelter, and their material culture and social organization was derived in some measure from a nomadic hunting and gathering existence, a cultural pattern that was itself derived from the introduction of the horse.

During the eighteenth century, the Sioux had been pushed progressively westward by the Ojibwa from the east, and they were fighting for survival. The horse, brought to the New World by the Spanish, probably reached the Sioux before the end of the eighteenth century. Along with the introduction of firearms, the horse was the catalyst in establishing Sioux military supremacy on the Plains and the ultimate pattern for their culture.[1] It was pastoralism that heralded the classic period of Sioux life associated with the mid-nineteenth century.[2] During this period, Sioux arts in particular enjoyed a great florescence.

Pastoralism determined to some extent the pattern of Sioux nomadism, for the maintenance of the increasingly large horse herds depended upon extensive pasturage, necessitating periodic camp movements. Another determining factor was the buffalo, for camps endeavored to remain within striking distance of the herds. Other considerations involved in camp movements included the availability of chokecherries, wild plums, and turnips, which were also important food resources and were collected by women.

Fig. 1. Painted muslin tipi cover, Sioux, probably South Dakota. Height:478.7 cm. No. 1. This detail of a tipi cover shows a painting of war exploits; in the midst of pitched battle with Crows, one Sioux runs off a fine herd of horses.

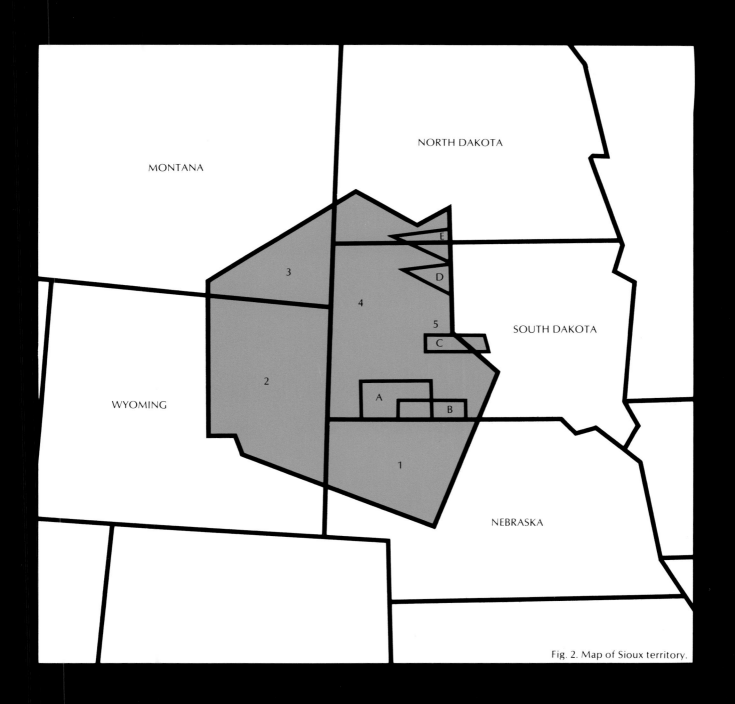

Sioux Territory ca. 1860

1. Brûlés
2. Oglalas
3. Hunkpapas
   Sans Arcs
   Blackfeet
4. Miniconjou
5. Two Kettle

Present Sioux Reservations

A. Pine Ridge
B. Rosebud
C. Crow Creek/Lower Brûlé
D. Cheyenne River
E. Standing Rock

MONTANA

NORTH DAKOTA

WYOMING

SOUTH DAKOTA

NEBRASKA

Fig. 2. Map of Sioux territory.

Buffalo hunting was usually a cooperative affair and was strictly supervised by the tribal police. On a given signal, each mounted hunter singled out choice animals from the herd and, riding alongside, dispatched them. The women followed the hunters to skin and butcher the buffalo and to pack the meat back to camp. After a successful hunt, large amounts of fresh meat were roasted and eaten immediately. The greater part of the meat was dried in thin strips for storage. Sometimes this dried meat was mixed with pounded chokecherries to make pemmican, which could be stored indefinitely. Elk, antelope, and bear were also occasionally hunted for meat and other products. Production in the Sioux economy was for subsistence and also for a surplus to be given away.

Early literature describes seven subtribes of a tribe referred to as the Oceti Sakowin or "Seven Council Fires." These included the Mdewakantons, the Wahpetons, the Wahpekutes, and the Sissetons, as well as the Yanktons, the Yanktonais, and the Titonwans. The first four of these subtribes, living east of the Missouri River, are now known collectively as the Eastern Sioux, or Santee. The Yanktons and the Yanktonais live today in the vicinity of Devil's Lake, North Dakota. The Titonwans were the largest subtribe, said to have constituted more than half the entire tribe and surpassing the others in wealth. The descendants of the original Oceti Sakowin speak the same Siouxan language with dialectic differences, principally in the use of consonants. The Santee speak "Dakota," the Yanktons and Yanktonais "Nakota," and the Titonwans "Lakota."

In the anthropological literature, all these groups have been referred to as Sioux. For the purposes of this discussion, "Sioux" will be identified with the seven divisions of Titonwans, or, as they have come to be known, the Teton Sioux: the Oglala, or "scatters one's own"; the Sicangu, or Brûlé, meaning "burnt thighs"; the Miniconjou, meaning "plant by the stream"; the Hunkpapa, "camp by the entrance"; the Sihasapa, or "blackfoot"; the Itazipco, or Sans Arcs, meaning "no bows"; and the Oohenupa, "two boilings" or "two kettles"[3] (see fig. 2). The term Lakota, the dialect of these seven divisions, means "friendly," or "allied," and it is used by these people to refer to themselves. Although "Sioux" is the commonly accepted designation today, it is not of Lakota origin. The term derives from the French mispronunciation of the Ojibwa word for these people—*nadoweisiwug*—meaning "lesser adders," or "snakes," signifying enemies.

Fig. 3. Painted hide shirt with decoration of human hair and glass beads, Sans Arcs Sioux. Length:124.5 cm. Width:157.5 cm. No. 6. This *Wicasas* shirt is painted with dots in mercury vermillion on grounds of blue and yellow, with classic beadwork strips and human hair scalplocks symbolic of the *Wicasas'* responsibility for all the people.

Social Organization

Each of the seven Teton Sioux divisions functioned more or less independently under the leadership of four *Wicasas*, or "shirt wearers." These *Wicasas* wore shirts ornamented in a special way, as symbols of their office (see fig. 3). Within each division there were two forms of social organization: small bands, or *tiyospaye* (local groups of cooperating kinsmen), and a number of men's military associations, which are referred to in the literature as *societies*. Members of the societies met frequently for feasting and dancing, which were accompanied by distinct ritual procedure. Although a society seldom went to war as a body, groups of friends in the same society might organize a war party together. Any one of these societies might be called upon by the leaders of the division to act as camp police. The various officers of the societies were entitled to wear or carry emblematic paraphernalia symbolic of their position. Most men belonged to at least one of these societies, and membership was offered by invitation.

During most of the year, the Sioux lived in small bands, under the leadership of headmen. Headmen were charismatic individuals who exemplified Sioux virtue, and bands formed around them. During the summer months, the bands from all the divisions aggregated for the annual Sun Dance and communal buffalo hunt, when acquaintanceships might be renewed and matters of tribal importance decided in council, because the entire tribe was together. At this time, a certain amount of Sioux identity was reinforced for all the bands, under the four great leaders of the tribe, the *Wicasa Yatapikas*. These leaders were selected by the people from among the most honored headmen of the seven divisions. Their position was one of authority through respect, not of absolute power. In Sioux cosmology, *four* is a sacred number, and the fact that four were selected as *Wicasa Yatapikas* may have insured both the dignity of the office and the character of the execution of their responsibility. While the prestige and authority of the *Wicasa Yatapikas* were unsurpassed, they conferred so infrequently that the greater part of government became the responsibility of the leaders, that is, the shirt wearers, of the various divisions and, ultimately, of the headman of each band. In fact, this system was an idealized one, which was never quite thoroughly realized. It was the product of the Sioux understanding that there was in nature a logical pattern which indicated the proper form for government. But the highly individual nature of Sioux society in general, and of the nomadic band way of life in particular, occasionally obscured this ideal.

Warfare

In Sioux culture, attitudes of self-reserve were juxtaposed with those of self-expression and individual ambition. On one hand, tribal police might punish individuals who broke formation during a communal hunt; on the other, young boys might sneak off to accompany a war party, without danger of reproach. The battlefield was the most important stage for achievement. The aggressor on the battlefield was a hero to be honored. The successful warrior earned privilege and distinction (and economic dividends as well, for Sioux warfare was the principal method of obtaining horses). Warfare contrasted the practical and economic aspects of Sioux life with the dividends of prestige. The reality of Sioux warfare is further complicated. In the ideal, warfare was regarded as a grand gambling game, with honor as the stake. The premier honor, or "coup," was not the slaying of an enemy but, rather, touching him with the hand or with a special stick employed for this purpose, called a *coup stick*.

The scenes in Sioux pictographs give us another perspective on Sioux warfare (see fig. 5). These depict men engaged in battles that are pitched and bloody. One man rides over his enemy at a gallop, lightly tapping him with his coup stick to add insult to injury; another rides past his enemy and fires his gun point blank; another dismounts and, pulling his foe's tonsure sharply back from the forehead, makes a clean slit and pulls the scalp away. Many men are depicted with mortal wounds, coughing blood. These scenes are rendered cooly and with proud demonstration. This is the definition of a warrior society.

Bravery, fortitude, generosity, and wisdom were the four virtues all Sioux men were expected to exemplify. Each of these moral qualities constituted a very real challenge, and in the Sioux schema they were all interdependent. The ideal of bravery, however, was foremost for men and women. The visionary precepts and formal songs of the Sioux were devoted to warfare, and the prescribed roles of the officers of Sioux military societies demanded extraordinary valor, to the point of death: "I am a Fox. I am supposed to die. If there is anything difficult, if there is anything dangerous, that is mine to do."[4]

Fig. 4. Painted drum of wood and hide, Sioux. Diameter:45.7 cm. No. 37. This is an unusual example: the painting appears inside the hand drum.

Fig. 5. Painted muslin dress, Hunkpapa Sioux, South Dakota. Length:125.7 cm. Width:127.6 cm. No. 13. Probably painted by Running Antelope (ca. 1880), the dress depicts war exploits in Hunkpapa Sioux battles with Arikaras. Dresses of this type are rare and may have been painted for women after the death of a son or husband on the battlefield.

Religion

One traditional means for the acquisition of prestige among Sioux men (and more rarely women) was participation in religious ritual. Young men were expected to endure a *hanbleceya*, or vision quest. During this rite, men fasted on a hilltop and waited to receive supernatural assistance. The power received from such a vision might require the observance of certain procedures, most commonly the making of medicine. "Medicine" refers to those material objects which expressed the "sacred," or *wakan*, for the Sioux. Medicine objects, sometimes wrapped in medicine bundles, had deep religious meaning and conveyed particular powers to their owner through their association with a supernatural helper: one object might afford protection in battle, another an advantage in matters of the heart. With the exception of tribal bundles, like the Sacred Calf Pipe, most medicine objects had significance only for their owner. Often he was the only one with complete knowledge of the symbolism, songs, and ritual procedures associated with a particular medicine object.

The Sioux believed that there were seven sacred rites and that the ritual procedures for these rites were given to them by the Sacred Buffalo Calf Woman.[5] Sponsorship of most of these rites was costly, entailing the distribution of large amounts of personal property and providing a feast for the participants and spectators. Consequently, the sponsorship of one or more of these rites contributed to the garnering of prestige.

The focus of Sioux religious life, and possibly the most important of the seven rites, was the Sun Dance. Participants in the Sun Dance fasted and endured self-torture, either in the fulfillment of a vow or to obtain supernatural help, for themselves or another.

The Sioux view of the cosmos gave to every aspect of daily life a religious significance, and everyday acts were often accompanied by ritual procedure. Smoking and eating, for example, were sometimes preceded by four feinting gestures, and prayer might accompany the preparation for an evening's gambling or an afternoon's journey to visit friends.

Historical Adaptations

For the Sioux, survival depended upon strict adherence to the traditional—in religion, politics, and social mores, among other things. Yet history occasionally demanded adaptations: survival through change. The European fur trade and the commercial goods that it brought to the Sioux introduced a new standard of living, which they accepted and enjoyed. In fact, the Sioux became dependent upon the gunpowder, firearms, metal cookware, and cloth that the fur trade provided. They incorporated these items of non-Indian manufacture into a way of life that was distinctly Sioux.

The classic Sioux way of life lasted scarcely a century before its decline. The westward expansion of non-Indians in the last century inevitably created insurmountable conflict. The virtual extinction of the buffalo and military engagements with the United States Army ultimately resulted in subjugation. The

Sioux made a valiant stand against the encroachment, yet within a year of the famous Sioux victory against General George Armstrong Custer on the banks of the Little Big Horn River, most Sioux had surrendered to the United States government, and by the 1880s, the Sioux were settled on reservations, principally in the present states of North and South Dakota.

The reservation system altered Sioux life in a basic way. Government agents assigned the chiefs and organized military police; warfare and hunting were no longer possible; and numerous religious rituals were proscribed. Still, the Sioux would not abandon the vision of old ways. The decades prior to reservation life were increasingly scrutinized and idealized; this earlier period was seen as a golden age, a classic period in which the Sioux were the lords of the Plains they surveyed. The reservation provided a way of life that most Sioux found depressing and demoralizing.

Late in the 1880s, Wovoka, a Paiute from Mason Valley in Nevada, initiated a religious movement that diffused rapidly among the Indians of the Great Plains.[6] The ethic of Wovoka's visionary message was to live peacefully in anticipation of the restoration of all old ways, the return of the buffalo, and the disappearance of white men. Wovoka gave instructions for dancing a "Ghost Dance," in which participants usually fell into a hypnotic trance and, upon recovering, recounted their own supernatural experiences. Wovoka provided a framework for the ritual that left room for variations in its expression. Because of the profound dissatisfaction among the Sioux with reservation life, the Ghost Dance doctrine was particularly appealing and found adherents almost immediately. Two Sioux men visited Wovoka at Mason Valley in the summer of 1890 and returned with the gospel, to which the Sioux added numerous innovations, including an element of militancy. On Pine Ridge Reservation, the government agent, confused and frightened by the Ghost Dance frenzy, called in the United States Cavalry. This action led to the massacre of a Lakota camp on Wounded Knee Creek in 1890 and effectively concluded the period of Sioux armed resistance to the United States in the nineteenth century.

Fig. 6. Painted muslin dress, Sioux. Length:134.6 cm. Width:172.7 cm. No. 12. The dress bears fine examples of pan-Plains Ghost Dance motifs, interpreted in a markedly Sioux fashion.

Fig. 7. Painted shield and cover with decoration of cloth, feathers and horsehair, Brûlé Sioux, probably South Dakota. Diameter:48.2 cm. Length of trailer:100.3 cm. No. 15. This elaborate shield is made of cut-up parfleche and may have been used as a dance ornament. The painting on the cover represents a mounted Brûlé Sioux man firing his gun at a Pawnee.

Art

While a great many of the salient features of Sioux political, economic, and social life were shared with other Plains tribes, tribal styles, especially in art, did vary and were occasionally quite distinct. The Great Plains was not, from an artistic viewpoint, a homogeneous area. The arts of the Plains Indians, and especially the Sioux, have attracted considerable attention in the popular and scholarly literature.[7] While the literature is replete with references to porcupine quillwork and glass beadwork,[8] painting as an art form has been explored to a lesser extent, and the social contexts within which all these arts operate are also largely unexplored.

Because Sioux art was not isolated from the rest of Sioux life and from the Sioux view of the world, the major factors influencing its development and changes of style were numerous. The complex Sioux pattern of self-expression and reserve, for example, created interesting concepts of security and change. Although Sioux art remained tenaciously conservative for decades at a time, individual variations in art did exist and sometimes altered existing traditions. It is also probable that type features emerged for each of the divisions of the Teton Sioux. For instance, while most Sioux shirts were painted with a horizontal median—the top half one color and the bottom half another—one Hunkpapa shirt was painted with a vertical median, and the same pattern appears for shirts rendered in Hunkpapa pictographs as well. A certain type of woman's dress, ornamented with pictographs, also appears particular to the Hunkpapa (see fig. 5). These examples might indicate a distinct Hunkpapa style. Further study may reveal specific types and applications of techniques for each Sioux division.

Among the Sioux, specialization was the exception rather than the rule. As in most egalitarian societies, each family unit was essentially self-sufficient. The act of decorating utilitarian objects, personal ornaments, and clothing may have been regarded in the same light as other household tasks. There were, however, certain individuals with exceptional ability in a specific craft. Without being full-time specialists, these individuals might satisfy requests for their products from other members of the band. A talented artist, for example, might be asked to ornament his neighbor's tipi with pictographs of war exploits.

If the manufacture of an article required no esoteric skill or knowledge, anyone with sufficient dexterity might practice the craft. The manufacturer of medicine objects, however, had to meet other requirements. The value of certain medicine objects depended on their magical potency. These objects, including shields, might be made only by certain individuals who had received their power in dreams. For others to employ such specialists usually required a certain amount of ritual, such as offering a pipe and sponsoring a feast, a process that was often costly.

Because much Sioux art was dictated by personal achievement and by visionary experiences, it displayed a high degree of individuality. Sometimes individual innovations became common ones through distribution by gift or purchase, especially if their magical power seemed effective. One occasion for this was the mourning period, for following an individual's death, his personal possessions were usually distributed to friends or relatives.

The Sioux artist worked confined within a set of stylistic conventions. The distinct types of Sioux painting have been regarded as a function of the sexual division of labor. A great deal of Sioux art is made up of a small number of geometric motifs combined in an often-complex variety of ways. This type of art was usually done by women (see figs. 8 and 10). Sioux art that consists of figures, rendered realistically with certain stylized conventions, was usually done by men. Sioux painting may also be understood in the social context in which it arises; that is, either sacred or secular. Art of the geometric type was generally considered by the Sioux to be decorative and was used to ornament largely utilitarian—that is, secular—objects. While these designs may have had a particular meaning for the artist who created them, for the Sioux, geometric art was largely non-iconic. Art of the realistically figured type is used usually in connection with religious articles or things associated with war (see fig. 7). Decorative and secular art was primarily the work of women, while art of a sacred character was created chiefly by men. The woman's role in Sioux life was characterized to some extent by her capacity to manufacture and maintain utilitarian objects. Men assumed responsibility for those facets of everyday life concerning hunting, war, and religion. Articles associated with these activities were usually manufactured and decorated by men. These articles acquired a somewhat sacred character. They were treated with reverence and often with rigid ritual proscriptions. Only the men were permitted to touch certain sacred objects. A woman's touch was considered to be contaminating and destroyed efficacy. Despite this, women occupied a high position of honor among the Sioux, derived from the values placed upon virtue, childbearing, industry, and craftsmanship.[9] Women who excelled in any of these attributes were frequently honored in society songs and dances. Young girls were often assigned roles in religious rituals, and *winyan wakan*, holy women, often effected supernatural cures.

Intertribal trade was another major factor in the development and change of style in Sioux art. The Sioux, who were at the nexus of the Plains trading network, were in contact with tribes in every direction.[10] From this vantage point, they could exercise discretion in adopting or ignoring a particular design trend crisscrossing the Plains. They themselves may be seen as trend setters, influencing design trends and combining pan-Plains traits—and returning them to the trade network revitalized and with a distinctively Sioux stamp.

Fig. 8. Painted hide parfleche, Hunkpapa Sioux, Standing Rock Reservation, Cannon Ball, North Dakota. Length:29.2 cm. Height:20.3 cm. No. 27. This is a miniature, probably a child's toy.

Painting

The technique of Sioux painting was complex, for the Sioux painted on a variety of surfaces and used a variety of materials. Dried paint was stored in small hide bags. Paint stored in a hard mass was ground for use in shallow mortars or dishes of rawhide. Artists often used a turtle shell cup to hold their prepared paint. Powdered paint was mixed with sizing made from hoof glue, beaver tail, or cactus juice. When prepared for a parfleche or robe, the sizing might be made from the boiled scrapings of the hide being painted. This sizing served as a binder and also helped the color adhere to the hide. Occasionally applied as a top coat, the sizing brightened colors as well. On later examples of Sioux painting, the designs were indicated in outline, sometimes with lead pencil. On some older examples of hides painted with geometric motifs, the outlines were pressed firmly into the hide with a small, peeled section of willow shoot. Brushes of bone, horn, or wood were used to complete the painting. Willow or cottonwood shoots were chewed to make a narrow, stiff brush; and a sharp piece of horn from buffalo or mountain sheep could be used for painting the outline. For applying color to large areas or for filling in designs, the leg-bone joint section of a buffalo or steer was used. This spongy joint material was ideal because it was porous and would hold a good deal of paint. The joint, cut up with an axe or knife, would yield several small, wedge-shaped brushes. The wide base of the wedge was used to apply paint to a large area, while the apex might be used for fine lining.

Before contact with Europeans, the Sioux used a limited palette of natural pigments. A few colors were obtained from various vegetable materials: bloodroot steeped in water yielded varying shades of orange; a black was sometimes obtained from rotten walnuts; and various berries were sometimes employed as color sources (principally blue and red) for paint. Red and yellow ochre were especially common pigments prior to the fur trade. The oldest Sioux hides seem to have been painted only with brown lignite and colorless glue sizing. This glue sizing was applied to a clean white hide, and, although colorless at first, it showed white as the hide became soiled or was smoked. Late in the eighteenth century, a mercury vermillion from China was introduced in the Indian trade. It was immediately very popular, and many early hides from the first half of the nineteenth century were painted in combinations of vermillion red, brown lignite, and white glue sizing. After the introduction of other commercial pigments, green, blue, and yellow were used freely by Sioux artists, in pleasing and whimsical combinations. During the last half of the nineteenth century and the early part of this century, lead pencil, colored pencil, crayon, and India ink were employed in Sioux painting.

Fig. 9. Ledger drawing: portrait of Red Crow by Red Dog, Sioux, probably Oglala, Pine Ridge Reservation, South Dakota, collected ca. 1884. Length: 19.1 cm. Width: 12.7 cm. No. 44. While it is improbable that Red Crow ever dressed this elaborately for battle, his friends and relatives would recognize his portrait by the details of his personal possessions.

A large number of drawings were made on paper in European notebooks and military ledgers (fig. 9). These drawings often commemorated specific incidents. They contain scenes of warfare as well as genre scenes of dancing or courtship. Sometimes they contain a series of accurate portraits. Individuals may be recognized by their personal possessions and accouterments, by distinctive face paint, or by some particular ornament or medicine known to have belonged to that person. These drawings articulate an enormous amount of detail. It is sometimes possible, because of this extraordinary attention to detail, to make observations about the distribution of a particular design element or the use of a certain trade item (see fig. 22).

With the beginning of the reservation period, some commercial developments took place in Sioux pictographic painting: a small number of Sioux paintings were made exclusively for sale. These included paintings on hides and on muslin and paper, as well as miniature tipi covers painted with pictographs.

Garments

The earliest examples of painting found on the Plains and attributable to the Sioux were rendered on tanned or untanned animal hide. The tanned hides of big game, principally buffalo, were used by the Sioux as untailored clothing in the form of robes. Robes for summer use were usually dehaired and sometimes scraped thin, while the hair was left on hides that were intended for winter use. These garments were often painted.

Five basic patterns have been described for the decoration of clothing in the Plains area.[11] At least three of these were widely employed by the Sioux. A sunburst pattern composed of concentric circles of featherlike elements, sometimes called a "feather shield" (fig. 16) or "black bonnet," seems to have been worn by men. A highly conventionalized design known as "box and border," sometimes said to represent the visceral organs of the flayed buffalo, was worn exclusively by women. Both these styles were painted only by women. Men painted robes with figurative forms in a distinctive pictographic style. These garments were the chronicles of Sioux warfare and they depicted the exploits of the wearer. Tipis and tipi liners were also commonly painted by individuals or groups of men, and they depicted war exploits in the same manner (fig. 1). These paintings may be regarded as a form of military medal or a badge of honor. The public display was a demonstration of pride for the owner and his family, and the voucher of public approval as well.

Although there were strict Sioux conventions for rendering, say, a horse or a buffalo calf, it was possible for different Sioux artists to vary their interpretations of these conventions enormously, and individual styles did emerge. The oldest hides show both men and animals drawn in relatively crude, "stick-figure" fashion. By the third quarter of the nineteenth century, however, the Sioux had developed a distinctive style, using elegant outline drawings and a considerable amount of detail.

It was possible for virtually any piece of clothing to be ornamented with painted decoration. Men's leggings (fig. 18), and often the upper portion of women's leggings, were commonly painted green, with a paint obtained from cupric oxide. A bright blue, sometimes obtained from commercial chalk, and a bright chromium yellow can also occasionally be seen on garments of this type. The color was applied either over the whole surface of the leggings or, sometimes, between narrowly spaced rows of beadwork. Occasionally, paint appears between the lanes of beadwork at the hem of Sioux women's dresses. The bodices and skirts of dresses were frequently whitened with the application of white clay. Women kept small balls of this white clay to rub on their dresses to clean them.

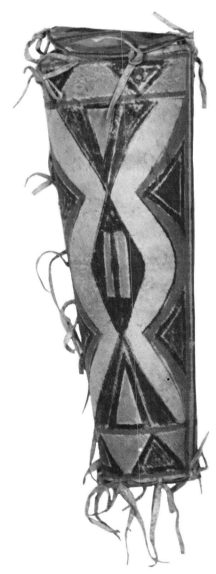

Fig. 10. Medicine bag of painted hide, Sioux, Standing Rock Reservation, North Dakota, collected by Frances Densmore. Length:39.4 cm. No. 29. This medicine case for a crow skin necklace is emblematic of the *Kangi-Yuha* or "Crow-owners" Society. It was collected from Eagle Shield.

Men's shirts are possibly the most striking articles of painted clothing. Shirts were occasionally painted with pictographs in the realistic style, which sometimes represented war exploits. Other shirts were painted with simple, conventionalized guns, pipes, or stripes, arranged in neat rows, usually down one side of the shirt. It is not uncommon to see both these types of painting on a single shirt. However, by far the most common painted decoration on men's shirts consisted of two fields of solid color, usually dividing the shirt on a horizontal median, a pattern that was possibly derived from the shirts worn as a badge of office by the *Wicasas* (color plate 2). In addition, many of these shirts were ornamented with numerous locks of human hair. While the locks on some shirts were certainly war trophies, the traditional symbolism of the locks on *wicasa* shirts dealt with the leader's responsibility for all the people of his division. These locks were usually obtained from wives or sisters. Many of these shirts were ornamented with strips of bead or porcupine-quill embroidery. While these shirts lost their political significance sometime during the nineteenth century, and many men wore them, they remain among the finest examples of Sioux painting.

Distinctive designs for men's shirts and women's dresses, as well as a particular type of face and body painting, were employed during the Ghost Dance. Individuals took a sweat bath, or *inipi*, and then were painted by a leader and the whole body was rubbed with sweetgrass. The forehead, cheeks, and the chin of a dancer might be painted with typical Ghost Dance motifs: circles, crescents, and morning stars. A special red ochre obtained by pilgrims to Wovoka, mixed with local red paint, was believed to give the supplicant some extra spiritual help in seeking a vision.

A recurrent theme in Ghost Dance visions was the visiting of deceased relatives and friends. Little Wound described one of his visions: "I would like to see my relations who have been dead a long time. . . . They appeared, riding the finest horses I ever saw, dressed in superb and most brilliant garments, and seeming very happy. . . . As they approached I recognized the playmates of my childhood . . . tears of joy ran down my cheeks."[12] Frequently, Ghost Dance visions inspired new design patterns for Ghost Dance dresses and shirts. However, all the inspired patterns usually conformed to a pan–Plains Indian design repertoire for the Ghost Dance, including stars, birds, dragonflies, and butterflies (fig. 6). These designs contrasted sharply with traditional Sioux motifs.

Some Sioux, such as Black Elk, the famous *wicasa wakan*, or holy man, preferred traditional Sioux patterns for Ghost Dance paraphernalia (fig. 11). In contrast to the traditional, a woman named Return From Scout painted, with a group of friends, standard dresses, all with the same designs. Perhaps the most striking innovation was the feature of the bulletproof Ghost Dance shirt. Kicking Bear, a respected warrior and pilgrim to Wovoka, conceived the idea for these shirts, and the Sioux adopted it. At the massacre at Wounded Knee in 1890, the inefficacy of the bulletproof shirts became tragically clear.

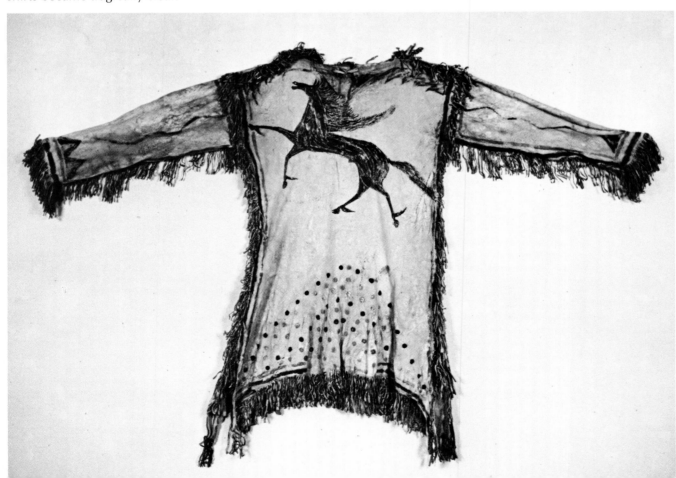

Shields

For many Sioux men, a shield was the paramount medicine in war. Traditionally, a circular-form shield was cut from the neck section of a buffalo hide. This stiff rawhide might deflect arrows that struck a glancing blow, but shields were seldom employed as practical protection. Sometimes only the painted cover, or a feather ornament from it, would be carried into battle. The soft hide cover of a shield was usually painted with designs that were indicated in an instructive vision (fig. 17). Sometimes an additional undecorated cover was employed as special protection for this powerful medicine.

Some shields were made for society dances, such as the Buffalo Society Dance (color plate 2). During the Ghost Dance, it seems, some men carried small shields of muslin painted with tempera, watercolor, or crayon (fig. 15). Later, these small shields became fashionable as dance paraphernalia and were carried as ornaments at secular celebrations. With the onset of the reservation period, one society activity known as the Grass Dance, or Omaha Dance, became an important and popular social event. It is very probable that young men rummaged through grandpa's old parfleches and adopted what they fancied for use as Grass Dance accouterments. As a result, old society and sacred items often lost their religious significance.

Shields were among the most original expressions of Sioux art, because individual visionary experiences were the inspiration for all the art associated with them. The palette was virtually unlimited, and many shields were ornamented in a multimedia fashion. Miniature shields were probably manufactured as charms, and it is possible that they were included in the contents of medicine bundles (fig. 14). Some of the Ghost Dance shields show the influence of the wider Ghost Dance movement on the Plains but interpreted in a decidedly Sioux way. The colors used on Sioux Ghost Dance accouterments and especially shields seem comparatively subtle. It is difficult to determine whether this is simply the result of fading. It is apparent that many were painted in a hasty fashion, with sketchy lines used to fill in broad areas. Among the Sioux, multiple production of Ghost Dance articles was certainly common, and this production in quantity may have affected quality to some extent. It must be remembered, however, that these items were regarded by the Sioux as medicine first, and as art in a strictly incidental way.

Fig. 12. Painted hide and trade cloth knife case for a woman, Sioux. Length:33.7 cm. No. 28. Probably new at the time it was collected, this knife sheath may have been produced as a commercial item.

Fig. 13. Swift Dog photographed by F. A. Rinehart ca. 1898.

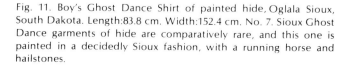

Fig. 11. Boy's Ghost Dance Shirt of painted hide, Oglala Sioux, South Dakota. Length:83.8 cm. Width:152.4 cm. No. 7. Sioux Ghost Dance garments of hide are comparatively rare, and this one is painted in a decidedly Sioux fashion, with a running horse and hailstones.

Fig. 15. Painted Ghost Dance shield decorated with feathers, Sioux. Diameter:45.7 cm. No. 23.

Fig. 16. Painted shield cover of hide and trade cloth, Sioux. Diameter:40 cm. No. 19. This was probably made from a man's robe. The concentric circles of feathers continue on the reverse, and the red stroud streamers have been added.

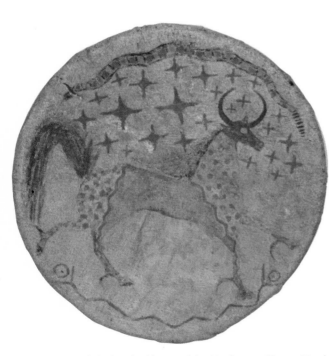

Fig. 14. Painted hide shield, possibly Hunkpapa Sioux, North Dakota. Diameter:24.1 cm. No. 25. This miniature shield cover on a wooden hoop is painted with a design of a horned horse, with stars and lightning.

Genuine Sioux shields are rare in museum collections. This is probably the result of two factors. First, because shield manufacture was limited to those who had received a requisite vision allowing them to practice this craft, Sioux shields may always have been scarce. Engaging such a specialist to manufacture a shield was costly, and many men might not have been able to afford the fees involved. Although one had completed a *hanbleceya*, or vision quest, and had obtained a strong medicine, the specialization of shield manufacture and the fees involved might preclude one from owning such an object. Second, because the Sioux carried on a long and ardent struggle for autonomy in the Indian wars, military paraphernalia was often destroyed by the United States government in battle and upon surrender. It is possible that many Sioux shields were destroyed by military personnel when various bands surrendered at local forts and agencies. Other items seem to have been popular as souvenirs, but relatively few shields have survived.

Among the Sioux shields in museum collections, a number have traditional covers but were not made in the traditional way with a heavy rawhide inner shield. Some of these are made of light rawhide, occasionally from a cut-up parfleche, sometimes with merely a wooden hoop to stretch the cover. These shields may have been made for dancing, and they do appear in photographs of the Wild West shows and in posed studio photographs (see fig. 13). It is also possible that a number of the shields in museum collections were manufactured for sale to non-Indians.

Fig. 17. Painted hide shield and cover, Sioux. Diameter:52 cm. No. 17.

Fig. 18. Painted hide leggings for a man, decorated with glass beads and cowrie shells. Length:76.2 cm. No. 3. The leggings are painted green and yellow, in the style typical of the last quarter of the nineteenth century.

Rawhide Containers

Numerous containers and other objects were manufactured from rawhide and painted with characteristic geometric motifs. Chief among these items was the parfleche. The term derives from the Old French *par-flèche*—"to parry and arrow"—and was formerly used to mean the material from which containers were made, the rawhide itself. The term now refers to those envelopelike containers, sometimes called "suitcases," used for storing virtually everything in the home, and especially dried meat or pemmican. This type of painted object was common throughout the Plains. However, there were distinct details of painting and a style that indicate a Sioux type of parfleche. The manufacture of rawhide, like other household tasks, was a woman's responsibility. The process included skinning, butchering, and removing excess flesh and fat from the hide (see fig. 20). When hides were prepared for painting, great care was taken to leave as few knife marks as possible. The hide was staked to the ground, flesh side up. It was then washed and scraped to achieve a uniform thickness. To help stretch the thick neck, or "hump," section to consistency, a hide was sometimes split in half before staking. While wet, the hide was painted and sized. Rulers of peeled willow shoot were used to execute lines that were both straight and uniform; when curved lines were desired, these shoots were bowed and then secured with cord or sinew. When dry, the hide was turned over and dehaired with a hoelike tool of elkhorn, called *wahintke*. In the final process, the hide was whitened by pounding on the hair side with a smooth stone. The parfleches might then be cut from the hide and folded for use.

A number of container types besides the parfleche were manufactured from rawhide. A wide variety of small bags made for storing paint, sewing kits, fire-making kits, and numerous other household items were common. Women manufactured for themselves rawhide knife cases (fig. 12). Both these and the small bags became popular items for sale to non-Indians at the end of the nineteenth century. Narrow saddle bags, made in pairs (fig. 19), most often were used to store clothing. Painted rawhide bags were sometimes used by women for gathering botanicals. Occasionally, religious paraphernalia were stored in bundles or containers that were painted by women with geometric motifs (fig. 10). When wagons became popular for transportation, the Sioux developed a rawhide wagon box for storage. Like parfleches, these boxes were customarily made in pairs and painted with geometric motifs. As European suitcases and other containers replaced the traditional Sioux rawhide containers, the latter remained popular for gift giving. These rawhide gifts often were immediately cut up and used for more practical purposes, especially for the soles of moccasins (see fig. 21).

Fig. 19. Pair of hide and canvas clothes bags, with painted decoration, Sioux. Length:63.5 cm. Width:27.9 cm. No. 35.

Fig. 20. Women tanning. The woman on the left is softening a hide, and the woman on the right uses a *wahinkte* as a fleshing tool.

Conclusion

It is difficult to obtain an absolutely accurate chronological perspective for Sioux arts. Because the central Great Plains were largely uninhabited by Europeans before 1850, very little early Sioux material is extant in museum collections today. As a result, very little is known about early styles. Also, the major part of the early material that is extant was collected in a manner that occasionally obscured the social context from which it issued. Explorers and military men on the Great Plains prior to 1850 collected a great deal of Plains Indian art, but unfortunately these collections are devoid of documentation with regard to tribal designations, dates, or geographical locations. There are a few very fine and well-documented early collections in this country and in Europe. Surely a comprehensive survey of these collections would provide some answers to questions regarding early tribal styles.

If any historical perspective may be obtained from a view of Sioux painting, it is that this is very much a living art form. Sioux painting did not end when the reservation period began. The Sioux today maintain an awareness of what is good and viable in traditional ways. A large number of contemporary Sioux people speak Lakota and maintain a very traditional social life. Numerous aspects of traditional Sioux religion persist today. The Sun Dance remains an annual event in several communities, and young men continue to fast for visions. Traditional games, social dances, feasts, and honorings remain popular pastimes. The Sioux values of cooperation, generosity, and bravery remain strong and pervasive. Sioux arts flourish in an atmosphere of increasing appreciation today—on and off the reservation. The variety of Sioux art commands the careful consideration of its aesthetic value.

Sioux painting is certainly among the highest achievements in Plains Indian art. Sioux artists have participated actively in the trends in contemporary North American Indian painting and in other forms of contemporary art as well. Contemporary Indian art continues the tradition of using non-Indian materials (tempera, acrylic, gouache, canvas) for expressing traditional attitudes and themes in an indisputably Indian way. Sioux artists have been among the contributors who have left a lasting mark on certain arts, and they continue to do so. The excellence of Sioux art has been recognized in numerous Indian and non-Indian competitive exhibitions and by major art museums as well. In less than two centuries, Sioux painting has undergone a number of striking developments, the most recent of which persist today. Sioux painting remains a visible and appraisable art—lasting and vital.

Fig. 21. Hide moccasin decorated with paint and glass beads, Sioux. Length:26.7 cm. No. 4. One of a fine pair of moccasins, this shows the use of cut-up parfleche for soles.

NOTES

1. Secoy 1953.
2. See Wissler 1934 for a comprehensive overview of Plains Indian culture.
3. See Hassrick 1964.
4. Wissler 1912:15.
5. See Brown 1953.
6. See Mooney 1896.
7. See Morrow 1975; Feder 1967, 1973; Dunn 1968; Blish 1967; Lyford 1940; Ewers 1939; Wissler 1904, 1907, 1912.
8. See Lyford 1940.
9. Hassrick 1964.
10. See Jablow 1952.
11. See Ewers 1939.
12. Utley 1963:90-91.

REFERENCES

Brown, Joseph Epes
   1953   The Sacred Pipe. Norman: University of Oklahoma Press.
Blish, Helen H.
   1967   A Pictographic History of the Oglala Sioux. Lincoln: University of Nebraska Press.
Densmore, Frances
   1918   Teton Sioux Music. Bureau of American Ethnology, Bulletin 61.
Dunn, Dorothy
   1968   American Indian Painting of the Southwest and Plains Areas. Albuquerque: University of New Mexico Press.
Ewers, John Canfield
   1939   Plains Indian Painting: A Description of an Aboriginal American Art. Palo Alto, Calif.: Stanford University Press.
Feder Norman
   1967   North American Indian Painting. New York: The Museum of Primitive Art.
   1973   American Indian Art. New York: Harry N. Abrams.
Hassrick, Royal B.
   1964   The Sioux: Life and Customs of a Warrior Society. Norman: University of Oklahoma Press.
Jablow, Joseph
   1952   The Cheyenne in Plains Indian Trade Relations. American Ethnological Society, Monograph 19. Seattle: University of Washington Press.
Lyford, Carrie A.
   1940   Quill and Beadwork of the Western Sioux. Lawrence, Kansas: Bureau of Indian Affairs.
Mooney, James
   1896   The Ghost Dance Religion. Bureau of American Ethnology, Fourteenth Annual Report, Part II.
Morrow, Mabel
   1975   Indian Rawhide: An American Folk Art. Norman: University of Oklahoma Press.
Secoy, Frank
   1953   Changing Military Patterns on the Great Plains. American Ethnological Society, Monograph 21. Seattle: Washington University Press.
Utley, Robert M.
   1963   Last Days of the Sioux Nation. New Haven: Yale University Press.
Wissler, Clark
   1904   Decorative Art of the Sioux Indians. Bulletin of the American Museum of Natural History 18:231-275.
   1907   Some Protective Designs of the Dakota. Anthropological Papers of the American Museum of Natural History 1(2):19-53.
   1912   Societies and Ceremonial Associations in the Oglala Division of the Teton-Dakota. Anthropological Papers of the American Museum of Natural History 11(1):1-90.
   1934   North American Indians of the Plains. American Museum of Natural History Handbook Series, No. 1.

ACKNOWLEDGMENTS

The author is indebted to a number of individuals without whose help this work would not have been possible; to John Ewers, for advice and commentary, to Royal Hassrick and to Dennis Lessard, who generously shared knowledge of Sioux material culture, to Paul Hadzima for Lakota usage, and to Tom Biolsi, whose enthusiastic support exceeded expectations. Pila maye yelo!

Fig. 22. Pencil and crayon (?) drawing on paper, Sioux, South Dakota. Length:16.5 cm. Width:26.7 cm. No. 41. In this portrait, a woman rides a bay horse with a silver bridle and a saddle blanket decorated with glass beads. She wears a dress of blue strouding and long, dentalium-shell earrings, as well as a woman's breastplate of bone. She carries an incised elk-antler quirt and wears a Navajo blanket around her waist, over her belt of silver conchos. Beaded leggings and moccasins complete her outfit.

the FEATHERWORKER
THE KARAJA OF BRAZIL

DAVID M. FAWCETT

Fig. 1. A Karajá man wearing a nimbus headdress, wrestler's belt, and knee bands. The nimbus, worn during ceremonies, is attached at the back of the head by tying it to a knot of hair.

When Europeans arrived at the Brazilian coast in the sixteenth century, they found it under the control of the Tupinambá, who dominated the area from the Amazon to what is today the state of São Paulo. The Europeans were struck by the feather ornaments of these Indians. Metraux[1] describes what they saw: "*The love for feathers was so great that men and even women glued them to their heads with wax or sprinkled chopped feathers all over their bodies, which they had previously coated with gum or honey. . . . They also pasted with wax on their temples patches of toucan skin covered with yellow feathers. Feathers, after use, were carefully collected, cleaned, and stored in bamboo tubes sealed with wax.*"

These traditions of featherwork continue among Amazonian Indians today. While there are many groups using feathers, a few, including the Urubú-Kaapor, the Bororo, the Tapirapé, and their neighbors the Karajá, are outstanding craftsmen.

The Karajá peoples are a linguistic and cultural group comprising the 865 speakers of Javahé, Shambioá, and Karajá-proper dialects.[2] They live on and around the 200-mile-long Bananal Island in the states of Goiás and Mato Grosso, Brazil. The three groups speak mutually intelligible dialects, yet linguists have found no affiliation of the Karajá languages with any other Amazon language.

Because featherwork is such an integral part of Karajá life, a brief history of European contact with the Indians and a description of traditional Karajá culture will provide a framework in which to place the role of feather ornaments.

History Of European Contact With The Karajá

Europeans first reported contact with the Karajá when Bartholomeu Bueno founded Santa Anna in 1682.[3] Shortly thereafter, in 1684, Antonio Pires Campos, a notorious *bandeirante,* led gangs into the area that raided Indian villages for slaves.[4] Other brief and violent contacts occurred during the eighteenth century[5] as Europeans attempted to exploit the interior of Brazil and take Indian captives. The Karajá resisted such exploitation and earned a reputation for fierceness in fighting their neighbors (the Sherente, Shavante, Yuruna, Tapirapé) and whites alike.[6]

In the early nineteenth century, Brazilian military posts were built along the rivers in order to hold criminals and control *bandeirante* activity in the area. The overall result, however, was not so much the control they sought as the transfer of European disease to the Indians, which reduced the Karajá population from more than ten thousand to a few hundred in less than a century.[7]

During this time, European exploration in the area increased. The French explorer Castelnau sailed up the Araguaya River, observing Indians and collecting artifacts in 1844; and in 1859, twelve Italian Capuchin monks, fleeing Rome because of their revolutionary activity, founded Santa Leopoldina (today, Leopoldina) and several other settlements in the area.[8] In 1863, Couto de Magalhães, governor of the province of

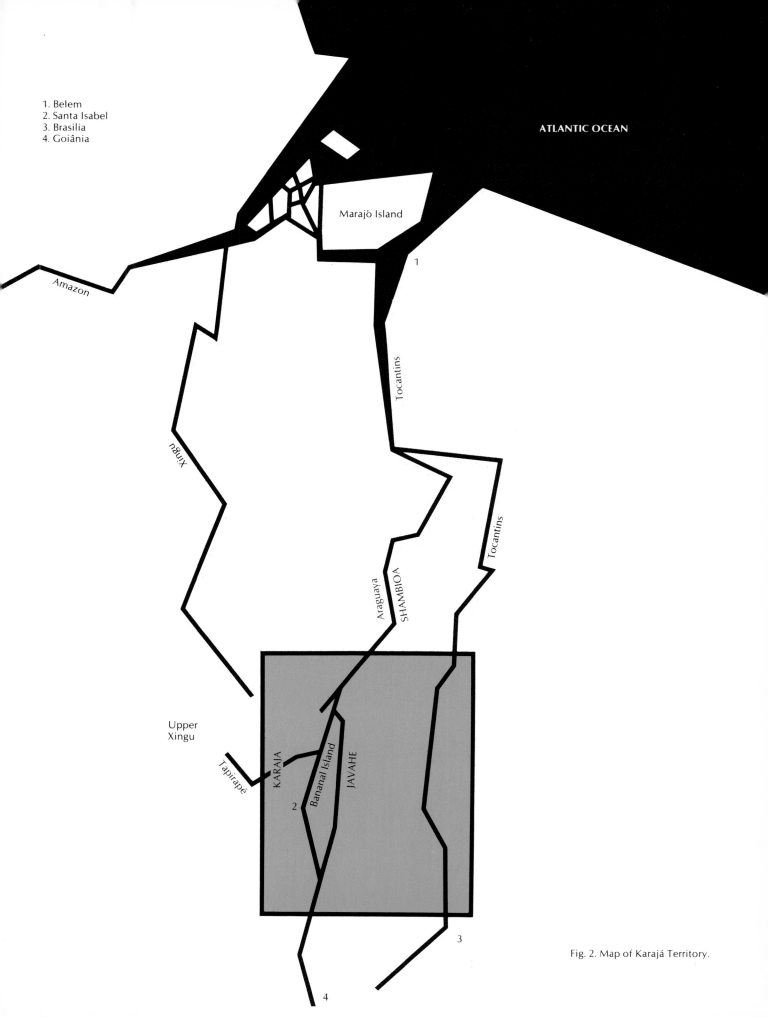

1. Belem
2. Santa Isabel
3. Brasilia
4. Goiânia

ATLANTIC OCEAN

Marajó Island

Amazon

Tocantins

Xingu

Tocantins

Araguaya

SHAMBIOA

Upper
Xingu

Tapirapé

KARAJA

Bananal Island

JAVAHE

Fig. 2. Map of Karajá Territory.

Goiás, developed a plan to run a steamship service from Leopoldina to Santa Maria Falls. Since this venture required the peaceful cooperation of the tribes en route, including the Karajá, the governor founded the Collegio Santa Isabel for Indian children, in order to "civilize" them, although the Karajá usually allowed only orphans to attend.[9] The governor did, however, get the cooperation of the Karajá for river travel, until the steamship service was voluntarily suspended in 1900. Throughout the nineteenth century the Karajá remained "half civilized" in European eyes,[10] accepting only those elements of European culture that appealed to them, such as iron knives and fishhooks.

The beginning of the twentieth century saw the maintenance of peaceful relations between the Indians and whites. Traditional Karajá patterns of hunting and fishing, as well as ceremonies and ritual life, continued despite a greatly reduced population. White contact increased with exploration by Europeans, especially Germans, who carefully described many varieties of feather ornaments and other objects, resulting in scholarly sources that are still, in many cases, the most important references for the region.

The current Brazilian effort to develop the Amazon region is exposing long-isolated cultures and forcing them to change at a rapid pace. Although many basic elements of Karajá culture remain intact, they have been altered and are continually threatened. The impact of such changes on the future of the Karajá will be discussed in the last part of this paper.

Karajá Subsistence

Karajá culture has long been centered on the Araguaya River and the many streams that feed into it. During the dry season, from May until September, the Indians camp in villages on the white sandy beaches, fishing, playing games, and dancing. In the rainy season they return to villages on higher ground to avoid the extensive flooding of the river. Smaller waterways, in addition to being arteries for travel throughout the region, are home to an abundance of turtles, water birds, and fish, including the dangerous piranha, as well as the pirarucu fish *(Arapaima gigas)*, the largest in the Amazon river system, commonly seven and eight feet long. Storks, herons, and spoonbills, whose feathers are prized for use in feather ornaments, also frequent the water to survive.

Fishing is a major source of food for the Karajá, who have developed a number of techniques. In communal fishing, *timbó*, a poisonous vine, is used to suffocate fish, which are then scooped into baskets.[11] At one time, the large pirarucu were struck with clubs, wounding them as they came up to the surface for air. Today, such clubs are rare, and individuals often use a bow and arrows or harpoons to kill these and other types of fish.

Fig. 3. Young men adorned with down and geometric body painting typical of the Karajá. The woven-cotton armspool bracelets and the knee bands indicate that the men are bachelors.

Fig. 4. Boy's head ring, Karajá, Brazil. Diameter: 22 cm. No. 18.

Fig. 5. Karajá feathered crown. Height: 27 cm. Width: 17 cm. No. 12. This type of head ornament is no longer worn by the Karajá. Feather petals are attached to a reed base, which is held together with cotton cord. The top of the crown is covered with feathers tied to netting.

Fig. 6. Karajá cap. Height: 34 cm. Width: 17 cm. No. 17. The base is constructed with reeds decorated by horizontal strips of liana-vine bark. Tall macaw feathers are surrounded by chicken feathers that have been dyed red. Chicken feathers are increasingly used as macaws become scarcer.

Thick galleries of forest grow intermittently along the waterways. Plots are cleared in the forests for gardens, which are an important source of food, especially for the Javahé, who live in the eastern portion of Bananal Island. Clearings are situated so as to be accessible by canoe in the dry season but not flooded in the rainy season. The most important crops are manioc, both bitter and sweet varieties, and maize, although beans, squash, peanuts, tobacco, cotton, potatoes, and numerous types of fruit are also cultivated.[12] Additionally, many plants are collected for use as food, medicine, and craft materials, including palm wood for bows (no. 38) and reeds for arrows. Collecting also provides two important delicacies: turtle eggs from the beaches and honey from the forest.

The patches of forest provide a home for various types of wildlife, including peccary, deer, jaguar, and monkeys, as well as tropical birds such as parrots and macaws that are so important for featherwork. Although there are hunts for deer, hunting in the forest is also undertaken to obtain feathers from these beautifully colored birds. Special bird-hunting arrows with blunt tips (no. 37) have been developed by the Indians in order to stun or kill a bird without harming its plumage.

Karajá Life Cycle

The life of every Karajá man and woman is organized around a cycle of age grades,[13] which mark successive stages in the growth of an individual, beginning with infancy and including childhood and adolescence. Each change in status from one grade to the next among the Karajá is marked by a rite of passage and a change in the type of personal ornaments and body painting associated with an individual. At puberty, for example, both boys and girls undergo an initiation ritual in which the symbol of the Karajá people, a small circle, is burned onto the cheeks with a heated smoking pipe.

During adolescence and until marriage, males spend a great deal of time together in the men's hut, which is set apart from the rest of the village. During their early years in the hut, boys spend their days doing errands for the older men, but as they grow older, they begin to pass more time hunting and fishing simply for pleasure, learning tribal songs, making feather ornaments, and wrestling.[14] Women are absolutely forbidden to enter the men's hut, which doubles as the storage house for the aruanã masks (color plate 4). Women are supposed to believe that spirits are visiting their village and not recognize the men when they don these masks in the aruanã dances, a ceremonial activity usually involving several villages. Should a woman even look into the hut where she could see the masks in storage, she could be held captive by the men and suffer punishment ranging from rape to death.[15]

In the age-grade system, young people move out of adolescence as they marry. A man is said to be ready for marriage when he is eighteen to twenty years old and owns a canoe,[16] though most young men cannot afford such an investment and so borrow canoes until they are older. Since the Karajá have no female equivalent of the men's hut, a girl lives with her parents until marriage, which for the female occurs at fourteen or fifteen years of age.[17] When a couple decide to marry, the man, if he has the resources, builds a new hut in the village with the help of his friends, while the woman begins work on sleeping mats and gathers household goods for their new home. If the couple cannot yet set up their own household, they will reside with the wife's relatives. Most marriages occur between individuals of the same village, but when husband and wife are from different settlements, normally the couple will reside in the wife's village.[18] On an appointed day, the man, having spent the morning hunting with his friends, calls for his bride at her parents' residence. On their wedding night they ceremonially remove each other's kneebands and spool bracelets and are thereafter considered husband and wife. Karajá marriages are predominantly monogamous.[19]

The status of a couple is enhanced with the arrival of children. The average Karajá family has three to five children[20] and the parents' pride is reflected by the fact that they are referred to as "father or mother of so-and-so," a practice called teknonymy. A final category in the age-grade system is "old age," including all people over forty-five.

Karajá Village Organization

The Karajá live in villages of up to one hundred people, which are located along rivers and streams. The population of any one village is quite fluid, especially between the Karajá-proper and the Javahé, and villages can be seen as the constant agglomeration and breakup of small factions. Within a village, families live in a row of huts on the beach, while a single structure, the men's hut, lies much farther back from the water. It is linked to the village by a wide path that serves as a dance track for ritual dances.

Each Karajá village usually has several different leadership positions, which are filled by males. Dance sponsors achieve status by hosting and providing food for celebrations; other leaders are chosen by the men of the village from those who are skillful in hunting and fishing, are strong, clever, and able to speak Portuguese.[21] Lipkind[22] writes that a third type of leadership position is inherited, passing from father to son, or through a daughter to her husband if there is no male heir. Such leaders probably function as arbitrators in intervillage conflicts. A fourth powerful figure in the village is the shaman, who has the primary role in Karajá ritual and health. A shaman is often paid to cure a sick person, but he can also be hired to cause illness or the death of an enemy. For this reason, shamans are much feared and often have more power in a village than anyone else.[23]

Karajá Featherwork

Among the Karajá, men are the sole featherworkers. Two general categories of featherwork can be distinguished: ornaments for personal adornment and masks used in ritual activities. Each man is responsible for the construction of feather ornaments for himself and his children, which takes place outdoors on woven mats. In contrast to this public activity, the large *aruanã* masks are assembled in secrecy in the men's hut, or sometimes even in another village. No feather craftsman claims a superior skill in constructing these feathered masks, for they are said to be actual spirits and are not supposed to be known to the Karajá women merely as *representations* of spirits. Krause[24] writes that every Karajá man had the knowledge to make them. While there is no specific period of apprenticeship for an individual, boys begin to learn the art of featherwork at puberty, when they move to the men's hut.

Fig. 7. Pair of Karajá knee bands, worn so that the tuft of feathers is just below the knee. Length: 36 cm. Width: 14 cm. No. 32. Such ornaments are markers of age-grade status and are often ceremonially removed at marriage.

Feathers are derived directly from both wild and tame birds and through trade. Harpy eagles, storks, spoonbills, and other birds are often hunted, while various types of parrots and the rare macaws are favorite pets of the Karajá and can be found in most villages.[25] Often, young parrots are taken from their nests in the forest at an early age and raised with a great deal of affection. They reside happily on posts around residence huts or on the roofs, occasionally returning to the forest to breed. Tame parrots and macaws are highly prized and are regarded as a continuing source of feathers, as they are harmlessly plucked twice a year.[26] Feathers are sometimes used as currency and are an important trade item, being readily negotiable in any Karajá village.[27] Because of their great value they are carefully stored in baskets (no. 36) which are hung in the hut roofs and guarded against theft. More recently, small suitcases have been traded to the Karajá, and these provide ideal containers for featherwork materials.

A great variety of plumage is incorporated into the featherwork of the Karajá. Most common are feathers of the various macaws: red-and-green macaw (*Ara chloroptera*), blue-and-yellow macaw (*Ara ararauna*), and the scarlet macaw (*Ara macao*). Turquoise-fronted parrots (*Amazona aestiva*) and other birds of the *Psittacidae* family are very common. White feathers of the Jabiru stork (*Jabiru mycteria*), Maguari stork (*Ciconia maguari*), great egret (*Egretta alba*), as well as the chicken are used. Black feathers are derived from the razor-billed curassow (*Crax mitu*), gray from the Cocoi heron (*Ardea cocoi*), and chocolate brown feathers from the hoatzin (*Opisthocomus hoazin*). Color is added with the lemon yellow feathers of the crested oropendula (*Psarocolius decumanus*), the yellow and black feathers of the yellow-rumped cacique (*Cassicus cela*), and the pink feathers of the roseate spoonbill (*Ajaja ajaia*). Striped feathers of brown, black, and white come from birds of prey, including the harpy eagle (*Harpia harpyja*) and the hawk family (*Accipitridae*). The irridescent green feathers are from the native domesticated Muscovy duck (*Cairina moschata*).[28]

Although the valuable feathers, especially those of the macaw, are always rare, they have at times been totally unavailable for use by the Karajá. Certain types of headdresses that were reported to be very common by Ehrenreich[29] were not found by Krause during his visit to the Karajá several years later.[30] Krause postulated that this was due to the deaths of many Karajá from a measles epidemic that swept through the Karajá villages at the turn of the century. Krause noted that he did not see ornaments, because none were made during the mourning period that followed these deaths. But it may have been the case that while Krause was in Brazil a scarcity of the feathers used in constructing these headdresses, especially those of macaws and parrots, not the mourning period itself, caused the absence of the ornaments. During an epidemic, trade networks that furnish macaw feathers, especially from the heavily forested region of the Shambioá, could easily break down. Similar shortages of red macaw feathers have been common since the 1960s, and the Karajá often use red cloth in lieu of red macaw feathers in constructing the ritual *aruanã* dance masks.[31]

While the natural color of Amazonian feathers is in many cases spectacular, techniques used by Amazonian Indians to artificially color feathers have been reported, although until recently these were never attributed to the Karajá. One process, known as *tapirage* (first noted by officials in French Guiana and called *tapirer*, "changing the color of bird feathers"), involves the use of various organic substances derived from fish and frogs, which are rubbed into the skin of young parrots.[32] When they have undergone such a process, the feathers contain more red and orange than normal, minimizing the greens and blues typical of parrot feathers.

Several recent examples of Karajá feather ornaments, however, show evidence of artificial coloration, not by tapirage, but by the use of a red aniline dye, which turns common chicken feathers into substitutes for red macaw feathers. Such dyed feathers are appearing with increasing frequency as the prized macaws become scarcer.

Once feathers have been obtained, the craftsman needs several other materials before he can begin his work: cotton, splints, bark cloth, and natural "glues." Cotton, which is grown in the village gardens of the Karajá, is spun into thread and used to secure small feathers to splints and to wrap and cover exposed areas of headdresses not decorated with feathers. Reed splints and midrib spines of palm leaves are used to construct the frames of various types of headdresses. Inner tree bark, which is beaten with flat stones and dried until it is soft and white,[33] is used to make bark-cloth fabric, which in turn is made into headbands to hold the large headdresses in place. Finally, down and feathers are often glued to an ornament or directly to the body, using various tree resins and beeswax.

Two general techniques of fastening feathers can be distinguished. The first involves tying feathers to cord, which is traditionally made of twisted palm-leaf fiber or cotton. The ends of the quills are trimmed and folded back over the cord and then tightly wrapped in order to secure them in position[34] (fig. 9).

A second technique involves wrapping the quills of small feathers onto reed splints to secure them.[35] In this manner, rows of single feather "petals" can be constructed (see crown headdress, no. 12), or single feathers can surround the splint to form flower-shaped rosettes (fig. 10). Both these techniques are incorporated in feather ornaments, which in turn play an essential role in the personal adornment and ritual activities of the Karajá.

Featherwork And Personal Adornment

Personal appearance on a ceremonial occasion is a matter of great importance to the Karajá, and much effort and care is given to it. The spectacular colors of the feathers in the Amazon lowlands make them an obvious material for personal adornment, and they are used in many ways, ranging from down that is glued to the skin with tree resins to headdresses three feet wide.

Such extravagant feather ornaments and feathered objects are usually reserved for the ceremonies that punctuate all important events, because feathers are difficult to obtain and are therefore valuable.[36] The feathered lances with the jaguar-bone tips, for example, are used only in ceremonies.[37]

Occasions for ceremonies include the visit of people from neighboring villages; success in war, fishing, or hunting; the initiation of a young boy into adolescence; or the capture of a young boy's first pirarucu fish or jaguar. In general, the use of feather ornaments for such ceremonies diminishes as a man grows older.

The largest of the Karajá ornaments is the head fan,[38] which is worn exclusively by boys and only on festive occasions, such as the reception of visitors or at wrestling ceremonies, the major intervillage sport.[39] These headdresses are flexible and when not in use can be folded into a small bundle and stored in the thatch wall of a hut. When they are to be worn, the wearer's hair is gathered at the back of his head into a knot, and the headdress is tied and secured to the hair with a chignon of bark cloth or palm wood. It is held in place by a bark-cloth band around the forehead in such a way that the back of the head is encircled with a multicolored fan of feathers (color plate 3B; nos. 2 and 3).

Fig. 8. Karajá nimbus headdress. Height:69 cm. Width:83 cm. No. 5. Long tail-feathers of the blue-and-yellow macaw contrast with white feathers of the great egret and dark feathers of the Muscovy duck. The U-shaped frame is made of reed splints fastened together with cotton cord that has been rubbed with white clay.

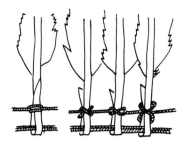

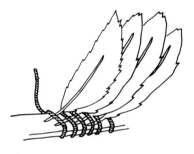

Fig. 9. One technique of fastening feathers involves folding the quill over a length of cord and tightly wrapping it to secure the feather in place. Cotton used for cordage is grown and spun in Karajá villages. After Ribeiro 1957:64.

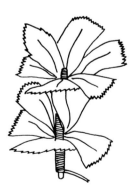

Fig. 10. Individual feather "petals" can be attached to reed or palm splints with cotton cord. When they are wrapped around such splints, feather "rosettes" are formed, which resemble flowers. After Ribeiro 1957:66.

The foundation for the head fan is made of cotton, which is grown and spun in Karajá villages. Splints of palm-leaf midrib spines are attached to this cotton base. Feather plumes are slipped over the midribs, presenting continuous bands of color on the front side of the fan. These contrasting zones of color are arranged so that light and dark areas alternate,[40] usually beginning with dark green Muscovy duck feathers closest to the head and building outward with white stork and egret feathers, the brown feathers of hawks and harpy eagles forming the outer zone. The palm-leaf midribs are covered with cotton cord toward the outer edge of the headdress. This accentuates the decorative feathers at the tips of the spines, usually brightly colored parrot, macaw, or spoonbill feathers.

The nimbus (color plate 3a) is another ceremonial headdress.[41] Its foundation is a double layer of U-shaped reed splints and palm-leaf midribs, between which the feathers are inserted in a radiating pattern. The rigid splint base secures these feathers tightly in place. The two layers of the base are tied together with cotton cord, which is often incorporated into the design of the headdress (nos. 6, 8, and 10). When craftsmen want to cover this essential cotton cord, they may insert clay between the splints (fig. 16; no. 4) or apply feather down over it with tree resin (no. 9).

Feathers such as those of the blue-and-yellow macaw are two-sided; that is, the front of the feather is often much more colorful than the back. Because the Karajá men, when wearing their best ceremonial attire, want to appear attractive when viewed from either front or back, the nimbus headdress is often made with a complete layer of colorful feathers on each side of the U-shaped base. The headdress therefore has no back side but two equally colorful faces decorated with feathers.

Like the head fan, the nimbus is tied to a bundle of hair at the back of the wearer's head. Feathers are again arranged in zones, but generally the nimbus is a smaller headdress. Its form is variable and includes those headdresses with a smooth rounded edge (no. 10), others with a three-cornered shape produced by long tail feathers (fig. 8; no. 5), and those with a spokelike effect caused by macaw tail feathers radiating directly from the U-shaped base (no. 7).

A third major type of Karajá headdress is the crown,[42] which consists of vertical splints attached to a circular base. Feather "petals" (fig. 10) and down are attached to these splints, and the top of the ornament is usually closed with a net, to which feathers are attached. The crowns (fig. 5; nos. 11, 12, and 13) are worn on top of the head and are usually made with red and yellow macaw feathers. Like other headdresses, they are worn on ceremonial occasions.

The Karajá use a variety of additional forms of head ornaments. One of these is a circular splint head ring (fig. 4; no. 18) with feather "petals." Ehrenreich writes that head rings are worn by young men when welcoming strangers to the village, as well as in everyday situations.[43]

Another very common type of headgear is the feather

cap, one of the few ornaments worn by both boys and girls.[44] For these caps, brightly colored feathers are tied directly to netting or on short reed splints in the form of feather rosettes (nos. 15 and 16.) The netted base fits snugly on the head and can be worn during most kinds of activity. When not in use they are turned inside-out and hung from the rafters for storage. Feather caps occasionally have a rigid basketry base in addition to netting (fig. 6; no. 17).

Although feather ornaments normally serve as decoration, they may function as marks of status as well. Among the Karajá, status is ordinarily derived from age and individual achievements, the different age statuses being denoted by varied personal ornaments. Among males, labrets (lip plugs) of a variety of materials and sizes denote elder or younger status.[45] Spool bracelets (fig. 24; no. 31), another status indicator, are made of woven cotton and are worn from infancy through adolescence. As a youngster grows, these bracelets are replaced with larger ones, which must be discarded at marriage. Spool bracelets may be worn again if the individual is divorced or the marriage partner dies and also while participating in wrestling matches.[46]

The age-grade status of children and adolescents is often marked by ear rosettes, which are worn in pierced ear lobes. Soon after birth the ears of infants of both sexes are pierced and ear rosettes are inserted. This first pair (no. 24) is made with parrot and macaw feathers and the very valuable incisor teeth of the capybara ("water pig"), which lives in the rivers of Amazonia. Although formerly abundant, capybaras have been hunted so intensively that they are now rare, and they are so valuable that two of the teeth can be traded for one canoe.[47]

According to Schultz, a few boys in the village, especially sons of shamans, traditionally wore capybara ear rosettes and other valuable ornaments every day.[48] Lipkind writes that these boys are said to have been members of a "chiefly lineage" and were given preferential treatment because they would one day take over leadership of the village.[49] Today, however, such boys dress up only for the benefit of outsiders, who must pay for the opportunity to photograph them.[50]

Fig. 11. A Karajá featherworker assembles a boy's head fan. This headdress, one of the most elaborate of Karajá ornaments, is made by an adult male for use by a younger relative at puberty.

Fig. 12. Karajá man's headband. Height:30 cm. Width:44 cm. No. 20. Two tail-feathers of the blue-and-yellow macaw are offset by yellow feathers of the crested oropendula. A single bird-of-prey feather is found in either half of the ornament. This headdress is worn by wrapping it around the head and tying it in place.

Fig. 13. Various ear rosettes worn in the pierced ear-lobes of children and adolescents. Length of longest:19 cm. Diameter of widest:7 cm. Smaller children wear ornaments decorated with the valuable incisor tooth of the capybara, *front*. No. 22. Adolescents normally wear ear ornaments adorned with pieces of shell and wax, *rear*. Nos. 21, 25, and 27.

The ear rosettes worn by adolescents differ from those of the younger children. A small disc of river clam shell, often decorated with a design of beeswax,[51] replaces the capybara teeth. In these ornaments, both red and yellow macaw feathers, as well as chicken feathers (no. 25), are often assembled in layers, resembling variegated flowers (no. 27). While the Karajá-proper place a wax dot in the middle of the shell disc (no. 21), the Shambioá have a wax cross in the middle (fig. 13; no. 25).[52] Reed ear ornaments of various colors continue to be worn after marriage, but they are not decorated with feathers.

One more ornament deserves mention: the belts worn by men while wrestling. These belts have a base of palm-leaf fiber or woven cotton, to which are attached many different types of feathers, as well as *Thevetia* nuts. Wrestling is the most important leisure-time activity for men and boys, and it takes place on the dance track. The atmosphere at wrestling matches is usually casual, and joking relationships prevail. Wrestling also often occurs when two villages get together and the best wrestlers from each village are given a great deal of acclaim.

Fig. 14. Wrestler's belt, Karajá. Length:55 cm. Height:19 cm. No. 29. Such belts are worn wrapped around the lower back and tied at the stomach. The cotton fabric has been painted, and various types of feathers and *Thevetia* nut shells hang from it.

Fig. 15. Wrestler's belt, Karajá.Length:76 cm. Height:16 cm. No. 30. This belt was made relatively recently, possibly for sale to tourists. Feathers of the cocoi heron, macaw, parrot, and cacique hang from a base of palm-leaf fiber.

Even when no ceremonies are taking place, the Karajá expend a great deal of energy on their personal appearance. Everyone bathes in the river each morning, and adults spend time combing and darkening their hair with palm oil. The combs (fig. 18; no. 34) are made of palm splints, which are tied together with cotton cord in a zigzag pattern and decorated with red macaw feathers and the shells of *Thevetia* nuts.

Personal appearance is also enhanced by the use of body paint of two colors: red from the covering of urucú seeds and black from juice of the genipa fruit. The same designs are used for men and women and consist of geometric lines on the torso, arms, and legs.[53] Paint is applied either with a fiber "brush" or with stamps cut in geometric patterns, made from the ends of reeds.

The Karajá, like other groups around the world, believe that ritual bleeding gives purity and strength to the body. Shamans claim that such bleeding allows them to "see farther, hear better, and catch more fish and game," as well as to be more lucky in love. To improve their health, every few months the legs and arms of men and some women are striated. The striator is made of a piece of gourd set with teeth of the dogfish. After this ritual bleeding, the wounds are cleaned with a palm leaf and rubbed with pepper juice, an astringent.[54]

Fig. 17. A Karajá feather headpiece of white stork feathers, tied to a splint of cotton cord. Height:32 cm. Width:20 cm. No. 14. Small yellow and red feathers have been tied to the larger feathers around the top of this ornament for additional color.

Fig. 16. Karajá nimbus headdress. Height:53 cm. Width:36 cm. No. 4. Like other feathered ornaments, this nimbus is worn by males. It is tied to the back of the head and held upright by a bark-cloth headband, shown in the picture, which wraps around the forehead. Two plumes adorn the top of the headdress, to which small macaw feathers have been tied as danglers.

Featherwork And Ritual

The importance of birds in the ritual life of Amazonia has been discussed by Zerries, who relates the spiritual world of many peoples in the lowlands closely to the bird world.[55] Karajá shamans have a soul that takes the form of a bird, and this allows them to fly to the place from which they derive their power.[56] Given the important spiritual role of birds, it is easy to understand that feathers take on significance. The red tail feathers of the macaw are commonly associated with shamanism throughout Amazonia, and many other types of feathers are also used in a ritual context.

Masks worn during the *aruanã* dances are an important ritual item made by the Karajá (no. 1). Such masks represent the spirits of different fish, reflecting their importance to the Karajá. Although sting rays and many types of fish are represented, the most common mask depicts the *aruanã* fish, identified by Dietschy[57] as *Osteoglossum bicirrhosum*. The dances are said to be rooted in the mythological origins of the Karajá, where it is said that a fish came to live with the people but then returned to its own element, the water.[58] After that, the people imitated the fish by creating elaborate dance outfits, consisting of the fish masks, buriti palm-fiber skirts, and rattles carried in the hands of the dancer, which are hidden from view by the fringe of the mask.

The *aruanã* masks themselves are considered very powerful and are never discussed with women,[59] who are not supposed to recognize the men of the village dressed up in the masks but are to believe that fish spirits are actually visiting their village. It is for this reason that the masks are often made in another village and assembled in secrecy, either inside or behind the men's hut. While being stored, they are the responsibility of one resident of the hut, the "master of ceremonies," who must above all protect them from the eyes of women.[60] Only men of adult status may wear the masks in the dances.

Fig. 19. A Karajá whistle, made from bird bone to which macaw feathers have been fastened; beeswax and cord were also used in constructing this musical instrument. Length:20 cm. Width:9 cm. No. 35.

Fig. 18. A Karajá comb. Height:15 cm. Width:24 cm. No. 34. Common in many parts of the Amazon, combs are made by wrapping palm-leaf midribs together with cotton, in the pattern shown. Further ornamentation is provided with *Thevetia* nut shells and feather tufts.

Each different mask has its own set of songs, as well as its own characteristics, normally ordered on an agelike scale:[61] some masks have youthful qualities reflected in energetic dancing and singing, while others appear to be older and require less vigorous dance steps.

The mask consists of a cylindrical bundle of reed splints decorated with tiny macaw feathers, which are applied in a mosaic pattern with beeswax. The pattern of this mosaic featherwork symbolizes the fish.[62] Under this bundle of splints is a basketry frame that supports the mask on the dancer's head. Above the cylinder are long decorative feathers and bark-wrapped projections also adorned with feathers. In preparation for ceremonies, the dancers are painted with red urucú and black genipa pigments, and they wrap their forearms with palm leaves.[63]

The aruanã dances are organized by pairs of sponsors, who, through their wives' kin, arrange to supply all the vegetable food for the ritual. Meat is obtained by communal hunting parties. Dancers often come from other villages to participate in an aruanã cycle, which may last from several days to several months. Tavener[64] notes that the dances may create a context wherein unmarried men have an excuse to visit a village for several months in the hope of finding a wife.

The men put on the dance masks secretly behind the men's hut (fig. 20). They are occasionally assisted by the wives of the sponsors, who must keep their eyes toward the ground and under no circumstances actually look into the hut itself. When the dancers are dressed, a special pair of dancers wearing masks without feathers are sent down the dance track calling the women of the village to assemble by the row of huts (fig. 23).

The aruanã dancers always leave the men's hut in pairs, shaking their rattles and singing songs while advancing along the dance track toward the women of the village, who have assembled near the huts or in the house of the wives of the sponsors (fig. 21). Once the masked dancers get near the group of women, they turn around and begin the journey back to the men's hut. Two women, their bodies painted in the geometric designs typical of the Karajá, follow the male dancers as they dance back toward the forbidden men's hut, never getting too close. When the masked dancers reach a certain point near the men's hut, they turn around and begin to dance back toward the village. The two women who had followed them begin dancing backward in the same direction, continuing to face the men's hut as they do so (fig. 22). When the male and female dancers get near the village, the two dancing females turn around and run to the group of women, ending the dance. The masked dancers, now far from the men's hut, walk back as another pair of men begin their trek. The aruanã dances take place almost every day and they last late into the night, or even through it, until the end of the dance cycle, when the entire masks are either destroyed by burning or disassembled, the feathers being stored for further use.[65]

Although children never participate in the aruanã dances, boys and girls learn their respective future roles by creating a model dance in the sand with dolls.[66] The boys stick tall hawk feathers in a circle in the sand to represent the forbidden men's hut. The aruanã dancers are represented by wooden or ceramic figures, which are placed within this circle. A second circle is drawn in the sand by the girls to represent the assembled group of adult women. Into this circle the girls place painted ceramic litjoko dolls.[67] The boys move their masked figures out of the men's-hut circle and make them "dance" toward the women while singing the aruanã songs. The girls make their dolls "dance," replicating the movements of adult Karajá women in real-life ceremonies. By playing this game, the children rehearse important aruanã dances and songs long before they are called upon to participate in actual ceremonies.

The Karajá And The Future

More and more Karajá are seeking livelihoods on ranches and in the commercial fishing industry that is developing in the area. As they become incorporated into the commercial economic system, the meaning of traditional life, ritual, and crafts changes or is lost. Many forms of headdresses no longer occur. Ear rosettes, once so important for marking age status, are now only occasionally worn by small children and are never made with capybara teeth. Aruanã dances still occur as often as before—perhaps more often. They are not officially discouraged, but they are often impeded by well-meant meddling by outsiders. A proposed fence, for example, designed to keep cattle from wandering into a Karajá village, was to be built across the dance track, cutting off the men's hut and making aruanã dances impossible.[68]

The Karajá are now considered wards of FUNAI (the Brazilian National Indian Foundation, previously SPI—Indian Protection Service), which set up the first post on Bananal Island in 1910 and in 1969 had five posts with a dozen employees.[69] In addition to their eight villages, many Karajá live at such posts or at church-related missions, preferring these areas to Brazilian towns or the ranches that are becoming numerous throughout the region.

In 1959, Bananal Island was made into a national park in order to preserve the environment necessary to maintain Karajá culture. The park itself is administered by the Parks Section of the Forest Service, not FUNAI. The Parks Section has only two officials in the area. Their job is to watch over eight thousand square miles of park land, but they are not provided with any transportation to do so. The result is the constant illegal grazing of tens of thousands of cattle on Indian land.[70]

Health is another very serious problem for the Karajá. Venereal disease, malaria, and tuberculosis are common. By 1969, only one post—Santa Isabel—had medically trained personnel. Two other posts lacked malaria pills; their medicine stocks consisted of free samples of medication for nerve disorders meant for urban doctors.[71]

Improved communication has opened the interior to outsiders. Weekly flights link the town of Santa Isabel with Goiánia and Brasília. Tourists from as far as Europe and North America come to stay at the hotel near Santa Isabel, where the Indians sell craft items including clay dolls, featherwork, and miniature canoes and weapons.[72]

The disappearance of the spectacular varieties of Karajá featherwork and their replacement by tourist items is one small element of the inevitable transformation of the Karajá peoples into an integrated portion of Brazilian society. Cultures being subjected to such rapid change have sometimes rallied and adapted to the new situation around them, and crafts have on occasion played important roles in maintaining an identity—the weavers of highland Ecuador come to mind. Where this process of change will lead in Brazil, however, remains to be seen.

Fig. 20. Men from several Karajá villages put on the costumes of the *aruanã* dance in secret behind the men's hut and an adjacent wall, shown here at left. The cylinder part of the mask is decorated with a feather mosaic, the pattern of which represents various fish.

Courtesy of Christopher Tavener

Fig. 21. View of a Karajá village showing huts and dance track as seen from the men's hut. Three pairs of men dressed in *aruanã* masks can be seen dancing. The dances take place year round, but they are especially frequent during the dry season and can have a duration of days or even weeks.

Courtesy of Christopher Tavener

Fig. 22. A pair of Karajá women and *aruanã* dancers on their final lap down the dance track. The women must continually face the forbidden men's hut, as they are doing in this picture. Because of this, they must dance backward in front of this pair of singing *aruanã* dancers.

Courtesy of Christopher Tavener

Fig. 23. A pair of women bring food in a gourd container to two masked dancers. The women are painted in typical geometric designs with genipa pigment and wear bark-cloth aprons. The masked dancers represent a special variety of *aruanã* dancer; they serve to make the dances go smoothly by bringing food, calling the village women to assemble, and so on.

Courtesy of Christopher Tavener

1. Metraux 1948:107.
2. Kietzman 1967:34.
3. Lipkind 1948:180.
4. Ehrenreich 1891:4.
5. Ehrenreich 1891:4-5.
6. von Königswald 1908:217.
7. Tavener 1973:443.
8. von Königswald 1908:217.
9. von Königswald 1908:217.
10. von Königswald 1908:218.
11. Lipkind 1948:181.
12. Lipkind 1948:181.
13. Hartmann 1973:16-21.
14. Krause 1908:108; von Königswald 1908:237.
15. Schultz 1961:81.
16. von Königswald 1908:237.
17. von Königswald 1908:237.
18. von Königswald 1908:237.
19. Lipkind 1948:186.
20. von Königswald 1908:238.
21. von Königswald 1908:237.
22. Lipkind 1948:186.
23. Lipkind 1948:186.
24. Krause 1908:108.
25. Schultz 1961:71.
26. von Königswald 1908:234.
27. Lipkind 1948:181.
28. Meyer de Schauensee 1966.
29. Ehrenreich 1891:21.
30. Krause 1908:98.
31. Tavener, personal communication.
32. Metraux 1944:252-253.
33. Lipkind 1948:184.
34. Ribeiro 1957:64.
35. Ribeiro 1957:66.
36. von Königswald 1908:223.
37. Lipkind 1948:181.
38. Baxter 1968:88
39. Krause 1911:234.
40. Krause 1911:232.
41. Baxter 1968:78.
42. Baxter 1968:93.
43. Ehrenreich 1891:22.
44. Krause 1911:232.
45. Krause 1911:220.
46. Krause 1911:226.
47. Krause 1911:224.
48. Schultz 1962:26.
49. Lipkind 1948:186.
50. Schultz 1962:26.
51. Krause 1911:225.
52. von Königswald 1908:219.
53. Krause 1911:214.
54. Schultz 1961:68.
55. Zerries 1977.
56. Zerries 1977:281.
57. Dietschy 1970.
58. Schultz 1962:22.
59. Schultz 1961:81.
60. Schultz 1962:25.
61. Tavener, personal communication.
62. Krause 1908:101.
63. Krause 1908:103.
64. Tavener, personal communication.
65. Krause 1908:108; Tavener, personal communication.
66. Krause 1908:99.
67. Hartmann 1973.
68. Tavener 1973:454.
69. Tavener 1973:433.
70. Tavener 1973:435-436.
71. Tavener 1973:440.
72. Tavener 1973:447.

Fig. 24. Karajá armspool bracelets decorated with glass beads and macaw feathers. Height:16 cm. Width:11 cm. No. 31. These bracelets, worn from infancy through marriage, are woven with cotton and painted with red urucu paint. After marriage, they may be worn only while wrestling, or if the marriage ends in divorce or in the death of the spouse.

REFERENCES

Baxter, David N. P.
　1968　Brazilian Feather Headdresses: A Type-Variety Classification of Specimens from Central and Northeastern Brazil. Unpublished Master's Thesis. University of Calgary.

Dietschy, Hans
　1970　Die Tanzmasken der Karaja-Indianer Zentralbrasiliens und der Aruanã-Fisch. *In* Schweizerische Gesellschaft für Anthropologie und Ethnologie Bulletin 47:48-53.

Ehrenreich, P.
　1891　Beiträge zur Völkerkunde Brasiliens. Veröffentlichungen aus dem Königlichen Museum für Völkerkunde, Vol. 2.

Hartmann, Günther
　1973　Litjoko, Puppen der Karajá. Veröffentlichungen des Museums für Völkerkunde Berlin, No. 23.

Kietzman, Dale W.
　1967　Indians and Culture Areas of Twentieth-Century Brazil. *In* Indians of Brazil in the Twentieth Century. Janice H. Hopper, ed. Pp. 1-68. Washington, D.C.: Institute for Cross-Cultural Research.

Königswald, Gustav von
　1908　Die Caraja Indianer. Globus 94:217-223, 232-238.

Krause, Fritz
　1908　Tanzmaskennachbildungen Vom Mittleren Araguaya. Jahrbuch des Museums für Völkerkunde zu Leipzig III:97-122.
　1911　In den Wildnissen Brasiliens. Leipzig: R. Voightländer Verlag.

Lipkind, William
　1948　The Caraja. *In* Handbook of South American Indians. Vol. 3. Julian Steward, ed. Pp. 179-192. Bureau of American Ethnology Bulletin 143. Washington, D.C.: Smithsonian Institution.

Metraux, Alfred
　1944　Tapirage, A Biological Discovery of South American Indians. Proceedings of the Washington Academy of Sciences 34 (8):252-254.
　1948　The Tupinamba. *In* Handbook of South American Indians. Vol. 3. Julian Steward, ed. Pp. 95-133. Bureau of American Ethnology Bulletin 143. Washington, D.C.: Smithsonian Institution.

Meyer de Schauensee, Rodolphe
　1966　The Species of Birds of South America and Their Distributions. Narberth, Pa.: Livingston Publishing Company.

Ribeiro, Berta G.
　1957　Bases para uma Classificacão dos Adornos Pulmarios dos Indíos do Brasil. Rio de Janeiro: Museu Nacional.

Schultz, Harald.
　1961　Blue-eyed Indian. National Geographic: 120 (1):65-89.
　1962　Hombu. New York: Macmillan & Co.

Tavener, Christopher
　1973　The Karajá and the Brazilian Frontier. *In* Peoples and Cultures of Native South America. Dan Gross, ed. Pp. 433-462. Garden City: Natural History Press.

Zerries, Otto
　1977　Die Bedeutung des Federschmucks des Südamerikanischen Schamanen und dessen Beziehung zur Vogelwelt. Paideuma 23:227-324.

ACKNOWLEDGMENTS

I am indebted to a number of people who enthusiastically shared with me their knowledge of the region and of the Karajá, including John Farrand of the Ornithology Department, American Museum of Natural History; Christopher Tavener, who generously provided unique information and photographs based on field work among the Karajá; and especially Gertrude Dole, whose insight and critical suggestions were invaluable to this paper. I remain, of course, responsible for any errors.

Fig. 25. Feather caps for use by children, and adolescents. *A*, cap right side out. Height:15 cm. Width:27 cm. No. 15; *B*, cap turned inside out. Height:24 cm. Width:20 cm. No. 16. These caps are common in Amazonia and are worn by both boys and girls. When worn, the netted base fits snugly on the head. When stored, the cap is reversed in order to protect the feathers.

Fig. 26. Man's nimbus headdress. Height:53 cm. Width:70 cm. No. 9. The U-shaped base of this ornament is constructed with palm-leaf midribs to which down has been fastened with an adhesive made of tree resin.

the CARVER

THE HAIDA OF THE NORTHWEST COAST

JAMES G. E. SMITH

The Pacific Northwest Coast was the scene of one of the most highly developed art styles to be found among any hunters, gatherers, and fishermen of the world. Without benefit of domesticated plants or animals, other than the dog, a complex society developed before the coming of the Europeans, characterized politically by chiefdoms, that was unparalleled in the ethnographic record. To understand the richness and meaning of the art, particularly as it was expressed in carving, it is necessary to view the artisan and his product in relation to the traditional culture as well as to the historical events in the nineteenth century.

Environment

The complexity of the Haida[1] culture that flourished in the nineteenth century was made possible by the extraordinary, lush habitat in which they lived. In the temperate climate of the Queen Charlotte Islands of British Columbia and Prince of Wales Island in Alaska, the Haida enjoyed a world in which the natural abundance of the land and sea provided them with the necessities of life and many of the luxuries as well. In the sea were many highly valued mammals, including several species of whale and seal, sea lions, and porpoises, which not only provided them with food and hides but such raw materials as bone and ivory. The pelt of the sea otter was of great value originally as a symbol of wealth among the Haida, but with the advent of the fur trade in the late eighteenth century the pelts became much desired in Europe and China and were thus extremely important in Haida society. The sea also provided a variety of fish, the most important of which were the halibut and salmon; but there were also cod, herring, and other species. The regularity of the salmon's spawning season provided a dependable and rich harvest. On rare occasions of food scarcity, shellfish, especially the clam, cockle, mussel, and crab, were an unfailing emergency resource. Big game animals, with the exception of the deer (until the early nineteenth century), were relatively scarce on the islands, but the bear was important for its meat and hide, although it was even more significant for its symbolic and ritual meaning. Beaver, ermine, and marten were killed for their valuable fur. A variety of berries was seasonally available, including cranberries, huckleberries, salal berries, salmon berries, strawberries, and others. Edible roots, seaweed, and the inner bark of the alder and spruce also served as food. Fowl were abundant and included geese, duck, heron, grouse, eagle, raven, and about one hundred other species.

The islands were covered with a magnificent forest, with many species of trees represented.[2] The most important to the Haida were cedar, hemlock, and spruce, but there were some willows, alder, pine, and yew as well.[3] The ocean currents were responsible for the moderate climate that permitted trees to grow to a great height—the raw material for the great houses, monumental sculpture, and the ocean-going canoes. It is not surprising, then, that wood was among the most utilized of natural resources and that it formed the basis

Fig. 1. Chief of Raven clan, Haida, Skidegate, Queen Charlotte Islands, British Columbia, Canada, E. S. Curtis, photographer.

Fig. 2. Map of Haida territory and neighboring groups.

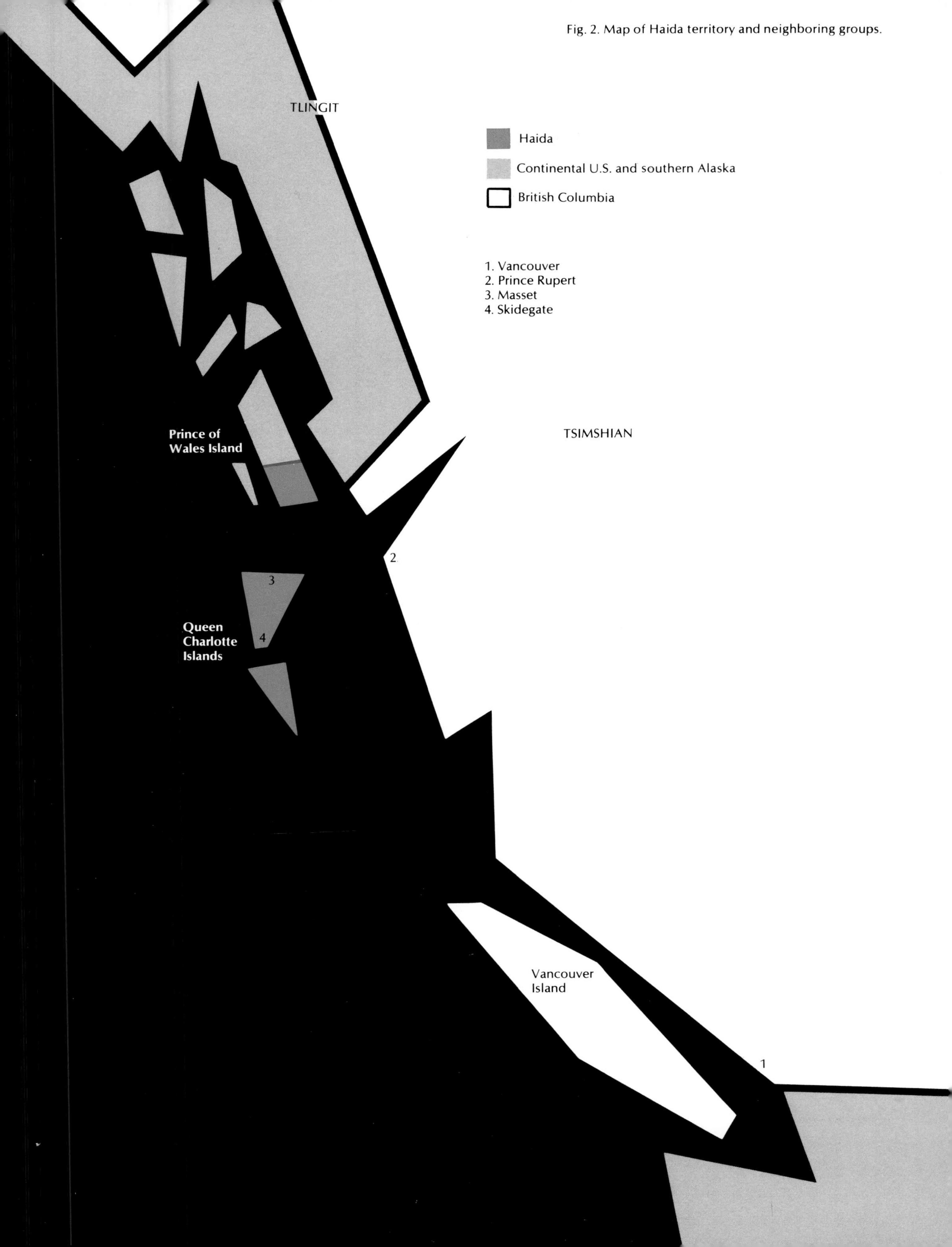

TLINGIT

■ Haida

■ Continental U.S. and southern Alaska

□ British Columbia

1. Vancouver
2. Prince Rupert
3. Masset
4. Skidegate

Prince of
Wales Island

TSIMSHIAN

2

3

Queen
Charlotte
Islands

4

Vancouver
Island

1

Fig. 3. Chief's house, Haida, Masset, Queen Charlotte Islands, British Columbia, Canada, R. Maynard, photographer, 1883.

Fig. 4. Model of a war canoe, with a carved and painted wolf on the bows, Haida, Prince of Wales Island, Alaska, U.S.A. Height:20 cm. Length:94.5 cm. Width:16.5 cm. No. 8. Full-sized war canoes measured up to seventy feet in length and eight in beam and were propelled by both a sail and paddles. Haida war expeditions ventured as far as present-day Victoria, on Vancouver Island.

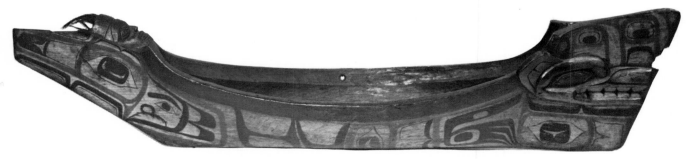

for the efflorescence of their art. Various types of igneous rock were utilized as tools and weapons, and argillite and nephrite were other valued materials for the craftsman.

Certain very highly valued raw materials, such as copper, blue haliotis shell, and the horn of mountain sheep and goats, did not occur in the islands but were obtained by barter: copper was found in the land of the neighboring Tlingit; and haliotis shell came from the California coast and, later, Hawaii. Chilkat blankets with elaborate designs, woven from mountain goat wool and cedar bark, were obtained from the Tlingit, and the highly prized candlefish (eulachon) oil came from the Tsimshian. Slaves were obtained by trade or were captured in war. With their trading partners the Haida exchanged their fine canoes, carvings, and other items.

As islanders, the Haida were adventurous seafarers, carrying on trade and warfare with their mainland enemies so that they were long termed the "vikings" of the coast.[4] Their raids went as far as Victoria, on Vancouver Island. Their fleets consisted of ocean-going canoes (nos. 7 and 8) up to seventy feet in length and eight in beam, capable of carrying thirty men and cargo, fitted with sails, made from a single log.[5] Even though they were perpetually at war with the Tlingit and Tsimshian (as well as other tribes), Haida chiefs maintained trading partnerships, similar to blood brotherhoods, with chiefs of their equivalent clans entitled to the same clan crests, in the enemy villages. The fictive kinship provided for mutual protection and hospitality. As seamen, some Haida accompanied American and British ships trading with Hawaii and China, and from the sailors they learned scrimshaw carving.

Seasonal Cycle

The seasonal cycle of the Haida was adapted to the habitat. Summers were spent at small, dispersed camps for hunting and fishing. Summer was the time of the salmon runs, and the salmon were taken by dragnets and weirs or with spears and harpoons. Halibut were taken in large numbers between March and November, with hook and line, the hook (no. 42) often carved with symbols appropriate to the task. Great quantities of fish were smoked or dried. The flesh and fat of bear and deer, and bark, berries, seaweed, and shellfish were preserved, and all were stored in handsomely carved and decorated boxes. Oil and grease from cod, herring, salmon, and marine animals, or the favored candlefish oil, were stored in special, elaborately decorated containers (no. 31) and served in special bowls. During the summer, the major effort of everyone was devoted to accruing a great surplus of food for the winter season and its ceremonials.[6]

For most of the year the Haida lived in villages located along the shore, often but not invariably in a single row. The individual houses were large, an average one measuring forty feet in depth and thirty in width, and those of important chiefs were considerably larger. The houses were made of cedar planks, split from the logs with stone wedges. The massive house posts that supported the structures were carved in the form of important legendary creatures, and other posts were carved and painted with the crests of the owners. From about 1840 to 1880 the imposing "totem poles"[7] were erected before the houses (fig. 3). These poles were elaborately carved and painted with the inherited heraldic crests of the house owner and his wife. Other carved and decorated poles were of a mortuary or commemorative nature. The interior of the house typically was excavated to provide three platforms within. The winter ceremonies and potlaches occurred in the great houses and along the shores.

Social Organization

Haida society was organized in an elaborate hierarchy, with every individual ranked in comparison to all others. The system of ranking, validated by the famous "potlatch," was the most important institution of the Haida and other Northwest Coast tribes. At the top of the hierarchy were the clan chiefs, who in aboriginal times were also the town chiefs. But the once-localized clans were dispersed following the advent of the Europeans, and the role of town chief was then given to the richest and most powerful chief of the largest and most important clan within the community, who combined the functions of town chief and clan head. Of somewhat lesser importance were the house chiefs, the heads of lineages within the clans, from whom the town and clan chiefs were chosen. The nobility, however, was not limited to the chiefs of town, clan, and house, for anyone who had inherited a title, crest, or name that was validated by one or more potlatches had status as a member of the nobility, without having chiefly authority. Indeed, it has been estimated that only ten percent of the Haida were commoners, and since the commoners were related to nobles, their lot was not necessarily poor, and at least some had the potential to enter the ranking system. Within the nobility, all were individually ranked, for no two people were completely equal. An individual's rank depended upon the prestige and number of inherited titles and crests, validated by the number and quality of the potlatches given by his parents.[8]

There were elaborate and ostentatious symbols of rank for the chiefs and nobility: already mentioned were the totem poles, house posts, and commemorative poles that stood within or outside the great houses; and wearing apparel also indicated rank. Carved helmets (fig. 12) not only provided some protection in warfare but proclaimed the important crests of the owner's lineage. The ceremonial headdress—often combining carved and painted wood inlaid with haliotis shell, surmounted with sea-lion bristles and eagle down, and backed with hanging ermine —symbolized clan chieftainship (color plate 5a). Ceremonial staffs were carved with the crests of the owner's lineage and were used in the formalities and dances of the potlatch (nos. 9, 10, and 11). The valuable and imported Chilkat blanket was another symbol of rank and status.

Descent and inheritance were based on exogamous matrilineal moieties, clans, and lineages. An individual did not inherit from his father but from his mother's brothers, and primary social affiliations were among kin based on descent through the female line. All Haida were divided into two moieties (from an Old French word meaning *half*), the Eagle and the Raven, which had as their principal function the regulation of marriage, for members of the same moiety could not intermarry. Each moiety was made up of about twenty matrilineal clans, which were, like individuals, ranked according to the titles and crests transmitted from generation to generation. A clan consisted of individuals tracing their social descent through the mother's line to a common ancestor, real or mythical, in the distant past. An individual was expected to marry a person of equivalent status from a clan of similar rank in the opposite moiety, with preference going to one standing in the real or classificatory relationship of father's sister's daughter or, in the case in which chieftainship was to be inherited, to the mother's brother's daughter. (A classificatory relationship is one in which a number of collaterally related individuals are classed together as if they were lineal kin; as, for example, father and father's brothers were termed "father," mother's sisters classed as "mother," or certain "cousins" called brother or sister. In other categories the concept of generation was disregarded.) Lineages, which consisted of persons who traced their genealogical connections to a common matrilineal ancestor, were ranked in a fashion similar to clans, as were the multigenerational extended families that occupied the great houses.[9]

Although clan and town chiefs enjoyed great prestige and *authority*, they held *power* only over the members of their own households. Their authority rested upon their wealth, prestige, and personality. Normally, the chiefs could rely on the support of their house chiefs, but they lacked the power to command them or to punish insubordination.[10]

At the very bottom of the social hierarchy were the slaves, usually war captives, although some were obtained by barter from other tribes and some were given as gifts in potlatches or in peacemaking activities.[11] Slaves were without rights and were committed to perform the menial tasks of the household, leaving their masters ample time for ceremonial and creative activities. To be enslaved was to receive a stigma that no ransom, however great, could entirely erase, and thus there was little incentive for many to attempt escape. Aside from performing menial activities beneath the dignity of the chiefs, the slaves were of great value as indicators of wealth and status. Some were killed at potlatches to demonstrate the wealth of the host, while others were given as gifts. Some were sacrificed at the time of construction of a new house, and, among the Northern Haida, others were crushed in the hole prepared for the erection of a new totem pole. Special knives (no. 32), usually of stone, were used to ceremonially dispatch slaves. It was estimated that in 1841 about one-third of the population of the Northwest

Coast were slaves.[12]

Within their localized segments, the clans had recognized rights to the exploitation of certain types of land. A clan may have had, for example, the right to certain hunting territories, berry patches, fishing areas, town and summer camp sites, or to beaches where whales drifted ashore. Far more important than material possessions was the right to incorporeal property. Most important of this form of property was the right of a member to use the crests belonging to the clan, but it also included a fund of personal names, ceremonial names, ceremonies, songs, and dances.[13] A man's personal property was inherited by his sister's son, following the matrilineal principle, but the deceased's successor was required to give a commemorative potlatch, in which the inherited property was distributed to guests of the moiety opposite that of the host.[14]

Standing somewhat outside the main hierarchy were the shamans, or medicine men. The shamans, who were sometimes women, typically received their calling from dreams and visions, followed by training from established shamans. The apprenticeship of a shaman was usually served, in the case of a man, with his mother's brother, real or classificatory; or by a woman, with her mother. Spiritual power was obtained through communion with spirit helpers, usually animals, in dreams and visions. These spirit helpers included the spirits of Otter, Mink, Hawk, Salmon, Bullhead, Bear, Moon, Sweathouse, and the Canoe (fig. 20). The distinctive regalia of the shaman (nos. 2, 48) included a fringed and decorated Chilkat blanket worn as a skirt, a bone charm through the septum, a rattle in one hand and another bone charm in the other. Over his head he wore the skin of a spirit helper. Unlike ordinary men, the shaman never cut his hair, for it was believed this would destroy his powers. The shaman's rattle (color plate 6b) was often elaborately carved and painted. The "soul catchers," bone tubes carved and inlaid with haliotis (fig. 11), were used to draw from the patient's body the evil spirit that was causing a disability or to capture the souls of the enemy when the shaman accompanied a war expedition. Special wands or staffs (no. 1) were carried by shamans, and other amulets (no. 4) and charms, often elaborately carved, were used in their rituals.[15]

As indicated above, Haida society placed a high value on the accumulation of wealth and, through wealth, the achievement of high status. Yet wealth afforded prestige only when it was given away in the institution of the potlatch; retained, it had no meaning and did not affect status.

The Potlatch

The potlatch as the mechanism of validating rank was central to Haida culture, and hence it requires some explanation. The potlatch was a ceremonial event in which vast quantities of wealth were distributed to the invited guests, most frequently to validate accession to a title, crest, or chieftainship. Among the Haida there were five different potlatches, ranked in order of importance. The most important of these was held on the occasion of the completion of a new house, for at this time the owner became a house chief. The potlatch often required many years of preparation, including the accumulation of the food for the guests and the gifts for distribution. The latter included otter furs, carved dishes (nos. 29, 30) and boxes (no. 35), coppers (fig. 21) in the form of a shield, and canoes and slaves. With the introduction of the fur trade, blankets from the Hudson's Bay Company, guns, ammunition, and other items of European origin were added to the inventory.

The potlatch was given by a man but on behalf of his wife. The preparations were elaborate. A year before the date established for the potlatch—following the basic accumulation of the wealth to be distributed—the wife lent blankets, furs, and other valuables to her kin, who were required to return them with one hundred percent interest at the time of the ceremony. Long before the established date, the host, on behalf of his wife, visited surrounding villages and issued invitations to the moiety opposite to his wife—that is, to members of his moiety. The guests would assemble at that time and remain the winter, working for their host and hostess, for it was the guests who contributed the labor for the construction of the house. During this period they were feasted by the hostess and her clansmen and entertained with dances, the ceremonial reenactment of legendary events, and other activities. When the house was completed, the formal potlatch was given. The guests arrived in formal attire, entered the new house in order of rank, and were seated and served in accord with strict protocol. After the feast, which was served in the finest and most elaborately carved dishes and vessels, the host and hostess in ceremonial dress conferred on their children the privileged names of their clan. The ceremonial names of the guests were then called out, in order of rank, and the property was distributed in quality and quantity according to protocol. By denuding himself of the accumulated wealth, the host had become a house chief, a man of political rank and great prestige. The children of the hostess were assured of social status, and her clan gained prestige.[16]

Other potlatches were somewhat less important. The erection of a totem pole following the death of a house chief symbolized the accession of the new chief, and the potlatch it occasioned was next in importance to a house-building potlatch. A lesser potlatch was given for the dedication of a mortuary pole in memory of a deceased chief and was hosted by his successor. Of still lesser significance was the vengeance potlatch, occasioned by a real or imagined slight or humiliation, for a Haida noble was very conscious of his social position. A face-saving potlatch was sometimes given by a person of high status to prevent his being ridiculed for a minor misfortune.[17]

Fig. 5. Oil dish of carved and painted wood, inlaid with bead and bone panels, with two bears facing one another, Haida, Queen Charlotte Islands, British Columbia, Canada. Height:19.5 cm. Length:48.4 cm. Width:19.5 cm. No. 31.

Early visitors to the Haida were aware of the potlatch, but few understood its significance and meaning in the social structure. With the arrival of the missionaries, it became thoroughly misunderstood. The first missionary to the Haida, W. H. Collison, who arrived in 1876 and remained for forty years, was aware of the pertinence of the potlatch to the system of crests but regarded it as wasteful and a barrier to industry and progress.[18] The positive aspects of the potlatch and ranking system were not comprehended. The early observers did not see a system of reciprocity that held Haida society together; they failed to note the economic redistribution that occurred; and they were unaware of how kinship ties were strengthened or of how hostility and tension were channeled into socially useful service.

The Coming Of The Europeans

In the late eighteenth century, when the Europeans arrived and provided firsthand accounts of Haida society, the culture and crafts were already highly developed, with the art style conventionalized into a standardized iconography.[19] There is evidence that carving in stone has a history of three millennia along the Coast;[20] and one may surmise that wood, bone, ivory, antler, and other materials were carved and decorated long before the advent of the Europeans, although evidence is lacking because of the rapid decomposition of these materials in the humid environment.

One remarkable aspect of Haida art was that it was created with a stone, bone, and antler technology.[21] Igneous rock was used for making maul heads (no. 40)—which were themselves carved—for adzes, wedges, and chisels. Nephrite or jadeite was used for pick-axe or planing blades, and bone and antler were used in a variety of tools. Iron was apparently known and in use before the first records of European discoverers were made,[22] perhaps obtained from sources in Siberia and the earliest Russian settlements in Alaska; and perhaps some was traded north from the Spanish outposts. With regular direct trade established toward the end of the eighteenth century, metal axes, adzes (no. 37), knife blades, and planes (no. 38) became abundant, and innovations in the carver's craft occurred. But if a new technology permitted the efflorescence of the arts and crafts, other features introduced by the Europeans ultimately had dire consequences for Haida society and its institutions.

Sea otter and several species of seal abounded in the waters around the Queen Charlotte Islands and led to a flourishing fur trade that temporarily enriched the Haida. In addition to iron and steel knives, axes, and other tools, in return for their furs the Haida obtained guns, ammunition, blankets, and cloth, as well as silver and gold. The scarce and valuable native copper used in the manufacture of fighting knives (no. 19) and ceremonial coppers was replaced by an abundant imported variety.

It was not only the furs that were valued by the newcomers, for the carvings attracted attention at an early date and were collected as curios by the naval

Fig. 6. Horn soapberry spoon, carved with the likeness of the Dogfish (shark) and a human face, Haida, British Columbia, Canada, and Alaska, U.S.A. Length:39.3 cm. No. 41. This flat soapberry spoon was used in eating the berries, which were whipped into a froth.

Fig. 7. Elaborately carved wooden ladle, probably most frequently used during potlatches, Haida, British Columbia, Canada, and Alaska, U.S.A. Length:72.7 cm. No. 21. This ladle is carved with the Bear, Hawk, Fish, and Hawk crests.

personnel, government officials, fur traders, and the crews of the trading and whaling vessels that visited the islands. By the 1820s the sea otter was virtually extinct, the fur trade dead; and the carved curios, now made for a commercial market and eventually for museums, became an important supplement to the traditional economy. By 1821 Haida carvers had begun to work in argillite, a soft slate that hardened with exposure to air. Argillite carving was made possible by the new steel tools and was stimulated by a rapidly developing market. About the same time, scrimshaw was adopted by the Haida from the sailors whom they accompanied on voyages to the Far East or observed aboard the ships in the islands. The splendid totem poles, for which the Haida were justifiably famed, are also of this period. They were descended from more modest posts recorded by the initial explorers and were probably due in part to the increased use of steel tools that made such monumental sculpture feasible.

While the economy and traditional institutions flourished for several generations after European discovery, other changes brought profound consequences. The earliest but continuing factor that induced demographic and social change was the introduction of epidemic diseases, particularly smallpox and the ubiquitous tuberculosis; and the native peoples possessed neither prior exposure nor immunity to any of them. Smallpox was probably first introduced from Russian Alaska, but there were recurrent epidemics introduced from the Coast.[23] The extent of these disasters is indicated by comparison of population estimates. In 1841 the Haida were estimated to number more than eight thousand, but by the end of the century only about eight hundred remained, many of whom were descended from mixed marriages.[24] The decline in population was probably even greater, for the estimate of 1841 was made after the initial epidemics had occurred. Through much of the nineteenth century the number of titles and crests remained constant, but as the mortality from disease reduced the population, they were inherited by an ever-decreasing number of heirs. Although the modest posts of the eighteenth century[25] gave rise to the great poles of the period 1840 to 1880, which has been referred to as the "golden age" of totem pole construction,[26] the evidence suggests that the enormous death rate required construction of new poles, some individuals inheriting so many crests that not all of them could be included on the modest poles of the past. Rather than a golden age, the apparent efflorescence of the totem pole carvers represents the last convulsions of traditional Haida culture. Moreover, the declining population meant the construction of fewer great houses with attendant ceremony; fewer chiefs, but each with more heraldic emblems; and more nobles and fewer commoners. Outside authorities prevented warfare and the enslavement of captives, and slavery was abolished. The abolition of slavery destroyed the economic basis for the leisure class, the producers of the arts and crafts for which the peoples of the Northwest Coast had become famous. Many villages were abandoned

throughout the Queen Charlotte Islands, and in the 1890s the remaining population largely resettled in the towns of Masset and Skidegate.

The last decades of the nineteenth century witnessed a final catastrophic blow to traditional Haida culture. In 1876 the Christian missionary Collison[27] began the process of religious conversion. His success as a missionary was aided by his possession of the vaccine against smallpox, which was successful in preventing the recurrent spread of the disease among the Haida. His success, where the traditional shamans had failed, led to the adoption of Christianity by many Haida and also undermined the authority of the shamans, who had naturally opposed the missionary effort. The rich symbolism of the inherited crests, the myths and legends associated with particular clans and lineages, became increasingly irrelevant to the social life of the Haida of the late nineteenth century. The traditional subsistence economy also changed, for by the end of the century the Haida of Masset and Skidegate were seasonally employed as wage laborers in the salmon canneries of the mainland.[28] Organization by moiety, clan, lineage, and extended family was further weakened by reorganization in the direction of the self-sufficient nuclear family oriented toward participation in the national industrial economy.

Fig. 8. Ceremonial "slave killer" knife of carved and polished stone, with a human face on the end of the handle, Haida, Queen Charlotte Islands, British Columbia, Canada. Length: 37.6 cm. No. 32. Knives such as this, or others in the shape of a pick axe, were used to dispatch slaves at the time of a potlatch and thus demonstrate the disregard for property on the part of the owner.

Fig. 9. A ladle made of carved mountain-sheep horn, with the handle representing the Raven, Haida, Queen Charlotte Islands, British Columbia, Canada. Length:59.3 cm. No. 24.

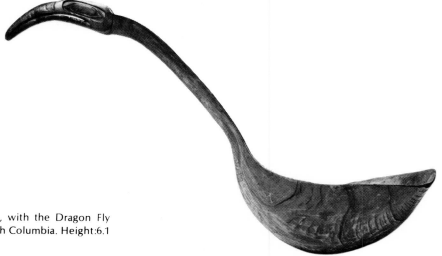

Fig. 10. Carved wooden child's feast dish, with the Dragon Fly crest, Haida, Queen Charlotte Islands, British Columbia. Height:6.1 cm. Length:35 cm. Width:12.5 cm. No. 27.

Fig. 11. Shaman's "soul catcher," made of carved bone inlaid with haliotis shell, Haida, British Columbia, Canada, and Alaska, U.S.A. Height:3.8 cm. Length:15.7 cm. Width:3.2 cm. No. 5. The "soul catcher" was used by the shaman on war expeditions to capture the spirits of the enemy.

Fig. 12. Carved and painted wooden chief's ceremonial helmet, Haida, Prince of Wales Island, Alaska, U.S.A. Height:53 cm. Diameter:53.5 cm. No. 15. Ceremonial helmets were worn by chiefs on occasions of war, when they provided some protection but primarily served to identify the leader, and in the villages as symbols of rank. This helmet is marked with the head of a Bear crest and the dorsal fin of the Killer Whale crest.

The Northwest Coast Art Style

The art forms of the Northwest Coast were fully developed at the time of European discovery, reaching an intellectual and aesthetic zenith among the northern tribes of the Haida, Tlingit, and Tsimshian. A fascinating aspect of the art was the extent to which it permeated all facets of material culture and was related to the social structure and the economy, to the sense of history and the rich oral tradition embodying myth and legend, and to the ceremonial cycle of the winter season. The same conventional symbols were carved, engraved, inlaid, and painted on antler, bone, copper, gold, silver, stone, and wood; they were woven into baskets, hats, mats, and raincoats, used in traditional cloth and European imports, and tattooed on the body. Almost all objects, from the great war canoes to the small amulet of the shaman, from the most utilitarian halibut hook or maul to the ceremonial headdress or totem pole, received decorative treatment from the skilled and gifted artisans.

The art of the Coast received attention in the period of initial European exploration. The earliest explorers in the late eighteenth century, whose pertinent comments have been extensively quoted by Barbeau,[29] were impressed by the "grotesque" figures of the stylized masks and other objects. Despite this, the high craftsmanship was immediately recognized. These objects immediately began to be collected as curios, and collection continued at an accelerating pace, with gradual recognition of their aesthetic qualities. Franz Boas,[30] the founder of academic anthropology in North America, was the first to provide detailed analysis of the style of Northwest Coast art. For decades, however, the products of the Coast remained primarily as ethnological specimens in museum exhibits or storage areas. It was not until 1946 that the first exhibit devoted exclusively to the art of the Northwest Coast was mounted in an art gallery, in which the objects were displayed as autonomous works of art, removed from their ethnological context.[31] Since then the art of the Northwest Coast has been available to the public on a much greater scale. Lévi-Strauss,[32] the preeminent French anthropologist, published an enthusiastic report on the Northwest Coast art in the exhibits of the American Museum of Natural History, combining the insight of the anthropologist with the imagination of the artist. Since 1950,[33] the art of the Northwest Coast has been made available to a larger public through particular exhibits, such as *Arts of the Raven*[34] or *Objects of Bright Pride*,[35] now traveling to major cities in North America, or as a significant part of other exhibits devoted to the arts of the American Indians in general.

Interest in the form and style of Northwest Coast art continued after Boas's seminal works of the early twentieth century. Marius Barbeau[36] was interested in the carvers of totem poles, in argillite carvings illustrating myths and legends, and in the representation of shamans and their activities. John and Carolyn Smyly[37] have documented the carved totem poles of one village, Skedans, in the Queen Charlotte Islands. More

important, Holm[38] and Holm and Reid,[39] the latter a Haida carver, have devoted themselves to studying the underlying principles of form, style, and aesthetics of this art tradition.

Some early explorers described the Northwest Coast objects as grotesque, but distortions from realistic or naturalistic representation followed strict rules. The rules, when understood, render most of the creatures readily identifiable and make possible an appreciation of the artisans' intent.

It must be emphasized that the art of the Coast is based on a tradition of carving and painting wood. This remains true regardless of the raw material used—ivory, bone, stone, woven material or whatever else is decorated. Haida art is essentially decorative and representational, and it is based on a two-dimensional concept, even when the object is three dimensional.

Fig. 13. Two spoons, with various crests carved on the handles, Haida, British Columbia, Canada, and Alaska, U.S.A. *A*, spoon of mountain-goat horn with haliotis inlay and copper studs, with Dragon Fly, and Beaver crests and unidentifiable figure. Length:25.5 cm. *B*, spoon of carved mountain-goat horn with the Dogfish, Wolf, Eagle, Bear, and Raven crests. Length:18 cm. Nos. 25, and 26.

Fig. 14. Ceremonial fighting knife, made of copper with a wooden handle, Haida, British Columbia, Canada, and Alaska, U.S.A. Carved with the crest of the Killer Whale. Length:40.6 cm. Width:3.4 cm. No. 19. Native copper was used before the coming of the Europeans, after which it was largely replaced by imported copper. The style of the knife indicates an ancient Asiatic origin.

The most important elements represented in traditional Northwest Coast art were the heraldic crests, which were of vital importance in the system of ranking and potlatching. Crests were carved, engraved, painted, or woven into every conceivable material to denote the rank or status of the owner. The crests were usually of animals, some being supernatural (such as *Thunderbird*) and all representing the lineage, clan, and moiety to which the wearer belonged. With a knowledge of the conventional representations, most, but not all, crests are identifiable.[40] Without this understanding, a face may not seem to represent anything specific; it is clearly identified as *Beaver*, however, by the long incisor teeth, paws, and flat tail. *Grizzly Bear* is denoted by distinctive, rounded ears, muzzle, nostrils, teeth, and claws. *Raven* is differentiated by a long beak, usually slightly open. *Eagle* is represented by a large, short, hooked beak, but if the great hook continues to the chin, it is *Hawk* that is indicated. *Killer Whale* is identified by emphasis on the teeth and the sharp dorsal fin, the latter often standing as a shorthand symbol for the whole. Sharp ears and teeth symbolize *Wolf. Frog* is identified by a wide toothless mouth and flat nose and is usually recognizable.

From the foregoing, certain principles of representation stand out: stylization or conventionalization takes precedence over realistic portrayal; and characterization of a whole is achieved through the accentuation of certain distinctive elements of the animal, such as *Beaver's* incisor teeth. Another principle has been described as *splitting* or *unfolding*, that is, depicting a three-dimensional object in only two dimensions. The artist attempted not only to provide a full frontal view, but also to show the sides, resulting in an expanded, horizontal rectangle or oblong shape. (One may think here of a world map as compared to a globe.) Dislocation of elements that have been *split* is a conventional distortion, dictated by the rules governing the use of space. Other principles of representation include depicting one creature with two profiles, emphasizing horizontal bilateral symmetry, reduction, and transformation of new elements from the old.[41]

Not every element carved or painted on a complex piece can be understood. In many cases, myths, legends, or events were portrayed by a representation that symbolized, in a form of shorthand, the entire story that was known to the owner and the carver. With the high mortality rate among the Haida and the decline of their traditional culture, the meanings were lost before anthropologists or serious collectors entered the scene. In other specimens, the degree of abstraction demanded by the need to fill all available space prevents unambiguous interpretation.

The Haida artist was for the most part attempting to realistically depict his subject, however formalized the result may appear. One cause for *our* perception of distortion frequently is the failure to recognize that the artist often was representing all sides of the animal. In addition, he was often attempting to provide an "x-ray" view of the creature through the use of conventionalized parts. Perhaps another barrier to our understanding has involved the use of space. Typically in Northwest Coast art, all space must be filled but in accord with the rules of composition, sometimes with fragmentary designs with meanings that can never be clear.

Holm[42] and Holm and Reid[43] have analyzed the principles of composition, as opposed to representation, that underlie the art. There are varying degrees of realism, which range from a *configurative* design, in which the essential animal outline is maintained; to an *expansive* design, in which the animal is rearranged to fit the available space but with the anatomical relationships maintained; to the *distributive* design, in which the body parts no longer have any discernible interrelationship and the identity of the animal is perhaps not even accessible.[44]

Perhaps the most important principle of the craft that sometimes lifts the product to the level of art is the concept of a continuous primary *formline*, a heavy black line of varying thickness, curve, and angle that delineates the main shapes and provides a sense of tension and movement. The main shapes were elaborated with secondary figures and isolated tertiary units used as fillers.[45] The placement of the three primary colors of the art style—black, red, and blue green—was formalized for the primary and secondary figures.[46] The style utilized a limited number of design units that could be arranged and varied in proportion to fit the requirements of representation and space. The most important of these units were the formlines that outlined the creature, and two formalized units, the ovoid and U-shape, which could be modified according to rules to represent various parts of the body, including those which served to characterize the creature.[47] A number of devices were used to join forms to one another, principally the tangential placing of forms and the overlapping of formlines.[48]

Among the other principles of form and organization, the most apparent is the total use of the space and the adjustment of the principal forms to the specific surface to be decorated. Conceptually, the Haida artisan thought in terms of total organization of the space before beginning his work.[49] Collison[50] describes the view of a skilled Haida carver who was engaged in carving a very elaborate totem pole: "I was surprised at the apparently reckless manner in which he cut and hewed away with a large axe as though regardless of consequences. 'Where is your plan?' I inquired. 'Are you not afraid to spoil your tree?' 'No,' he replied; 'the white man, when about to make anything, first traces it on paper, but the Indian has all his plans here,' as he significantly pointed to his forehead."

The Carver

The technology of the carver was impressive, even before the advent of the European metal technology. Heavy stone mauls (no. 40) were used to hammer stone or antler wedges into the log, which was usually cedar, splitting it into appropriate segments. An adze that doubled as an axe and a plane was then used to create the outline of the product, which was finished with knife blades and drills. Fine detail work was done with the fine points of flint burins or gravers, obsidian microblades, and the important curved knife, which was made from the curved incisor of the beaver. Final smoothing was done with flat slabs of sandstone or the rough skin of the dogfish shark. Some of the stone used, such as nephrite and obsidian, was obtained from the coastal tribes with which the Haida had trading partnerships. Wood and antler were employed as hafts or grips for the various tools.

The carver had to be very skilled before he could begin his independent career, for his labor and the labor of those working with him were too valuable to be risked. Moreover, in the highly sensitive rank-and-status system of the potlatch, an incorrectly drawn crest or the failure of a mechanical mask to function properly could humiliate the chiefly host, requiring an additional expensive potlatch to remove the stigma.

In the execution of his project, the carver began by painting the design on the wood. The overall plan, complete in its detail, was carried in his head and sometimes based upon a vision. The all-important primary and secondary formlines that defined the major figures were applied first. Bark templates were used in the application of paint for the basic design elements, such as the ovoid and U-forms, that were fundamental to the portrayal of the creature or to fill space.

Fig. 15. Feast dish of carved and painted wood inlaid with shell and representing the Killer Whale, Haida, British Columbia, Canada, and Alaska, U.S.A. Height:18.8 cm. Length:47 cm. Width:45 cm. No. 29.

Fig. 16. Wood seal club carved with the Killer Whale crest, Haida, Queen Charlotte Islands, British Columbia, Canada. Height:8.5 cm. Length:56.3 cm. Width:5.5 cm. No. 43. Seals were usually hunted with bows and arrows or harpoons, and when the animal was exhausted, the death blow was given with a club of this type.

Fig. 17. Carved argillite sculpture of grizzly bears and a woman giving birth, Haida, Queen Charlotte Islands, British Columbia, Canada. Height:13.9 cm. No. 47. The carving represents the legend of the woman berry picker who was captured by and married to a grizzly bear. She is shown giving birth to their offspring. Characteristic of argillite carving, legendary events, myths, and creatures were portrayed, in contrast to the scrimshaw carving that embodied nontraditional elements.

Fig. 18. Feast dish, carved to represent the Seal crest and inlaid with shell, Haida, British Columbia, Canada, and Alaska, U.S.A. Height:18.5 cm. Length:56 cm. Width:27.5 cm. No. 30.

Fig. 19. Carved stone shaman's charm with zoomorphic figures, Haida, British Columbia, Canada. Height:9.2 cm. Length:25 cm. Width:4 cm. No. 4. The shaman or medicine man was the important religious figure on the Northwest Coast, as well as being responsible for curing through medical practices, which included a knowledge of the medicinal qualities of herbs and of setting fractures.

Fig. 20. Argillite carving of the Spirits of the Canoe, inlaid with ivory, Haida, Queen Charlotte Islands, British Columbia, Canada. Height:17.8 cm. Length:36.2 cm. Width:7.9 cm. No. 6. The Canoe Spirits were supernatural beings who aided the shaman.

The overall effect of the Northwest Coast art style was to provide a strong impact through the division of the shape of the given object. The various divisions of that shape were given unity through the controlled, interlocked formline patterns that were related in form, color, and scale. The effect is the same whether it is on a totem pole of monumental size, a miniature argillite pole, or the carved horn handle of a spoon. The sensitivity of the artisan working within the strictures of the style frequently raised a craft product to the level of true art.

The Haida carver was not a "carver" in the sense that the term is used in Western European tradition. He was not limited to wood—although that raw material formed the basis of the style—but worked in antler, bone, copper, ivory, stone, and other material, and he painted as well as carved. After the advent of the Europeans he added the categories of goldsmith and silversmith (no. 51) to his already large repertoire. Manual dexterity, mental framework, and training were not the only requirements for the craftsman, for he had to understand the traditions and legends of the Haida in general and the crests, names, and titles of the clans and lineages in particular. Since the objects portrayed were inherited private property, the carver necessarily had to have the right to use them and to have authorization to use those of other lineages. In Haida society he was, therefore, a man of high rank or status, a chief or noble. Niblack[51] noted that every chief kept a "carpenter" [a lesser chief?] to construct and repair canoes and to make ceremonial masks and other objects. According to Barbeau,[52] "A craftsman's calling was not the lot of the common folk (according to Alfred Adams), but of the chosen few in the highest lineage, and it behoved [sic] the holder of such a privilege to train the fittest and most gifted among his nephews as his successors."

Of the carvers discussed by Barbeau,[53] all for whom status is indicated were holders of a chiefly title, although this undoubtedly reflects the demographic catastrophes of the nineteenth century, which caused the numerous titles to be passed to the few surviving inheritors.

Training for the craft of carver was through the apprenticeship system. A boy who was believed to be talented was apprenticed to his mother's brother for training, and he moved to his uncle's house, usually at about the age of ten. Here he was at home, for his lineage was traced through his mother's family line. As an apprentice he was also commonly the successor to the title of house chief, and hence he often served concurrently as an apprentice chief of the house in which he now lived. Unfortunately, detailed accounts of the apprenticeship system among the Haida do not exist.

As a noble member of a chiefly lineage, the carver was, of course, entitled to use the crests of his lineage and clan for objects of his own use or the use of other members of his lineage. The complex reciprocity of the Haida potlatch system, however, required that certain work be done for those of the opposite moiety. For example, at a potlatch given for building a house or constructing a totem pole, the guests (who were of the moiety opposite that of the hostess and of the same moiety as the host) were responsible for the construction. The leading guest, a chief, was responsible for carving the crests for his hostess, for which he had implicit authorization. If the visiting chief was not a skilled carver, he designated one to act in his stead, chosen from those who in the Haida kinship system[54] stood in the relationship of "father," i.e., a "father's brother." A chief was richly rewarded for his labor (or that of his surrogate) at the time of the potlatch, but also as a chief or noble he was bound in time to give a potlatch for those whose guest he had been.

Fig. 21. A ceremonial "copper" used as a symbol of wealth. Engraved and polished, this specimen's major features are two Eagle crests facing outward, Haida, Queen Charlotte Islands, British Columbia, Canada. Height:84 cm. Width:59 cm. Thickness:0.4 cm. No. 33. Coppers made originally of native, beaten copper were major symbols of wealth and status. At potlatches they were often destroyed or given away to display the wealth of the owner and his disregard for material possessions.

The carver was a specialist, with necessary control over those involved in the construction of major sculptures, such as totem or house poles or house and mortuary columns. For example, he chose the great cedar that was to become a totem pole, and he supervised the felling of the tree and its transportation to the spot where it was to be carved, painted, and erected. He was then responsible for the plan of execution, including the selection, ordering, and scaling of the various crests and other design elements that were to be included. In the actual carving of the pole, he was presumably assisted by his apprentices. For the erection of the pole a greater labor force was required, and the winter's work culminated in a great feast and potlatch.

The construction of a great house was of even greater complexity. Numerous cedar logs had to be selected, cut, and moved to the construction site, split into boards, hewn into appropriate sizes and shapes, and finished. The often elaborate and massive house posts that supported the weight of the structure were carved into representations of creatures and crests significant to the lineage. Finally, with construction completed, the house front was painted with the important crests of the chief's lineage. In many cases, outer house posts were carved, painted, and mounted beside the door; indeed, in some houses the entry was through a circular hole in a central house post. Because the construction of a house required several winters of work and an enormous output of energy by numerous workers, there was ample reason for the final feast and potlatch, the house potlatch, to be the most important and lavish.

European Influence

With the collapse of the fur trade, caused by the virtual extinction of the sea otter, the Haida craftsman began to produce curios for a newly developed commercial market. The objects produced were known as *scrimshaw*, a term that has been questionably extended to the argillite carving developing at the same time. These products differed as much from the traditional creations in subject matter and freedom of style as they did in function. The scrimshaw specimens (fig. 24) were derived from the models of the visiting seamen and they embodied European elements and stylistic freedom, in contrast to the formal style and subject matter of tradition. The argillite carvings, however, largely belong to a new and innovative category that graphically expressed legendary creatures (fig. 20), events, or other topics not found in the traditional style.[55]

By 1870 the whaling industry, which had been a primary market for the curios, began to decline. Northwest Coast masks and other items had also been marketed through the trading posts of the Hudson's Bay Company, but after about 1880 the trade was directed to the developing tourist outlets. Correlated with these developments was another change in the commercial art of the Haida, for scrimshaw production gradually declined and the innovative carving in argillite was largely given up to be replaced by the carving of miniature totem poles (fig. 23). This return to traditional form and style, albeit for a commercial market, has been interpreted[56] as an indication of the stabilization of the Haida social system following the stresses and strains introduced by the fur trade and the whaling period. However, this interpretation is subject to question on a number of grounds: smallpox continued to ravage the population; conversion to Christianity was taking place; intermarriage with Europeans was occurring; wage labor was developing as Haida were employed in mainland salmon canneries; the kinship and clan system was being replaced by an emphasis on the nuclear family; and other consequences were resulting from the impact of modern industrial civilization and the incorporation of once-autonomous societies as ethnic groups within the Canadian federal state.

The craft of the carver did not become extinct in spite of these great changes. The few remaining Haida carvers were, however, working almost completely in argillite for a commercial art and craft market, not in the social and cultural context in which the style had been developed and nurtured. Much of the subtlety and understanding of the principles of the style were lost as the artisan copied old pieces but without, for example, recognition of such an important element as the formline in defining the chief figures of a work.[57] In many Northwest Coast Indian communities there has been an increased interest in and renewal of activity in traditional crafts. Among the Haida this is manifest in the products of such carvers as Bill Reid, whose analysis and application of the original principles result in works that are surely to be classed as art. The revival of the apprenticeship system, a return to traditional principles, a reawakened interest in original culture, and a desire to further probe the potential of the style augur well for the future of the carver's craft in the Queen Charlotte Islands.

Fig. 23. Carved argillite miniature totem pole, with representation of a bear on the head of a shaman, above the Bear and Frog crests, Haida, British Columbia, Canada, or Alaska, U.S.A. Height:15 cm. No. 46. Carving in argillite began about 1821, after the advent of the Europeans and about the same time as scrimshaw. Intending their work for the commercial market of curio seekers, carvers in argillite produced works of great freedom from traditional style; but about 1870, miniature totem poles became the primary product in this medium. The change represented a return in miniature scale to traditional forms.

Fig. 22. Carved sandstone pipe, with design elements including those representing the Octopus, Haida, Queen Charlotte Islands, British Columbia, Canada. Height:5.7 cm. Length:8.7 cm. Width:3.4 cm. No. 49. Tobacco was known to the Haida before the coming of the Europeans, but it was only chewed. The newcomers taught them to smoke, and pipes of various materials were then produced for their own use or for sale as curios.

1. The term "Haida" (*Xa'ida*) is their own term for themselves, meaning "people" or human.
2. Rowe 1972:83.
3. Murdock 1934a:221-225.
4. Collison 1915:88; Murdock 1934a:241.
5. Murdock 1934a:229.
6. Murdock 1934a:224-226, 1936:3-4.
7. The so-called totem poles were not strictly totemic, as the Haida did not believe they had any direct spiritual relationship or identification with the creature portrayed; nor were there any special taboos or rituals associated with the animals of one's crests. The crests should be interpreted in a manner similar to the heraldic devices of the European nobility.
8. Murdock 1934a:245-247, 1936:15-20; Niblack 1888:250, 251.
9. Swanton 1909:66-71; Murdock 1934a:235-237.
10. Murdock 1934a:237; Niblack 1888:250.
11. Collison 1915:225.
12. Niblack 1888:252-253.
13. Murdock 1934a:236; Swanton 1909:107-121.
14. Niblack 1888:224-225.
15. Barbeau 1958; Murdock 1934a:257-261; Swanton 1909:38-46.
16. Murdock 1936:3-12.
17. Murdock 1936:13-15.
18. Collison 1915:131-134.
19. Barbeau 1929:192-209.
20. Duff 1975.
21. Stewart 1973:34-122.
22. Barbeau 1929:192-209.
23. Chief Weah, head of the Bear clan at Masset, quoted in Collison 1915:107.
24. Hodge 1907:I:522.
25. Barbeau 1929:15-26.
26. Harrington 1949:201.
27. Collison 1915.
28. Hodge 1907:I:521.
29. Barbeau 1929:192-209.
30. Boas 1897:123-176, 1927:183-298.
31. Carpenter 1975:12.
32. Lévi-Strauss 1943:180, quoted in Carpenter 1975:10-12.
33. Inverarity 1950.
34. Duff, Holm, and Reid 1967.
35. Wardwell 1978.
36. Barbeau 1929, 1950, 1953, 1957.
37. J. and C. Smyle 1973.
38. Holm 1965.
39. Holm and Reid 1975.
40. Boas 1927:186-212.
41. Boas 1897:123-176, 1927:183-298; Holm 1965:8.
42. Holm 1965.
43. Holm and Reid 1975.
44. Holm 1965:11-13.
45. Holm 1965:35-37.
46. Holm 1965:26-35.
47. Holm 1965:37-57.
48. Holm 1965:58-66.
49. Holm 1965:67-91.
50. Collison 1915:138.
51. Niblack 1888:254.
52. Barbeau 1957:156.
53. Barbeau 1953, 1957, 1958.
54. Murdock 1934b.
55. Barbeau 1957, 1958.
56. Gunther 1956.
57. Holm 1965:80-82.

Fig. 24. An example of scrimshaw carving representing a "steam-boat" pipe, made of carved and painted wood with ivory panels, Haida, British Columbia, Canada, or Alaska, U.S.A. Height:10 cm. Length:40 cm. Width:4.2 cm. No. 45. Scrimshaw carving was adopted and adapted by the Haida from the example of sailors aboard ships involved in the fur trade or in whaling, as well as those on voyages of discovery. These carvings were produced as curios for commercial purposes, not for use in the Haida community.

Barbeau, Marius
    1929   Totem Poles of the Gitskan, Upper Skenna River, British Columbia. National Museum of Canada, Bulletin 61.
    1950   Totem Poles. National Museum of Canada, Bulletin 119. 2 vols.
    1953   Haida Myths Illustrated in Argillite Carvings. National Museum of Canada, Bulletin 127.
    1957   Haida Carvers in Argillite. National Museum of Canada, Bulletin 139.
    1958   Medicine-Men of the North Pacific Coast. National Museum of Canada, Bulletin 152.
Boas, Franz
    1897   The Decorative Art of the Indians of the North Pacific Coast. American Museum of Natural History, Bulletin IX:123–176.
    1927   Primitive Art. Cambridge: Harvard University Press.
Carpenter, Edmund C.
    1975   Introduction. *In* Indian Art of the Northwest Coast: A Dialogue on Craftsmanship and Aesthetics, by Bill Holm and Bill Reid. Seattle: University of Washington Press.
Collison, W. H.
    1915   In the Wake of the War Canoe. London: Seeley, Service.
Duff, Wilson
    1954   A Heritage in Decay. Canadian Art 11:56–59.
    1975   Images:Stone:B.C. Seattle: University of Washington Press.
Duff, Wilson, Bill Holm, and Bill Reid
    1967   Arts of the Raven: Masterworks by the Northwest Coast Indian. Vancouver: Vancouver Art Gallery.
Gunther, E.
    1956   The Social Disorganization of the Haida As Reflected in Their Slate Carving. Davidson Journal of Anthropology 2:149–153.
Harrington, Lynn
    1949   Last of the Haida Carvers. Natural History 58:200–205.
Hodge, F. W.
    1907–10
        Handbook of the Indians of North America. Smithsonian Institution Bureau of American Ethnology, Bulletin 30. 2 vols.
Holm, Bill
    1965   Northwest Coast Indian Art: An Analysis of Form. Thomas Burke Memorial Washington State Museum, Monograph 1.
Holm, Bill, and Bill Reid
    1975   Indian Art of the Northwest Coast: A Dialogue on Craftsmanship and Aesthetics. Seattle: University of Washington Press.
Inverarity, R. B.
    1950   Art of the Northwest Coast Indians. Berkeley: University of California Press.
Lévi-Strauss, Claude
    1943   The Art of the Northwest Coast at the American Museum of Natural History. Gazette des Beaux-Arts 24:175–182.
Murdock, George P.
    1934a   Our Primitive Contemporaries. New York: Macmillan.
    1934b   Kinship and Social Behavior among the Haida. American Anthropologist 36:355–385.
    1936   Rank and Potlatch among the Haida. New Haven: Yale University Publications in Anthropology 13.
Niblack, A. P.
    1888   The Coast Indians of Southern Alaska and Northern British Columbia. United States National Museum, Reports:225–386.
Rowe, J. S.
    1972   Forest Regions of Canada. Department of the Environment, Canadian Forestry Service, Publication 1300.
Smyly, John, and Carolyn Smyly
    1973   The Totem Poles of Skedans. Seattle: University of Washington Press.
Stewart, Hillary
    1973   Artifacts of the Northwest Coast. Saanichton, B.C.: Hancock House.
Swanton, J. R.
    1909   Contributions to the Ethnology of the Haida. American Museum of Natural History, Memoirs 8:1–300.
Wardwell, Allen
    1978   Objects of Bright Pride: Northwest Coast Indian Art from the American Museum of Natural History. New York: Center for Inter-American Relations and the American Federation of Artists.

ACKNOWLEDGMENTS

The author wishes to thank Dr. Edmund Carpenter, of New York City, and Dr. George MacDonald, of the National Museums of Canada, for their helpful comments and criticism.

the GOLDSMITH

THE COCLE STYLE OF ANCIENT PANAMA

ANNA CURTENIUS ROOSEVELT

Fig. 1. Cast-gold Bat God pendant, Costa Rica. Height:5.2 cm. Weight:33.9 grams. No. 36. The pendant, which is of the Coclé style, may have been traded to Costa Rica from central Panama. It shows a great deal of attrition from wear, especially on the suspension loops at the back. Most pendants were apparently worn around the neck on a cotton cord. Fragments of cord have been found in the loops of several pendants that have been excavated (Doyle:1960:48; Sander and Mitchell 1960).

The hole at the breast of the figure was caused by the formation of an air lock during casting (Sonin, personal communication). The stubs of cut-off pouring channels or vents can be seen at the head and heels.

The Bat God holds two curious tubes at the corners of his mouth. Their function is not known. The Crocodile God also is sometimes shown holding the same kind of tubes.

During the last thousand years before the conquest of the New World, there flourished in central Pacific Panama a group of paramount chiefdoms known for their highly developed style of goldworking. The remains of these societies are found in the states of southeastern Veraguas, Los Santos, Herrera, Coclé, Panama, and the Canal Zone. The style is named Coclé, after the central state in the region, because the first scientific finds of gold were made there. The ancient chiefdoms were closely linked to each other by marriage, trade, war, and alliances, and they shared a similar religion, economy, and sociopolitical structure. Their art was closely related in technique, style, and iconography. The chiefdoms arose during the first five hundred years after Christ, when populations burgeoned on the basis of seed-crop cultivation and competition over land became intense.[1]

The aboriginal culture is defined archaeologically by a group of elegant polychrome pottery styles characteristic of Pacific coastal Panama in late prehistoric times.[2] Vessels and sherds of these styles have been found in substantial quantities in archaeological sites of the coastal plain and islands of central Pacific Panama (fig. 2).[3] Some of the better-known sites of the prehistoric occupation are Venado Beach in the Canal Zone, Sitio Conte and El Caño in Coclé Province, and El Hatillo near Parita in Herrera Province.[4] The archaeological finds have been made by a variety of discoverers, including grave robbers, amateurs, and professional archaeologists.[5] The discoveries, both scientific and unscientific, have revealed the existence of earthen mound complexes, great alignments of carved stone columns, statues, and altars, and vast cemeteries. There is also a hierarchy of habitation sites in the region, ranging from small village middens to the refuse of large towns.[6]

The polychrome ceramic styles that define the ancient culture are some of the most complex and sophisticated produced anywhere in the ancient New World (fig. 4). Their rich palette is duplicated nowhere else and includes a true purple, in addition to white, red, brown, and black. The subject matter of the ceramic art is predominantly zoomorphic, and at the height of its iconographic development the art portrayed a legion of diverse animals—the preeminent crocodile, and frogs, crabs, sharks, turtles, snakes, bats, worms, rays, insects, many kinds of birds, and animal-human combinations. The polychrome ceramic styles make up a regional tradition of considerable temporal variability, the chronology of which is just beginning to be worked out. The tradition spans the time from about A.D. 400 to the period of European conquest in the beginning of the sixteenth century. Three periods of development have been worked out by study of ceramic sequences, cross-dating, and a few radiocarbon dates: an early period, from A.D. 400 to 700; a middle period, from 700 to 1100; and a final period, from 1100 to about 1520.[7] The tradition begins with an emphasis on realism, passes through a phase of growing stylization and complexity, and ends with an emphasis on geometric motifs. Only future work will reveal the

1. Nata
2. El Caño
3. Sitio Conte
4. Penonome
5. Chame
6. Venado Beach
7. Panama City
8. Miraflores
9. Tonosi
10. Macaracas
11. Las Palmas
12. El Hatillo
13. Parita

Fig. 2. Map of central Panama, showing archaeological sites and modern settlements.

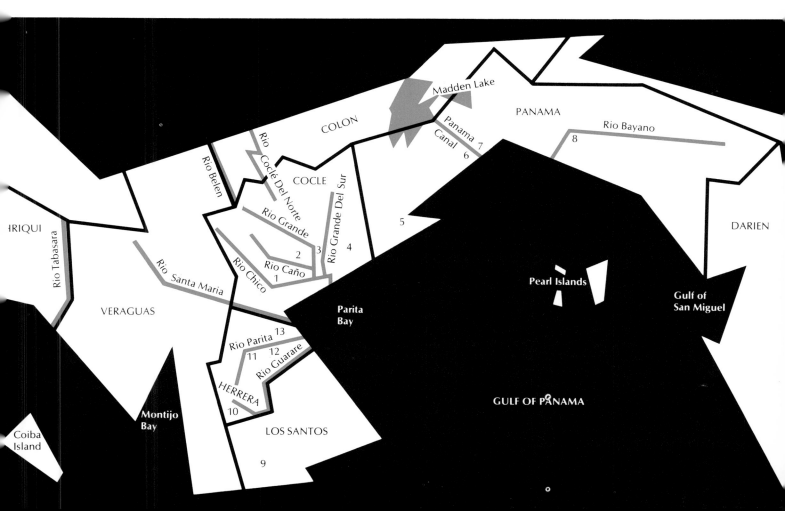

Fig. 3. *A*, nose ring of green stone with embossed caps, temple site, El Caño, Coclé Province, Panama, collected by A. H. Verrill. Diameter:3.4 cm. No. 24; *B*, small nose ring of cast and hammered gold, with crimped caps, Madden Lake, Canal Zone, Panama. Diameter:2.5 cm. Weight:12.5 grams. No. 13; *C*, large hollow nose ring of hammered gold with crimped caps. Madden Lake, Canal Zone, Panama.

"Both Men and Women at solemn Meals or Feasts, when they wear their large Plates or Rings, take them out, and lay them aside til they have done Eating; when, rubbing them very clean and bright, they put them in again. At other times, when they eat or drink, they content themselves with lifting up with the left Hand, if need be, the small Plates or Rings they then wear . . . while they use their right Hand in taking up the Cup or feeding themselves. . . . Neither the Plates nor Rings hinder much their Speaking, tho' they lie bobbing upon their Lips" (Wafer 1903:141).

significance of the development and change of the polychrome ceramic styles, but it is likely that they were closely related to the changing political and military fortunes of the prehistoric chiefdoms.

An important feature of central Panamanian culture was the manufacture and use of gold artifacts. The Coclé gold is considered to be one of the most elegant and complex of the regional goldworking traditions of the prehistoric cultural sphere comprising the present nations of Panama, Costa Rica, and Colombia. What is known of the methods of the central Panamanian goldworking is derived from study of artifacts; there are no contemporary descriptions. The Coclé goldsmiths have been called "the most affluent and skillful artisans of the Isthmus."[8] They used a great variety of manufacturing techniques. They were masters at high-relief embossing, or repoussé, the art of pressing designs into thin gold sheets. Their lost-wax casting was of consummate artistry and included some exceedingly delicate cast filagree. Like many of the smiths in their cultural sphere, the Coclé artisans cast numerous ornaments of gold-copper alloy and decorated the surfaces with coloration gilding, by etching away surface copper with acids. Many artifacts were made in one piece, but clinching and a simple kind of welding were used to join separate pieces. Most unusual in the traditions of New World metalworking is the Coclé practice of setting precious and semiprecious stones in cast-gold ornaments and their use of sheet gold to sheathe carvings of ivory, bone, wood, resin, and stone.

Most Coclé-style gold objects were made to be ornaments for the body. There are headbands, helmets, and gold ornaments for cloth or feather-and-basketry headdresses. For the neck there are figurine pendants, collars, and gold-bead necklaces. Gold spools and gold-tipped rods were worn as ear ornaments, and some of the most common ornaments are the rings, plaques, and clips that were made for the nose. There are also adjustable finger rings of cast or hammered gold. The early reports of Panamanian Indians mention gold penis sheaths and a kind of golden breast support for women. Hammered discs of all sizes were made for the decoration of clothing. Among the very few tools are chisels and awls, as well as tweezers for plucking out hair.

Gold also had certain important functions over and above personal ornamentation. It was an important source of wealth for the elite in central Panamanian communities, and it served as a symbol of rank. Gold was an important medium for the depiction of religious subjects and had a significant funerary role. The gold of a chiefdom was hoarded in the chief's house, stored there in cane and deerhide treasure chests or hung on the mummies of the chief's ancestors in the mortuary rooms.

The Panamanian Chiefdoms

The use and manufacture of Coclé gold is closely tied to the workings of the aboriginal societies and cannot be understood isolated from them. The societies were stratified chiefdoms, small but populous state societies.[9] Their characteristics have been determined from the information given in the records of the conquest of what is now central and eastern Panama and from the archaeological remains.[10] There were several distinct chiefdoms in central Panama in the sixteenth century, according to the Spanish descriptions, and several different languages were spoken within the area.[11] Each chiefdom centered on a large village or town of as many as fifteen hundred people, or more, where the chief had his establishment (see fig. 5).[12] One chief's capital, Nata, apparently had an area of four square kilometers.[13] Its size came as quite a shock to the commander of a Spanish force that entered it in 1516. He wrote, "So many were the houses there that I believe that there was no one of us who was not fearful to see such a great town."[14] Some of the lesser noblemen had their lands and houses away from the paramount chief's town, and many people lived in small settlements in the countryside. Overall, settlement was very dense, to judge from the comments of the Spanish and the extent of the archaeological refuse.[15]

The subsistence economies of the Panamanian chiefdoms were based on the intensive cultivation of maize and other crops, hunting in the savannas and gallery forests, and fishing in the rivers and coastal waters. The climate of central Panama is tropical, with moderate, irregular rainfall and a long dry season.[16] The region has had a cover of manmade savanna since about 5000 B.C. Only the riverbanks and hilly land had forest on them at the time of the conquest. The rich soils of the coastal alluvial plain supported large fields of maize and beans (both of which have been found in ancient garbage), manioc, sweet potatoes, and various tree crops. Fish are said to have been the main source of animal food in the region, but white-tailed deer were also very important, and archaeological finds show that many other animals were hunted or collected. These include many birds, both aquatic and terrestrial, and peccaries, frogs and toads, iguanas, turtles, crabs and other shellfish, and sharks. Some areas had saltworks, which apparently belonged to the chief, and many seem to have had superficial deposits of alluvial gold.

Also very important in the economies of the Panamanian region was the brisk trade in produce, salt, basic raw materials and manufactured goods, slaves, precious materials, and luxury goods.[17] The trade was based on regional specialization of production. Hunters and fishermen came to the big towns with their dried meat and fish to trade for the maize grown in the agricultural districts. Slaves were a very important part of the trade, as were the pearls, raw and worked gold, pottery, cotton thread, and clothing that were traded in return. Weapons were important articles of trade. Some materials were traded very long distances: archaeological sites have yielded manatee bone from the Caribbean and gold and emeralds from Ecuador or Colombia. The traded goods moved both on men's backs and on water. Fifty- to sixty-person canoes are described in this area. The intense trading seems to have been conducted in the central towns, under the control of the paramount chiefs, all apparently by barter, with no true medium of exchange.

Fig. 4. Polychrome ceramic jar depicting the Crocodile God, Veraguas Province, Panama. Height:25 cm.

Fig. 5. House in Nata, Coclé Province, Panama, the center of a sixteenth-century chiefdom. After the manuscript of Fernández de Oviedo.

"In our Western terms, the seat of the chief was the palace, court of law, and temple, the center of authority. . . . The great house also held the main treasure of the native state, a good part of it on the mummies of the ancestors, the accumulation of generations" (Sauer 1966:240–241).

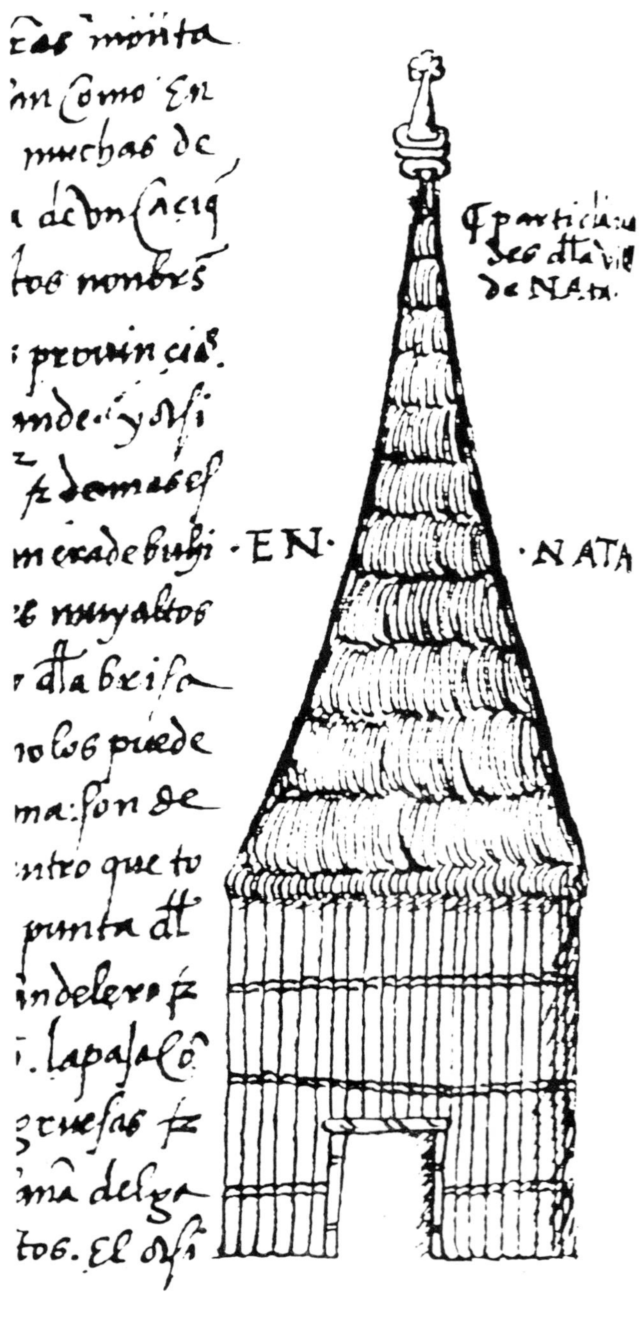

The Paramount Chief

The hereditary ruler of a Panamanian chiefdom, called *Quevi* or *Tibi*, according to the Spanish accounts, was a man of considerable power and wealth (fig. 8).[18] His position and property were inherited from his father, and in many cases they had been passed down through a long line of chiefly ancestors. He had political, military, and economic control over a number of subchiefdoms, and he ruled over large areas of land.[19] He had the right to exact from his people the labor to supply him with gold, game, fish, agricultural products, housing, and assistance in war, in return for their food and drink. Members of the elite classes had to serve him in administrative and military capacities, and subchiefs had to make the gold in their treasuries available to him in certain circumstances.

The chief's house or palace was a large, well-built structure of many rooms, provisioned with large quantities of smoked and dried fish and game, maize and other crops, and beer in great jars set in the ground.[20] Also stored in the chief's house was his treasury of gold and other precious materials, as well as various tools and weapons. It may also have served as a workshop for specialized craftsmen, such as goldsmiths, as it did in Darien.[21] His entourage, consisting of his family, servants, and slaves, must have been considerable.

The chief and people of high rank had certain privileges in dress and ornament. They had the right to own and wear gold ornaments; and certain kinds of ornaments, such as gold breastplates, crowns, and helmets, were apparently reserved for the use of the chief alone.[22] The chief also had the privilege of funeral rites and furnishings not available to others. The Spanish accounts and the archaeological excavation of cemeteries make it clear that the obsequies of members of the ruling class were highly distinctive.[23] Much effort and resource were spent on the preparation and accouterment of a chief's body for burial. His body was mummified through slow and careful smoking and drying over fires. It was arrayed with large quantities of gold and precious stones and wrapped in many layers of fine fabric.

De Espinosa, one of the Spanish commanders of the exploration of central Panama, entered the chief Parita's house on the eve of his funeral. He opened up his mummy bundle and later wrote a report describing what he found.[24] He wrote:

> . . . the mummified body of the dead man inside the covers . . . was all armored in gold, and on his head there was a great basin of gold like a helmet, and at his neck, four or five necklaces like collars, and on his arms armor in the shape of tubes . . . and on his chest and shoulders were many pieces of gold and large, gold medals and thin plates of metal, and a belt of gold, girded with gold bells, and his legs were also armored with gold, so that the body of the chief appeared as if it were armored in a coat of mail or braided corselet.

The booty of gold that the Spanish got from Parita's house came to almost four hundred pounds.[25] In many regions, the chief's mummy was kept for a time in a special mortuary in the chief's house, to be brought out occasionally and feasted. Eventually, the chief's mummy was buried; there are very rare mentions of cremation. The excavations by Lothrop in the cemetery at Sitio Conte are a rich source of information about the burial of chiefs. Their graves are distinguished from others by many features, but particularly by their large quantity of grave goods. In these graves there were large amounts of ceramic vessels, baskets, feather ornaments, clothing, tools, weapons, food, and jewelry, all apparently intended for the use of the chief in the afterlife. Many of the artifacts had been broken, apparently ceremonially "killed," so that they could accompany the dead. One of the most striking things about the burials is the great quantity of gold ornaments that they contain, displayed about the body of the chief or piled in caches.[26] Many gold ornaments, in fact, seem to have been made for burial and have never been worn or are not finished.

To accompany the chief to the next life, from ten to fifty people might be buried with the chief. According to the Spanish, they were either smothered when drunk from the funeral drinks or were given poison to take. The chief's grave companions were said to be slaves or servants in the chief's household, his favorite concubines, or war captives. The chief Parita had two mummified noblewomen with him, and there were captive prisoners tied up in the house, who were to be sacrificed at the funeral festivities:

... he had at his head a dead woman, and another at his feet. They had on just as much gold as he. . . . A strange thing happened. . . . In truth this chief had in his house up to twenty Indians tied with ropes around their throats, who had been brought from the provinces of Descoria and Cheru, with whom this chief was at war . . . all of whom were to be killed the following night.[27]

There is much archaeological evidence of mass forced burial of retainers or war prisoners in central Panama.[28] In one famous grave, 26 of Sitio Conte, twelve bodies were placed around a central mummy body, which appears to have been the mummified body of the chief.[29]

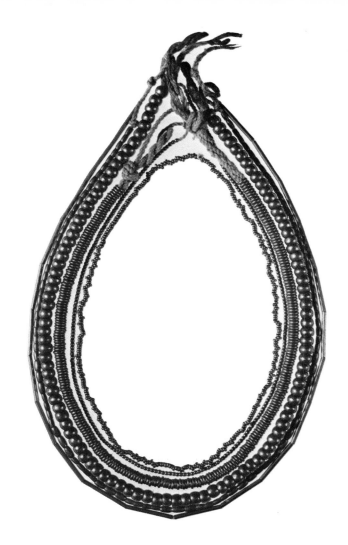

Fig. 7. Group of necklaces of hammered and "welded" gold beads (restrung), Rio Grande, Coclé Province, Panama. Length:52 cm. to 72 cm. Weight:.02 to .72 grams. No. 1.

Fig. 6. Tweezers of embossed and burnished gold, Coclé Province, Panama. Length:4.5 cm. Weight:12 grams. No. 64. It was the custom in Panama to pluck out facial hair (Wafer 1903:132, 134; Lothrop 1948b:254; Stone 1966:233).

The Panamanian chief was paid elaborate forms of respect.[30] In the region of the Panama Canal, the subjects of an acceding chief saluted him by kissing his feet as he lay in his hammock. He also had special forms of transport at his disposal. He traveled in a hammock-litter carried by relays of slave bearers. He had privileged access to woman, also. He could take a principal and legitimate wife, called *hespode*, whom he married with great ceremony and whose sons were heirs to his realm and his possessions. In addition, a chief could take a number of other women.[31] These women were taken into his household without any ceremony, and their children had no rights of inheritance from their father. It was from this group of concubines that women were chosen to accompany the chief to the afterworld. In Panamanian societies, the legitimate children of the ruling class apparently had burial privileges similar to those of their elders. For example, in the cemetery at Venado Beach, a three-year-old child was found richly adorned with gold ornaments, some of which bore motifs connected with the Crocodile God, a deity associated with rulership.[32]

In certain situations, the chief had the power of life and death over the people in his domain.[33] Both the Spanish accounts and the archaeological record attest to the murder and forced suicide of slave-retainers, war captives, and concubines for the burial ceremonies of chiefs. The chief pronounced and in some cases carried out sentences of death for the crimes of murder and robbery, a role not permitted to any other. People accused of crimes were taken in charge for the chief by sherifflike officers.

Fig. 8. Lacenta, a seventeenth-century chief in Darien Province, Panama, with his retinue. After Wafer 1903:136–137.

War

The chief was the leader in war. Military diplomacy, an art highly developed in this region according to the Spanish, was the prerogative of the ruler and his group of noble advisors.[34] Although conditions within a particular chiefdom were peaceful in general, there was fierce and continual war between chiefdoms. The purpose of war is said to have been the conquest and defense of territory and subject populations and the acquisition of slaves and gold.[35] Gifts of gold were given to win and cement military alliances.

There were fortified strongholds on elevations, and large settlements were stoutly palisaded.[36] The war parties of great chiefs were very large—the chief Parita is reported to have met the Spanish with an army of three or four thousand—and may have been organized in regimentlike groupings.[37] Movement of troops was facilitated by the use of canoes.[38] In some areas there were special barracks to house fighting men and fortress-houses for people to withdraw to during wartime.[39] There were special weapons and apparel for war, including bows and arrows, lances, atlatl darts, wooden "swords," and padded cotton armor.[40] Men of high rank wore their gold ornaments to battle.[41]

A warlike and cruel cultural ethic is reflected in the terrible mutilations that had been performed on some of the people buried in ancient cemeteries. Aside from the traumas probably received in battle, there was much evidence of decapitation for war trophies in the finds of headless bodies and bodiless heads, and there were examples of cut-off limbs and fingers and uprooted teeth.[42] The impact of war on demography must have been substantial. A necklace of human teeth found in a grave at Venado Beach represented the teeth of at least two hundred people, and the site of a single battle is said to have had pavements and towering piles of human heads.

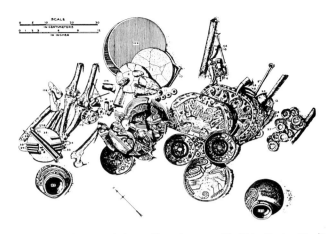

Fig. 9. Plan of some of the artifacts in grave 26, Sitio Conte, Coclé Province, Panama. After Lothrop 1937:275, fig. 247.

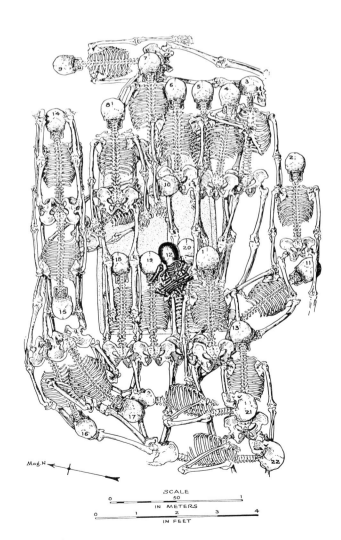

Fig. 10. Plan of skeletons in grave 26 at Sitio Conte, showing twenty-one extended burials arranged around a central flexed, seated burial. After Lothrop 1937:50, fig. 31.

"In Panama, Nata, and Pacora, and other provinces of the Cueva language, on the coast of the South Sea and its vicinity, it is the custom, when the chief dies (or a principal lord), for all the laborers and domestic servants of his household . . . to be killed. Because they believe . . . that the person who is killed when the chief dies will go to heaven with him and there will serve him, give him food or drink, or do whatever job he did for the chief in his house when he was alive" (Fernández de Oviedo 1853:III:154).

"It was the custom in the land that when a chief died, the wives who it was supposed he loved best should voluntarily be buried with their husband, and if the chief had pointed them out, this was done whether they liked it or not" (de Andagoya 1865:15).

Religion

Not much is known about religion beyond that which can be gleaned from the archaeological remains, the iconography of art, and the vague descriptions from the Spanish conquerors.[43] Great marriage feasts and funeral ceremonies are said to have taken place in and around the chief's house, and there were special huts for shamans and houses for the gods. It is not known exactly what observances were held in the ceremonial colonnades. Presumably, the altar stones were used to make some kind of offerings.

People of the general area are reported to have worshipped the sun and moon, but the art—especially the goldwork—is characterized by representations of mythical combinations of humans and animals. According to the Spanish, there was an important "devil" that appeared to people as a beautiful boy with clawed feet. That the aboriginal people considered the creatures worked in gold to be deities is confirmed by a passage in de Herrera's work about the people of the vicinity of Panama City.[44] He wrote: "They called their Idol *Tabira*, and cloath'd him as he appeared to them and talked to him and had him in several Shapes of Gold cast." There seem to be two major anthropomorphic gods. The most important one in terms of frequency of representation is the Crocodile God, a creature with human body and crocodile head, hands, and feet. His presence is pervasive in central Panamanian art. The other major deity is a Bat God, with the body of a man and the head of a bat. The Bat God, less prominent in the iconography, is associated with the ethic of war. He is sometimes shown as a warrior, with weapons and occasionally trophies of human heads.[45] In addition to their belief in animal-human deities, it is clear from the conquest accounts and the excavations of cemeteries that they believed in an afterlife. The high-status people were equipped with food, clothing, tools, jewelry, weapons, slaves, servants, farmers, and women—all that they might need in the afterlife. It was believed that the people who were killed to accompany the chiefs would gain immortality with their rulers.

As to religious functionaries, there were shamans, who had a special hut and who practiced divination, exorcism, and curing, and who spoke with the gods. It is also possible that the chief had an important role in religious matters. Cooke writes about the ceremonial enclosure at El Cano, Coclé Province:

> . . . we cannot say exactly how the precinct was used but one can conjecture that at the time of the construction of the "temple," magico-religious ideas in the central provinces had passed from tutelary shamanism or naturalistic polytheism . . . to a more hierarchical system, suggesting the association of some divine personages with temporal power.[46]

It may be that the chief was closely associated with the principal god of central Panamanian religion. Most of the archaeological gold ornaments depicting the crocodile deity were found in apparent chiefly graves. It is interesting that there are hints in the conquest-period literature of the existence of ancestor worship in the chief's class.[47]

Fig. 11. Two stone sculptures discovered by Verrill at the temple site, El Caño, Coclé Province, Panama.

Fig. 12. View of Verrill's excavations at the temple site, El Caño, Coclé Province, Panama. (Verrill's dig should not be taken as a model of excellent archaeological technique.)

Fig. 13. Plan of stone monuments in the ceremonial precinct of the temple site, El Caño. After Verrill 1927a:plate IV.
"The symmetrical and apparently radial plan of the precinct and the existence of probable altars carved with zoomorphic and anthropomorphic figures suggest a well-established ceremonial rite, although we have no indication whether they were correlated with human sacrifices, movements of the astral bodies, or honors to specific chiefs" (Cooke 1976d:451).

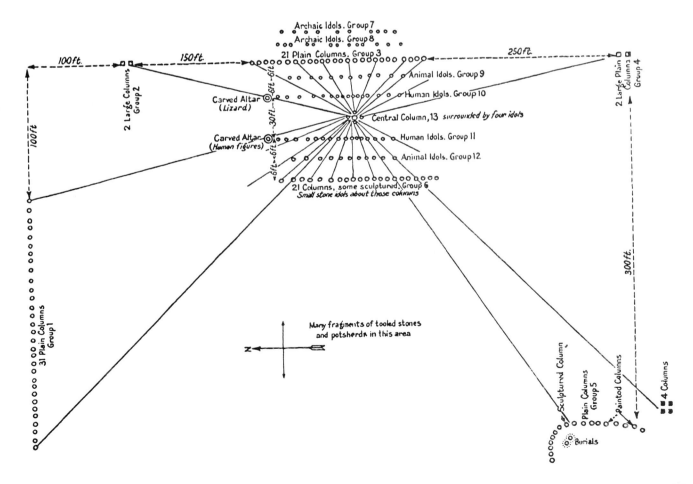

Social Stratification

In this province they call the principal men who have vassals and are inferior to the chief, saco. The saco has many other Indians subject to him, who have land and estates and are called cabra, who are like knights or noblemen, separate from the common people, who order others about. Fernández de Oviedo.[48]

The structure of society was distinctly stratified and hierarchical, and positions of rank or occupation could be inherited as well as won by achievement.[49] At the top of the society was the chief, whose functions and privileges have been described above.

Subchiefs and the relatives of the paramount chief seem to have made up a hereditary noble class. In some areas they were called *sacos*, or *piraraylos*. The *sacos* seem to have ruled the lands and vassals of the chief and to have acted as leaders in war. They formed an advisory council for the chief. They also were obliged to supply both gold and manpower to the chief when he needed them. The *sacos*, with the lesser nobility, had certain sumptuary privileges.[50] Their women, for example, got to wear longer skirts than others and had golden breast supports. Noblemen wore long, fringed cotton robes for special occasions and golden penis sheaths. They also had jewelry of gold and precious stones, which ordinary people did not have. By committing capital crimes, noble people could lose their rank and with it their privilege of burial.[51]

In addition to those who had noble rank by inheritance, there was also a class of nobles called *cabras*, who rose by achievement in war. By showing great bravery and success in battle for the chief, they could win titles, land, and slaves. They acted as captains, organizing fighting men for the chief and commanding them in battle during wartime.[52] They had administrative authority over commoners, and they acted under the direction of the hereditary nobles.

Little is written about these commoners in the Spanish accounts. Most people must have belonged to the class of food producers, either fishermen or farmers, or both. Many commoners may actually have been attached closely to the establishments of the chief and nobles. Some farm hands were buried with the chief, along with seed corn and their digging sticks, to grow food for him in the afterworld.[53]

More is written about the slave laborers and servants.[54] They were acquired by capture in war or were traded for commodities or luxury goods, and they bore cruel marks of servitude, such as brands, face paint, tattoos made with gold chisels, or knocked-out front teeth. The slaves apparently worked as goldminers, hunters, farm hands, domestics, personal servants, and bearers.

Among the occupational specialists, there were shamen. There were also apparently prostitutes and homosexual male transvestites for the use of chiefs.[55] There may also have been an occupational class of merchants or traders, as is mentioned in the literature on Colombia.[56] Finally, there seem to have been several types of specialized artisans who made luxury items, of whom the goldsmiths were a very important group.

The Coclé Goldsmiths

The patrons and employers of the Coclé goldsmiths were apparently the paramount chiefs and members of the noble classes, whose privilege it was to own and dispose of gold. The working of gold seems to have been highly specialized in the Colombia–Panama –Costa Rica cultural sphere, and a division of labor existed within the craft. Intensive gold mining in mountains and seasonal placer mining in alluvial deposits were done by slaves, or by commoners to fulfill their debts of tribute; in this sphere there was a division of labor by sex: men dug up the gold-bearing gravel and bearers carried it to a stream, where women carried out the panning.[57] A household of cooks and servants was maintained by the chief near the site of the mining to provide food for the specialized miners. In Colombia the actual working of the gold into artifacts was often done by an entirely distinct group of people, who were located near population centers where there was a market for gold.[58] In Panama, some chiefdoms had no mines or goldsmiths and they obtained gold ornaments by trade.[59] Other chiefdoms without gold mines specialized in the manufacture of gold ornaments, both for trade and for local use.[60]

The Coclé goldsmiths must have received long training in their art, but the accounts of the period of conquest are silent on this point. It appears that accomplished smiths were in great demand in parts of Colombia, and chiefs would compete for their services.[61] It has been suggested that master Panamanian smiths traveled extensively throughout the region and beyond, and the distribution of objects, styles, and techniques supports the idea.[62] Throughout the larger region, smiths were closely associated with trade.

It is likely that the smith's workshop was attached to the chief's establishment. The central Panamanian goldsmiths seem to have been closely identified with the chief and may actually have been members of the ruling class. A Spanish administrator wrote of the Panama Canal area, "the present cacique of Panama is called Coti. He and all his ancestors are great smelters of gold and masters of working it and very handsome articles are made there."[63] The organization of labor in the goldsmiths' workshops is not known, but it is likely that the smiths had assistants to provide fuel and lung power for the blow pipes. The chief whose capital town was an important gold emporium in Darien is said to have had over one hundred men working full-time in his house on the manufacture of gold ornaments.[64]

Fig. 14. *A*, hollow ear rod of embossed and "welded" gold. Length:11.5 cm. Weight:12.5 grams. No. 18; *B*, ear rod with embossed gold caps (reconstructed). Length:13.2 cm. No. 21; *C*, ear rod with one pointed cap of cast gold and one embossed gold cap (reconstructed). Length:16 cm. No. 20; *D*, ear rod with one gold cap of embossed and incised gold (reconstructed). Length:14.6 cm. No. 19. Temple site, El Caño, Coclé Province, Panama. Ear rods have been found *in situ* at the sides of skulls in ancient graves (Lothrop 1937:fig. 223; Mason 1942:107).

Fig. 15. Men in long, fringed cotton robes, seventeenth century, Darien Province, Panama. After Wafer 1903:108–109.

Origin Of The Coclé Tradition Of Goldworking

Little is known of the origins of the Coclé goldworking tradition. One of the minor stylistic components of the Coclé gold is clearly derived from the Quimbaya gold style of the upper Cauca Valley in Colombia, and the Panamanians imported and copied the best of the goldwork of many other regions. Nevertheless, the Panamanian styles are not just extensions of Colombian styles,[65] and there is no evidence to suggest that the Coclé tradition was derived from a particular tradition in any other region. In fact, recent archaeological work in central Panama reveals that goldworking was carried on in the early first millennium A.D.[66] The hammering of gold appears earliest in Peru during the second millennium B.C., and the Coclé styles of hammering and embossing may well be offshoots of the Peruvian tradition.[67] It is likely, however, that the technological complex of lost-wax casting, gold-copper alloying, and coloration gilding developed in the Colombia–Panama–Costa Rica sphere, rather than in Peru.[68] Lothrop wrote: "It might be urged that the Colombian region and adjacent territory represent a center of metallurgical invention . . . but we have no chronological data to prove it." As yet today, the small amount of scientific excavation that has been done in the larger region has not revealed much concrete information about the history of metallurgy.[69]

Gold Mining

Some of the gold worked by Isthmian smiths probably came from local alluvial deposits and was recovered by placer mining and panning; some was undoubtedly imported, probably from the rich mines in Colombia.[70] Spanish explorers heard of many rich deposits of gold in the Isthmus, and Vasco Núñez de Balboa himself found surface gold deposits in several places. There were at least three quite productive gold-bearing deposits in Panama: one on the upper Rio Grand de Coclé, one to the west in Veraguas, and one to the east in the Bay of San Miguel. Overall, however, the amount of placer, or alluvial gold, in Panama was probably small.

This system of mining exploits gold that has been removed from veins and transported by water.[71] The physical weathering of gold-bearing rocks in river headwaters dislodges particles and nuggets of gold, which are washed downstream with the alluvium. The gold-rich sediments were collected by the Indians and panned.[72] In some regions the Indians diverted streams to make the alluvial gold easier to get at. In 1515 Vasco Núñez de Balboa described the gold-mining methods of eastern Panamanian Indians in a letter to the Spanish government. He wrote, "The Indians assured me that there were very rich rivers near the houses of these caciques. . . . Their method of collecting gold is by going into the water and gathering it in their baskets. They also scrape it up in the beds of streams when they are dry."[73] In panning, the heavier gold is separated from the earth by agitation of the alluvium in water. Oviedo describes how the female washers would squat by the stream and flip water expertly in and out of their panning trays until the gold was washed clean of earth.

Copper was probably mined from superficial deposits of copper carbonate (Malachite).[74] It was probably imported from Colombia, where the only rich deposits were to be found.[75] The precious and semiprecious materials used in gold ornaments were apparently both imported and obtained locally. The emeralds set in cast-gold ornaments found at Sitio Conte are believed to have come from Ecuador or Colombia.[76] Pearls for setting in gold could be obtained in the Gulf of Panama.[77]

Fig. 16. Panning for gold in the sixteenth century, Colombia–Panama region. After the original edition of Fernández de Oviedo 1851–1855.
"*. . . they put certain Indians to mining the earth, and they heap up soil in wooden trays or troughs, and other Indians have the job of taking these trays to the water to be washed; but those who carry the trays don't wash them, rather, they go back for more soil. That which they leave is put in other trays for the women who do the washing. . . . These washers are seated on the edge of the water up to their knees in water . . . and they take the tray in both hands by the handles . . . and shake it, taking in water and putting it in the current with a certain dexterity, so that no more water enters the tray than that which the washer needs, and with the same skill they empty it. The water that leaves the tray floats the earth out little by little. The tray is concave and about the size of a barber's basin and about as deep. After all the earth has been thrown out, the gold is left in the bottom of the tray, and they set it aside and turn to take more soil and wash it.*" (Fernández de Oviedo 1950:250–251).

Gold And Tumbaga

Gold was the major metal worked in central Panama. Analysis of the gold in ornaments of Isthmian style reveals the presence of such impurities as silver, copper, and iron, indicating that local smiths did not refine gold.[78] The only ornament of completely pure gold appears to be an imported Ecuadorian piece. The gold of most of the Coclé-style artifacts that have been analyzed has been found to contain very little silver as an impurity, usually just over three percent. In contrast, gold ornaments of Colombian styles usually have a silver content of over sixteen percent, and those of styles indigenous to western Panama have between six and ten percent. The regional differences in silver content of gold have helped in the definition of local styles in a culture area that is characterized by much trade in gold artifacts.

In addition to the base metals that are present as impurities, about half the Coclé-style gold ornaments contain copper added as an alloy.[79] The copper content of the alloyed metal ranges from about eleven to eighty-nine percent. The gold-copper alloys of about ninety-percent gold are comparable to our twenty-one to twenty-four-carat gold; metal of sixty-percent gold is like fourteen-carat gold; and that with only thirty-percent gold compares with seven-carat gold.[80] The gold-copper alloys of New World metallurgy are called *tumbaga*, a word derived from the Malay word for copper; the alloys were called *karocol* in the Carib language and *guanin* in Arawak.[81]

The alloy *tumbaga* has several advantages over unalloyed gold and copper. First, when *tumbaga* is hammered, it reaches a much greater hardness than can

Fig. 17. Embossed gold finger ring with geometric decoration, Parita, Herrera, Panama. Diameter:1.9 cm. Width:2.1 cm. Weight:2 grams. No. 11. The ring is adjustable and has holes for fastening.

be achieved with gold or copper alone, a hardness that is similar to that of hammered bronze.[82] Second, use of *tumbaga* permits very delicate casting at relatively low temperatures. Its melting point is much lower than those of gold and copper. While copper melts at 1,083°C, and gold at 1,063°C, an alloy of eighteen-percent copper and eighty-two-percent gold has a melting point of about 800°C.[83] The lower melting point would make some varieties of *tumbaga* much more economical than unalloyed gold and copper because of a saving of fuel, an important consideration in aboriginal Panama, which the Spanish conquerors describe as treeless in many areas. Walter Ralegh's informant about goldworking in the mysterious lake of Manoa (somewhere in northern South America) certainly was aware of the eutectic (Greek for "easy to work") properties of gold-copper alloys when he said, "they gathered it in graines of perfect golde ... and they put to it a part of copper, otherwise they could not work it."[84] However, many of the Coclé artifacts of gold-copper alloy have a copper content above the fifteen to twenty percent that is required for the lower melting point.[85] It may have been difficult for Coclé smiths to achieve the desired copper content;[86] the balance scales that were used by Colombian smiths to weigh out the proper proportions are not mentioned in the literature on central Panama.

Fig. 18. Embossed gold helmet, Parita, Herrera Province, Panama. Length:22 cm. Width:19 cm. Weight:317.4 grams. No. 17. The helmet is apparently unfinished. On the outside, in the central and side panels, there are incisions and punch marks outlining a complex curvilinear design that was never embossed. The edge of the helmet is pierced, perhaps for the attachment of a fabric lining.

Gilding

A third useful property of *tumbaga* is that it can be surfaced with pure gold by depletion gilding, or coloration gilding (see fig. 19; no. 39).[87] Coloration gilding gives a pure gold surface to alloyed metal by removing a layer of base metal. There are two methods of coloration. One involves heating and acid treatment. When an object of gold-copper alloy is heated, a layer of black copper oxide is formed on the surface. The oxide can be dissolved away with acid, leaving a surface of pure gold on the artifact. Repeated alternation of heating and acid treatment creates a thicker layer of gold, which can be hammered and burnished to bring up the gold color. In a slightly different method, an alloyed object can be placed in a corrosive bath for a time, wherein surface copper is removed, leaving a dark, spongy layer of gold that can be consolidated by heating in an oxygen-free atmosphere and then hammering and burnishing.

Gold-copper alloys can be coloration gilded by the use of vegetable acids, such as oxalic acid. The technique is called *mise-en-couleur* ("coloration" in French). López de Gómara wrote about Colombian gilding: "There is in Santa Marta much gold, which they gild with a certain herb that is mashed and squeezed of juice; they rub the copper with it and dry it at the fire; the more of the herb they put on it, the more color it takes on, and it is so fine that it fooled many Spanish at first."[88] Oviedo wrote of the Colombia-Panama area, "the Indians know very well how to gild the pieces that they make of copper and very low gold; they give it such a lustre that it appears to be as good as twenty-three carat gold. . . . This they do with certain herbs."[89] The published sources of the conquest refer specifically to the use of plant juices for depletion gilding, but, as several scholars have pointed out, the ammonium carbonate in urine could have been used as well.[90]

An obvious economic advantage of gilding is that objects of alloyed metal can be made to look like objects of high-grade gold, and the Spanish believed that the Indians gilded *tumbaga* artifacts to dupe them. Studies of ancient Colombian metalworking show that a preference for gilded *tumbaga* over high-grade gold is most characteristic of regions that lack their own gold sources.[91] This suggests that in some regions where gold was scarce, *tumbaga* did function as a substitute for high-grade gold. However, it does not appear that the Coclé gilded *tumbaga* was made to conserve gold supplies, since gold was apparently more abundant than copper in the area.[92] Whatever the reason might have been for using *tumbaga* in the first place, the Coclé smiths may have gilded it to preserve the integrity of the metal alloy.[93] Although almost pure gold is highly resistant to corrosion, alloys of gold and copper corrode rapidly.[94] Corrosion of the alloy can be prevented by depletion gilding, since the surface of pure gold seals off the alloy from moisture and the air. Nevertheless, study of the gilded *tumbaga* ornaments from the metallurgical region shows that little attempt was made to renew gilding that had worn off.[95]

Hammering And Embossing

Many of the Coclé gold ornaments were made of hammered sheet metal. There are discs of all sizes, pierced for suspension as pendants or ornaments for clothing. Hammered gold strips were made into headbands, cuffs, and ear ornaments.

The process of manufacture probably began with a nugget or ingot of gold or alloy. By repeated hammering with stone or metal hand-hammers, the lump of metal could be stretched and thinned into a sheet (fig. 20). The sheet was probably cut into shape with stone points or metal chisels, and the edge smoothed with stone files and abraders.

Copper, gold, and gold-copper alloys become brittle after protracted hammering and have to be annealed to permit further hammering.[96] *Annealing* is the heat-treatment of metal to restore flexibility during hammering. The process is difficult, because too-great temperatures cause the metal to collapse and melt, and hammering metal that has not been sufficiently heated may cause it to crack. Laboratory analysis has shown that some of the hammered *tumbaga* discs from Sitio Conte had been annealed.[97]

High-grade gold stays soft much longer when subjected to hammering, and it is almost pure gold that the Coclé smiths used most often for large, deeply embossed and chased sheet-metal artifacts. Coclé embossed gold stands out in New World metalworking for excellence of design and technique. The hammered and burnished sheet gold to be embossed may have been worked over anvils of wood or stone into the desired shape. In some cases the artisan first traced the designs on the outer surface of the sheet gold with incision and punchmarks (see fig. 18). The goldsmith embossed the designs by pressing or tapping the sheet gold from behind, with an awl or punch, while bracing the sheet against a soft but resilient layer of leather or resin. (The pressure of the embossing tool stretches the sheet gold into the desired contours.) Coclé smiths supplemented embossed designs with chasing, or tooling, from the front of the sheet, and they sharpened the designs with incision.[98] Incision was used as a primary decorative technique only rarely.[99] The finished embossed artifact was often polished and burnished until it had a mirrorlike sheen (see figs. 6 and 27).

Fig. 19. Cast and gilded *tumbaga* pendant depicting a pair of curly-tailed animals, Las Palmas, Herrera Province, Panama. Length:3.7 cm. Height:2.9 cm. Weight:39.5 grams. No. 40.

Fig. 20. Hammering gold, Peru. After Benzoni 1857:251.

Fig. 21. *A*, monkey pendant of plant resin and embossed gold sheathing (one leg missing). Height:7 cm. No. 6; *B*, monkey pendant of agate and embossed gold sheathing. Height:6 cm. No. 5. Parita, Herrera Province, Panama.

Joints in sheet-gold artifacts were made either by clinching or a variety of welding.[100] Coclé smiths used clinching for the joints of telescoping earspools. The technique consists simply of folding and crimping the two sheets of metal to be joined. The "welding," or fusion of two sheets of metal by repeated heating and hammering, was used to join the edges in sheet-gold beads, pendants, and ear ornaments. So expert were the Coclé smiths that the welded joint is almost invisible and very difficult to find on the finished side, even under magnification.

The Coclé artisans made a great variety of objects by the technique of embossing. The best known are the deeply embossed "Crocodile God" plaques (see color plate 9*b* and fig. 31), which were worn as breastplates or sewn to clothing. There are also helmets (see fig. 18), greaves,[101] rings (no. 17), nose ornaments, and ear ornaments.

Sheathing

The Coclé goldsmiths used hammered and embossed sheet gold in an ingenious and unusual way to sheathe parts of pendant figurines and ornaments of stone, bone, whale-tooth ivory, resin, and wood (see figs. 21 and 29).[102] These delicate composite ornaments are seldom found outside of central Panama and seem to have been an art form particular to the Coclé style. The small figures of animals or animal-humans were carved or, in the case of some of the resin figures, mold-made. The face, ears, tail, legs, or paws were overlain or sheathed with gold. The smiths made the overlays by embossing hammered sheet gold into the shape of the part to be covered. Various nonrepresentational elements were also sheathed in gold, such as the "cusps" of the nose ornaments made of stone and the tips of some of the stone ear rods.

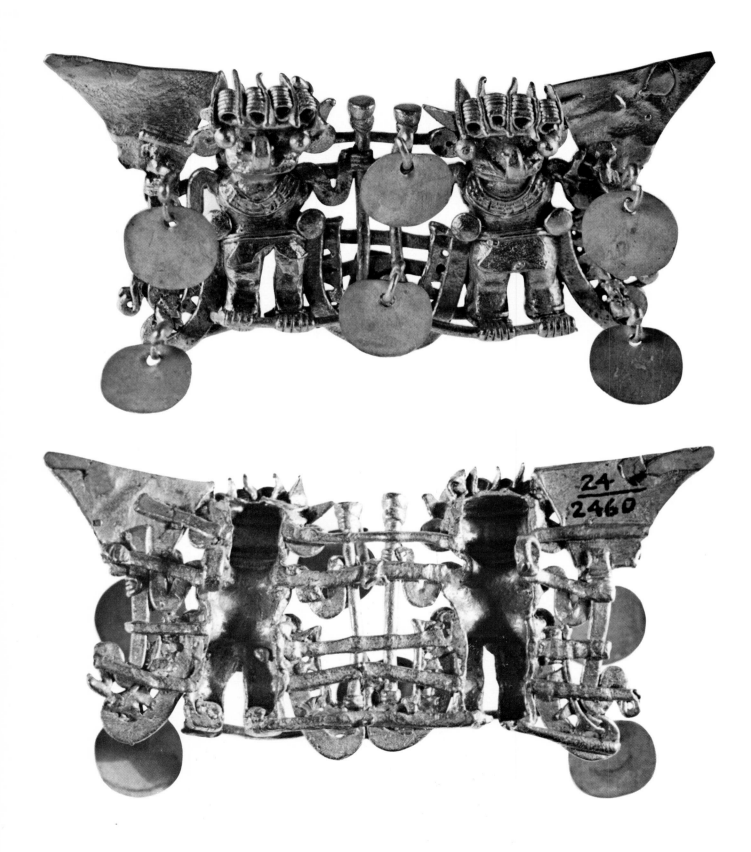

Fig. 22. Cast-gold pendant representing twin Bat Gods, Parita, Herrera Province, Panama. Height:4.5 cm. Width:9 cm. Weight:85.5 grams. No. 28. The pendant is decorated with six circular hammered danglers suspended from hooks. The clubs or standards in the figures' hands have been hammered to flatten out the stubs of the pouring channels or vents. The belt streamers of the figures are profile crocodile heads.

Casting

Gold casting is a major technical component of Coclé metallurgy. Coclé cast artifacts are exceptional in the tradition of New World metalworking for their richness of crisply executed detail (see fig. 22). Coclé smiths used both high-grade gold and *tumbaga*. The predominant technique of Coclé casting is the lost-wax method.[103]

The essence of lost-wax casting is the use of a wax model, which is melted and replaced in a clay mold by molten metal. In Coclé casting, the process began with a core of charcoal and clay, carefully fashioned in the shape of the artifact to be cast, minus surface details. A wax model of the artifact was built up on the core by the addition of wax sheets, threads, and nubbins. The Coclé smith might possibly have added resin to the wax to make it firmer. The most delicate of the Coclé castings were made up entirely of fine wax threads, a kind of cast filagree (see fig. 24). For a hollow casting in the round—a Coclé specialty—a wax model encircled the core.[104] For an open-back casting, the model was built up on one side of the core only. Funnel and rod-shaped pieces of wax were added to the model to provide vents for air (risers) and pouring channels for molten metal (runners, or gates).

In the light of the exquisite detail of Coclé cast gold, it is likely that the wax model of the artifact was finished off with a coating of finely ground charcoal, a measure which increases the delicacy of detail that can be achieved. The smith then would have enveloped the wax model with a layer of clay to form a mold. In preparation for casting, the smith would have heated the mold over a charcoal fire to remove the wax and permit the entry of the metal in its place. Gold or gold-copper alloys, melted in ceramic crucibles (see fig. 23), would then be poured into the mold to fill the space left by the wax model and to form the artifact. When the mold had cooled, the smith would break it and then cut and file off the protruberances left by the flow of gold in the vents and channels (figs. 1 and 33). The charcoal and clay core of a casting-in-the-round would be broken up and removed through a slit or hole in the artifact. Coclé smiths usually burnished the surface of cast artifacts and sometimes stretched and modified portions of them by hammering (see fig. 22). Cast artifacts of low-grade gold were depletion gilded and then burnished.

The delicate and intricate Coclé castings are a triumph of technique and design, but the Coclé jewelers were not content with plain casting. Many of the Coclé cast-gold ornaments that have been recovered from archaeological sites are set with precious and semiprecious stones. The most magnificent of these are the emerald settings found by Lothrop and Mason at Sitio Conte, but beautiful settings of pearls, quartz, and serpentine have also been found (fig. 37; nos. 30 and 46).[105]

Fig. 23. Melting gold in crucibles with blowpipes, sixteenth century, Colombia–Panama region. After Benzoni 1857:73.

Tools

The tools that the Coclé smiths used to make their *tumbaga* and gold masterpieces were apparently very rudimentary indeed. The metalworkers of the New World had in common a set of very simple tools (see fig. 25).[106] They dug in gold-bearing alluvial deposits with the fire-hardened tips of wooden sticks and possibly with stone hoes. Clay provided the material for cores, molds, braziers, and crucibles, and charcoal was the tempering material and the fuel. Blowpipes of ceramic or reed served, with human lung power, for bellows. Urine and plant juice were available for gilding. The wax for models came from wild, stingless bees, and the resin for models, figurines, and embossing supports came from trees.

For hammering tools the smiths relied on stone or metal hammers, and they worked on stone or wood anvils. Embossing, chasing, and burnishing would have been done with bone, antler, stone, and wood tools against the base of wax, resin, wood, or leather. The heavy leather could have come from wild animals, such as the tapir, peccary, or manatee. All incision, cutting, scoring, and modeling had to be done with chisels, awls, or spatulas made of metal, stone, wood, shell, ivory, or bone. The technical strengths of the region's smiths lay not in their development of tools, but in their creative use of knowledge about the physical and chemical properties of metals.

Fig. 24. Nose clip of cast-gold "filagree," Panama, collected by Samuel K. Lothrop. Diameter: 2.4 cm. Weight: 8.5 grams. No. 31.

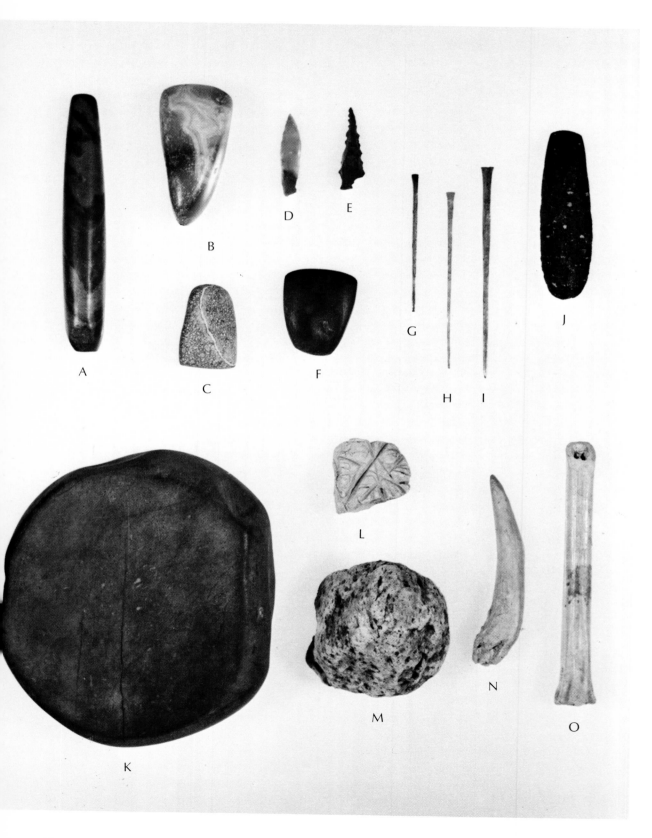

Fig. 25. *A*, cylindrical implement of ground and polished stone, temple site, El Caño, Coclé Province, Panama, collected by A. H. Verrill. Length:14 cm. No. 50. One end of the tool is rounded. The other is squared and shows flaking from use. It may have been used both as a hammer and as an embossing tool; *B*, agate burnishing stone, Coclé Province, Panama, collected by A. H. Verrill. Length:7.5 cm. No. 51; *C*, hammerstone, Coclé Province, Panama, collected by A. H. Verrill. Length:4.5 cm. No. 52; *D*, chipped agate point, Venado Beach, Canal Zone, Panama. Length:4.5 cm. No. 53. A stone point would have been useful for scoring and cutting sheet gold (Sonin, personal communication); *E*, chipped stone point, Rio Coclé, Coclé Province, Panama. Length:4.5 cm. No. 54. Possibly this point was used as a drill; *F*, ground stone celt, Venado Beach, Canal Zone, Panama. Length:4.6 cm. No. 55. A possible woodworking tool, the celt might have been used to shape wooden anvils for embossing and hammering; *G*, cast and hammered gold chisel, Panama. Length:7.5 cm. Weight:3.5 grams. No. 56; *H*, cast and hammered gold chisel, Panama. Length:9.8 cm. Weight:2.75 grams. No. 57; *I*, cast and hammered gold chisel, Panama. Length:11.6 cm. Weight:10 grams. No. 58. The chisel blades have been hardened by cold hammering (Sonin, personal communication). They may have been used to cut and incise metal or to shape wax models and clay cores and molds; *J*, chipped and polished stone chisel, Venado Beach, Canal Zone, Panama. Length:9 cm. No. 59. The chisel may have been a woodworking tool; *K*, ground-basalt anvil stone, west bank of the Rio Grande, Coclé Province, Panama, collected by A. H. Verrill. Diameter:14 cm. Height:5.75 cm. No. 49; *L*, sharpening stone, Coclé Province, Panama, collected by A. H. Verrill. Diameter:4.6 cm. No. 60. The stone could have been used to sharpen bone or stone cutting tools; *M*, lump of pumice, temple site, El Caño, Coclé Province, Panama, collected by A. H. Verrill. Diameter:7.5 cm. No. 61. Pumice could have been used for polishing metal; *N*, antler-tine awl, possibly used in embossing, Parita, Herrera Province, Panama. Length:10 cm. No. 62; *O*, bone tool, possibly used for embossing and burnishing, Rancho Juan Calderon, Parita, Herrera Province, Panama. Length:14.3 cm. No. 63.

Fig. 26. Cast-gold nose ring with decoration of four miniature frogs, Venado Beach, Canal Zone, Panama. Diameter:2.5 cm. Weight:11.3 grams. No. 32. The nose ring could never have been worn, as the ends are fused together. It may have been made for burial.

Style

There are a number of stylistic components in the Coclé goldworking tradition, but their temporal, geographic, and sociological significance is uncertain. Some of the stylistic distinctions within Coclé goldwork seem to have a technological basis, in part. For example, the designs on the famous large, embossed plaques have a sinuous quality of line very similar to that of designs painted on pottery and carved on bone, ivory, and stone. This style of representation is not found in contemporaneous cast artifacts. Its qualities seem to derive from the fact that the designs rendered in embossed gold, paint, and carving are drawn, rather than modeled. Cast artifacts have their origin in modeled sheets, lumps, and threads of wax. Accordingly, they have an entirely different quality of form than the depictions that began as drawings.

One style of goldwork seems to be restricted geographically. There is a group of very delicate cast-filagree ornaments, most of which apparently come from the area of Venado Beach in the Canal Zone.[107] The group may represent a subregional stylistic specialization in goldworking.

Some styles of Coclé goldwork are now known to have a temporal significance. Forty years research into the distribution of polychrome pottery in prehistoric garbage and graves has produced a chronological seriation, or ordering, of styles. Since the gold ornaments are almost always found in graves with pottery vessels, dating the pottery makes it possible to date the gold. Unfortunately, most of the Coclé-style gold in museums and private collections was excavated unscientifically, with the result that the associations between gold and pottery were not recorded. Fortunately, however, the scientific excavations at Sitio Conte, Coclé Province, uncovered numerous elite graves filled with abundant polychrome pottery and gold ornaments.[108] The ancient practice of robbing old graves to furnish new ones and the relatively small number of gold-bearing graves cause some difficulties in dating their contents, but the outlines of a chronological sequence of goldworking styles is beginning to emerge.

Fig. 27. Square embossed gold plaque with geometric decoration, Parita, Herrera Province, Panama. Length:12.3 cm. Width:11.4 cm. Weight:47 grams. No. 10.

According to ceramic associations, the Sitio Conte graves 1, 2, 31, and 32 of Lothrop's excavations date between A.D. 400 and 700, while Lothrop's graves 5, 6, 24, and 26, and Mason's 11, fall into the period A.D. 700 to 1100. There are considerable differences between the goldwork of the two periods. For example, the large, deeply embossed plaques of the early graves are quite realistic in representation and the iconography is variable, while the later plaques are more stylized and standardized in iconography. Certain kinds of objects seem to be restricted to one period, like the openwork cast-filagree nose clips and concentric-pattern nose rings of the early period, and the ear rods and cast-gold settings of the later period.

The characteristics of the goldwork styles of the period A.D. 1100 to 1520, the last period of prehistoric occupation, are not yet well-known. Farther west, in western and northern Veraguas State, the gold of the last few centuries before the conquest has an iconography that emphasizes "eagles," large birds with flat, outstretched wings and tail.[109] It has been suggested that such birds might also have been typical of the central Panamanian goldwork of the same time period.[110] The birds, however, are exceedingly scarce in central Panamanian collections,[111] despite the fact that the burials of the last period of occupation were placed in urns in conspicuous artifical earthen mounds, readily accessible to both archaeologists and grave robbers. It seems that the "eagles" make up a western regional type not necessarily diagnostic of the central Panamanian goldworking styles.

There are, however, other known styles of central Panamanian goldwork that may exemplify the gold of the last period. The Museum of the American Indian has a group of gold artifacts from central Panama that are unlike the published artifacts from Sitio Conte. These gold artifacts lack the characteristic represensative designs of the Sitio Conte gold and have instead geometricized decoration of zigzags, wavy lines, and dots (figs. 17 and 27; no. 14). Cooke has suggested that the iconography of late-period pottery, and this group of specimens in the Museum of the American Indian, seems to fulfill the prediction. Cooke also posits, on the basis of finds at El Canō, that there was a miniaturization of animal images in goldworking styles during the period A.D 1100–1520.[112] Interestingly, the museum's collections include several central Panamanian gold rings with decoration of rows of minute frogs (figs. 26 and 28; no. 33). It is possible that these artifacts exemplify the miniaturization that Cooke hypothesizes.

Iconography

There are several formal concepts that are highly developed in the ancient art of central Panama. One is the concept of doubling, or twining, images. Another important concept is the combination in one image of the features of several animals or of animals and humans, a convention that in its simplest form involves substitution of the parts of one creature for the same parts of another. An example is the endowment of a

Fig. 28. Adjustable cast-gold finger ring with decoration of three miniature frogs, Parita, Herrera Province, Panama. Diameter:2 cm. Width:1.5 cm. Weight:7.5 grams. No. 34.

human figure with the feet of a crocodile (fig. 31). A more complex expression of the concept is the substitution of one part of one kind of animal for another part of another animal. Examples are the substitution of birds' heads for the legs of a frog or the substitution of small crocodile heads for the legs and torso of an anthropomorphic crocodile.[113] An even more complex expression of the concept is the combination of two different images in one depiction. An example is the Sitio Conte embossed plaque that shows the Crocodile God when held right-side up and a grotesque face when held upside down.[114] A third important iconographic convention in Coclé art is the addition of animal parts to the dress of an animal or animal-human. For example, the anthropomorphic crocodiles and bats often wear belt tassels or headdresses of profile crocodile heads, and one rare example of crocodile man wears a headdress of deer antlers (color plate 9B; figs. 22 and 31). It is not possible to tell whether the additions represent apparel or actual appendages.

The different techniques of Coclé-style goldwork do not share an identical iconography. All, however, have a strong emphasis on animals. Human images with no animal features are quite rare, being mostly restricted to a minor style of cast figurine highly derivative of the "Quimbaya"-style figurine from Colombia.[115] A Coclé-style anthropomorphic deity, however, will occasionally be depicted in a wholly human guise, complete with characteristic dress and accouterments.

The gold-sheathed figurine pendants usually represent animals naturalistically, without mythological references.[116] Monkeys are very common (fig.21), but there are also birds, curly-tailed animals of uncertain identification (no. 8), crocodiles (fig. 29), and massive quadrupeds (no. 7).

The cast-gold objects have the most varied subject matter. They depict crocodiles (color plate 9a; fig. 30), crabs (fig. 37), insects (no. 39), monkeys, and possible dogs and seahorses. The main anthropomorphic image of cast work is the Bat God (color plate 9c; figs. 1 and 22). The creature is sometimes called the "warrior god" because he often holds a sort of club or standard, sometimes with trophy-head tassels.[117] The creature's batlike features consist of small, triangular ears and an upturned nose. The images vary in their degree of "batness." Some examples appear as normal humans.[118] Like many of the other images cast in gold, the Bat God is often shown doubled or with two heads. He seems to be associated with the Crocodile God and often has crocodile appendages (see fig. 22). Occasionally, a crocodile's head is substituted for the bat head.[119]

The Crocodile God, per se, however, is almost never rendered in cast goldwork.[120] His depiction occurs mainly in the embossed goldwork and in the ceramic art (color plate 9B; figs. 4 and 31). A complex combination of human and animal,

this deity is represented full face, with arms extended and feet turned out. The face is square, the eyes round and staring, the mouth bristles with teeth. From the top of the head sprout great crests with sharply pointed appendages which have been interpreted as plumes or scales. The body, while not realistically rendered, is distinctly human but the hands and feet are armed with claws. Around the waist is a belt with a pattern suggesting some woven material, from either side of which depends a flowing streamer. . . . [121]

The identification of this creature with the crocodile is reinforced by the addition of profile crocodile heads as tassels on decorative streamers (fig. 22)[122] or as headdresses (color plate 9b) and by the transposition of paired crocodile heads for the creature's head or legs. One unique depiction seems to wear on his head the antlers of a deer (fig. 31).

Other images executed with embossing are frogs, birds, nonanthropomorphic crocodiles, spiders, and rare sharks. There are also ingenious imitations of animal teeth and shell ornaments in embossed gold (color plate 8a; fig. 38). Geometricized motifs consist mainly of dots, wavy lines, and serrations (figs. 17 and 27; no. 14). The serrations may actually represent the crest of the crocodile.[123] The serrated pattern also occurs in cast goldwork as well, on the necks of crocodiles (color plate 9a), and as a device decorating other animals (no. 46). The Crocodile God and the Bat God are thought to have been gods in the ancient mythology because they do not occur in nature and thus must be the creation of religious imagination. The Crocodile God may have been the central figure in central Panamanian religion, for depiction of him or apparent visual references to him are found in many media and with great frequency. André Emmerich has written:

The crested alligator is a major motif that runs through all of Coclé art, often in a highly stylized form that becomes a kind of iconographic shorthand. . . . Judging by its frequency and widespread appearance in the art of Coclé and also to the west in Veraguas, Chiriqui, and the Diquis region, it seems almost certain that the design represents a dominant, all-pervasive deity or religious concept. [124]

The gold objects on which the Crocodile God is represented are almost entirely restricted to the rich, multiple burials, which suggests that this deity may have been part of a cult of rulership.

Linares[125] has attempted to find a psychological significance in the iconography of central Panama. Citing the frequent representation of stinging insects and dangerous animals and the supposed lack of common edible animals, she argues that the symbolic system of animal motifs was used to express the aggression and hostility characteristic of the aboriginal societies. A problem with these interpretations is that common edible creatures are in fact important in the ancient iconography. Study of archaeological refuse in central Panama reveals that many of the "hostile" and "cryptic" animals were eaten by the ancient people. In the light of the distinctly zoomorphic character of Coclé iconography, it is likely that the representation of images is linked to a mythological explanation of the native ecological adaptation.[126] However, a valid ecological analysis of central Panamanian art will require a detailed reconstruction of the cultural adaptation.

Trade And Influence In Goldworking

Within the cultural sphere to which the Coclé chiefdoms belonged, there seems to have been exchange of much gold, gold artifacts, goldworkers, and technological, stylistic, and iconographic information. Artifacts were traded widely, probably passing from person to person by barter. Some artifacts left their regions of manufacture when the treasury of a defeated chief was raided by the victors. Some of the influence that people of different regions had on each other can be explained by the movement of finished artifacts, which were valued and copied by local smiths. Some of this influence, however, has to be due to the movement of goldsmiths. As Bray has written: "Trade, looting, and pilgrimage can account for the spread of manufactured articles over a wide area, but the transmission of complex techniques like metalworking involves the actual movement of traveling smiths and specialists."[127]

Fig. 29. Crocodile pendant of carved stone sheathed with embossed gold, Veraguas Province, Panama. Length:12 cm. No. 43. There are microscopic chisel cut marks on the metal sheathing (Sonin, personal communication).

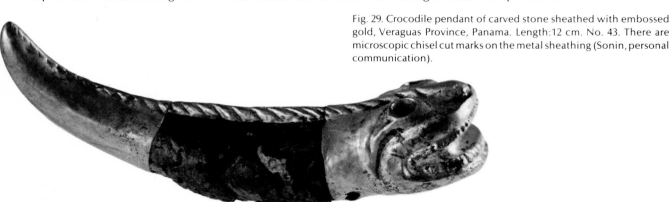

Fig. 30. Cast-gold double bell pendant with a pair of crocodiles on top, Panama. Height:2.8 cm. Weight:38 grams. No. 47.

The gold ornaments made by Panamanian smiths were apparently much valued in the other chiefdoms of the region and beyond. Panamanian artifacts have been found in Colombia, Costa Rica, and the Yucatan, and apparent copies of Panamanian artifacts have turned up in Colombia and Costa Rica (see figs. 1 and 34).[128] Similarly, artifacts by some of the most accomplished foreign smiths were imported into the Panamanian region, and local smiths copied some of the styles with which they came into contact.[129] Despite the openness of the central Panamanian smiths to influence from the foreign goldworking traditions, the local smiths maintained an outstanding, distinctive tradition of their own.

The End Of The Tradition

What thing, then is this, Christians? Is it possible that you set a high value upon such a small quantity of gold? You nevertheless destroy the artistic value of these necklaces, melting them down into ingots. Martyr[130]

It is sad and ironic that the very richness of the central Panamanian chiefdoms brought their doom at the hands of the Spanish. Upon hearing of the chiefs' rich treasuries from their neighbors, the Spanish set out to seize the gold, gain possession of any mines, and secure slaves to work them. It took them several years to subdue the central Panamanians, from about 1516 to 1520. The Indians had the advantage of greater numbers and had a highly developed military art. Biese has written: "Pedrarias [a Spanish administrator] . . . did not reckon with the fierce opposition the Indians would display in resisting the seizure of their precious metal. The Spanish had to mount at least four expeditions against the chief known as Parita . . . and were able to occupy the territory only after his death."[131]

Despite their valiant resistance, the chiefdoms could not withstand the European military, and one by one they fell. The death toll was tremendous; it is said that forty thousand Indians died during one Spanish campaign.[132] The chiefs were forced to give up their treasures under torture, and they persuaded their allies to do likewise.[133] The land was pillaged, and houses and fields were razed. The Spanish sometimes mutilated captured Indians by cutting off their hands or noses.[134] Fernández de Oviedo wrote at the time, "there is not space or time to express wholly that which the Spanish did to devastate the Indians and rob them and destroy their land."[135] An historian of the conquest has written: "The malignant cruelty and vicious depravity displayed by the Spanish under Pedrarias is almost beyond belief."[136]

Soon after the defeat, there was a rapid decimation of the Indian population, due partly to the impact of the new diseases and partly to the labor policies of the Spanish.[137] De Andagoya wrote at the time: "As each Cacique had to give nearly all to his Indians, who were required to till the ground and build houses, and those that remained were taken off to the mines, where they died, in a short time neither the chiefs nor the Indians were to be found in all the land." By the 1620s speakers

Fig. 31. Embossed gold disc representing the Crocodile God with antlers on his head, Coclé Province, Panama. Height:10 cm. Width:11 cm. Weight:37.5 grams. No. 4.

Fig. 32. Pair of ear spools of embossed and clinched gold. Diameter: 3.6 cm. Weight: 13 grams. No. 22. The spools come apart for insertion.

The destruction of the Panamanian societies by war, disease, and enforced labor spelled the end of the tradition of goldworking. The tradition had developed in service to the chiefdoms and could not survive without them. The manufacture of ornaments ceased when they were no longer needed for the chiefs' treasuries, for symbols of noble status, for trade goods, or for diplomatic bargaining. The Indian chiefs and nobles were not replaced by Europeans as patrons of central Panamanian artisans because there was no European market for these products. None of the Indian arts survived the conquest of this area. Cooke has written, "No trace of the polychrome pottery, colored textiles, goldworking has survived, but the system of agriculture was adopted by the mestizo peasant and still remains an integral part of production in the region."[145]

In more recent years, the ancient goldwork has found a market because of the rising interest of art collectors in pre-Colombian art. As Emmerich has pointed out, the commercial interest in the gold artifacts as art objects has saved a great many from being melted down for the gold.[146] Nevertheless, the search for marketable gold artifacts is a major cause of the destruction of archaeological sites. This wholesale ruination of the sites is the main cause of the lack of knowledge about the ancient chiefdoms of central Panama and the wonderfully skilled goldsmiths who worked for them.

of native languages had practically disappeared from the land.[138] In this way a population of as many as two million was drastically reduced in the space of just a few years.

Most of the gold that the Spanish got in Panama came from artifacts seized from the Indians.[139] The amount of this booty was sizable. Peter Martyr writes of the first expedition to the heart of central Panama, "during their journey they had collected piles of gold, girdles, women's breast ornaments, earrings, headdresses, necklaces and bracelets, to the value of eighty thousand castellanos."[140] The booty from Parita's house alone amounted to almost four hundred pounds of gold, and the four trunks of gold he gave to buy off the Spanish earlier may have contained as much as five hundred pounds.[141] Despite the large amount of gold that they got by melting down ornaments, the Spanish were really only interested in finding productive gold mines.[142] The nature of the European economy determined that the gold had a much higher value than the artifacts. Panama, however, had no rich gold veins, and the placer mines did not last long. According to Sauer, "The accumulations of placer gold were slight, as the natives knew and the Spanish would not believe."[143] When the rich metal mines of Mexico and Peru were discovered, the Spanish speedily abandoned Panama.[144] They had destroyed the native societies in a search for rich gold mines that did not exist.

1. Cooke 1976b:23-32, 1976c:314-332, 1976d:452, 1977:23; Cooke and Camargo 1977:154-157.
2. Lothrop 1942, 1966:205; Stirling 1949b:376; Ladd 1964. The cultural tradition associated with the polychrome pottery styles is often called Coclé, because the pottery, like the goldwork, was first recovered scientifically in Coclé Province. It is customary to name archaeological styles and cultures in this way. Archaeologists who study Panama, however, are loathe to use the term, fearing it might imply that the culture was confined to Coclé Province or that it first developed there. Unfortunately, they have not supplied an alternate term, and one is left with the cumbersome and inaccurate designation: central Pacific Panama. It is hoped that the archaeologists will work out a terminology soon, for the convenience of scholars, students, and interested nonspecialists.
3. Over the years there has been much argument over the meaning of the geographic distribution of polychrome pottery. The existing archaeological evidence suggests to this author that the pottery was made throughout Pacific Panama, from Montijo Bay to the Pearl Islands and beyond the Canal Zone almost to the border of Darien Province (Linné 1929:266-269; Lothrop 1942, 1948a, 1950; Dade 1959, 1961, 1970, 1972; Wassen 1960; Mahler 1961; Biese 1964; Ladd 1964; Linares 1968:87-89; Cooke 1972a, 1976a, 1976c, 1976e, 1979). The polychrome pottery found outside of this region would presumably have been traded there. Lothrop, however, felt that the actual manufacture of the pottery was confined to the central provinces of Herrera, Los Santos, and Coclé. Cooke, on the other hand, feels that the boundaries of the region of polychrome pottery manufacture extended as far west as the Tabasara River, but no farther east than Chamé. The disagreements will probably remain unresolved until further archaeological survey is done in Panama.
4. Lothrop 1934, 1937, 1942, 1948a, 1954, 1956; Ladd 1957, 1964; E. Lothrop 1948:145-234; Mason 1941; Stirling 1949a, 1949b, 1950; Bull 1958, 1961, 1965a; Sander et al. 1958; Mitchell and Acker 1961; Elliott 1965; Cooke 1972a, 1972b, 1976d; Verrill 1927a, 1927b, 1928, 1929:72-93, 1942.
5. Bull 1965b; Cooke and Camargo 1977.
6. Cooke 1972a:I:447, 1977:9.
7. Lothrop 1942, 1959a:88, 1959b:169, 1960, 1966; Ladd 1957, 1964; Linares 1968:87-89; Cooke 1972a, 1976a, 1976b:29-30, 1976c:316; Cooke and Camargo 1977:149; Haberland 1978:413, 415-419.
8. Kubler 1962:216.
9. Some anthropologists (Linares 1977:31; Cooke 1977:10; Cooke and Camargo 1977:155; Helms 1976) have pronounced these societies to be "rank" societies, according to the typology of Morton Fried (1960:718-719, 721-722, 728, 1967:110-115, 129-133, 183, 189-190, 1978:36-39). In Fried's scheme, in rank societies the chief rules by authority, not physical force. Kinship is the organizational basis for the ranks of society, and there are no occupational or economic classes or full time specialists, except for the chief and possibly the shaman. Thus no important differences in access to life-sustaining resources exist between people other than those determined by sex and age. In states or stratified chiefdoms, on the other hand, the ruler can use force to control people. Society is organized in economic or occupational classes, and there are great differences between people of different classes in their access to life-sustaining resources. As the discussion will document, the ethnohistory and archaeology show clearly that the aboriginal societies of central Panama and parts of eastern Panama were not rank societies but small states, a conclusion put forth in the earliest interpretations of aboriginal Panamanian society (Lothrop 1937; Baudez 1963; Sauer 1966).
10. The conquest-period descriptions of aboriginal societies in both central and eastern Panama are considered applicable to the reconstruction of the prehistoric societies of central Panama. The Spanish writers made it clear that the structure of economy and society were the same throughout the region, despite differences in language and dress. They did note, however, that populations were denser, towns larger, chiefdoms more extensive, chiefs stronger, war more intense, and food and gold more abundant in central Panama than elsewhere (Sauer 1966:271-272).
11. de Andagoya 1865:24-25, 29-31; Martyr 1912:I:406; de Herrera 1725:II:136; Lothrop 1948b:253.
12. de Espinosa 1864:488, 1873:41-42; Lothrop 1948b:254.
13. Cooke 1972a:I:447.
14. de Espinosa 1864:488. All translations from Spanish works cited are by the author.
15. de Andagoya 1865:25, 28; de Herrera 1725:II:87; Verrill 1927a:53-54; Cooke 1977:7-8.
16. The aboriginal mode of cultivation is sometimes identified as *swidden* or *slash-and-burn* cultivation (Cooke 1976c:314, 1978; Cooke and Camargo 1977:155), a method in which the forest is cut and burned so that the land can be farmed. After a few years of cropping, the fields are left fallow so that the forest can grow back to support further cultivation. The archaeological evidence and the conquest reports, however, indicate that aboriginal agriculture was a highly intensive system of annual and semiannual cropping, not swidden.
    For information about the central Panamanian landscape and aboriginal subsistence see: de Espinosa 1873:42-43, 1864:485, 488, 506, 512, 519; de Andagoya 1865:17-18, 25, 28-31; Martyr 1912:I:225, 409-410; Fernández de Oviedo 1851:I:355, 1853:III:136, 142, 1950:117-118, 136; Wafer 1903:69-172; Lothrop 1937:3, 15-18; Sauer 1966:285-287; Stone 1966:220; Cooke 1972a:I:420-428, 439-440, 463-465, 1976b, 1977, 1978; Cooke and Camargo 1977:145-146; Ranere and Hansell 1978:53-55.
17. de Andagoya 1865:xi-xii, 10-11; Fernández de Oviedo 1853:III:140; de Espinosa 1864:490-491, 508; Martyr 1912:I:221; Stone 1966:229; Sauer 1966:246, 271-276; Cooke 1972a:I:448, 1976b:26, 1976d:457, 1977:9.
18. Much has been made of the flexibility and instability of the aboriginal political systems of central Panama (Linares 1977:31; Helms 1976). Scholars have imagined that the tenure of chiefs was most uncertain and that there was little continuity of rule through time. Nonetheless, the chiefs described by the early Spanish observers were clearly hereditary rulers, often preceded by a long line of chiefs, whose bodies were kept reverently in mortuary chapels in the chief's palace (for example, Martyr 1912:I:219, 222; Fernández de Oviedo 1950:130-131; de Andagoya 1865:15).

Fig. 33. Trophy-head bell of cast gold, Parita, Herrera Province, Panama. Diameter:2.3 cm. Weight:20 grams. No. 38. Remnants of two pouring channels (runners) or vents (risers) can be seen on either side of the suspension loop.

19. de Andagoya 1865:12–13, 25, 30; Martyr 1912:I:310, 405; Helms 1976:25–26; Fernández de Oviedo 1853:III:132, 1950:129; de Herrera 1725:II:131, 136; de Espinosa 1864:490, 519, 1873:25; Lothrop 1937:10–12.
20. Fernández de Oviedo 1853:III:131; de Espinosa 1864:488, 512; Martyr 1912:I:219, Lothrop 1948b:254.
21. de Andagoya 1865:x–xii.
22. Wafer 1903:140–144; Mason 1940:17, 1941:263; Lothrop 1937:125.
23. Fernández de Oviedo 1851:I:134, 1853:III:154–156, 1950:128–133; de Espinosa 1873:23–25, 27–28; de Andagoya 1865:15–16; Martyr 1912:I:219–220; Lothrop 1937:43–64, 1954, 1956; McGimsey 1959; López de Gómara 1922:I:165; de Herrera 1725:II:6, 100–101, 133–134; Mason 1940:15–16, 1941, 1942, 1943:56; Stirling 1949a:378, 394; Stone 1966:226–227.
24. de Espinosa 1873:24.
25. Lothrop 1937:8.
26. Lothrop 1937:64.
27. de Espinosa 1873:24–25, 27.
28. Some of the richly dressed bodies in the archaeological chiefly graves may be those of noblemen killed in battle with the chief (Mason 1942:105; Linares 1977:43).
29. Lothrop 1937:269–277.
30. de Herrera 1725:II:101; Fernández de Oviedo 1853:III:126, 1950:142.
31. Martyr 1912:I:219; Fernández de Oviedo 1950:120; de Andagoya 1865:13, 15, 26; de Herrera 1725:II:133; Wafer 1903:154.
32. Lothrop 1956:35–36.
33. Fernández de Oviedo 1853:III:129–130, 142; de Andagoya 1865:13; de Herrera 1725:II:131; Lothrop 1937:26, 1954:234; Torres de Arauz 1972b:32.
34. de Andagoya 1865:26–27, 30; de Espinosa 1864:495–496; Martyr 1912:I:407; de Herrera 1725:II:91–92, 137, 1726:III:30–31; Lothrop 1937:4–8, 22; Anderson 1911:195; Biese 1967:204–205.
35. Martyr 1912:I:221–222, 306, 406; de Andagoya 1865:16–17, 25, 30–31; López de Gómara 1922:I:163; Fernández de Oviedo 1853:III:129, 1950:123; Torres de Arauz 1972b:32; Linares 1977:31.
36. de Herrera 1726:III:135; Fernández de Oviedo 1950:136; de Andagoya 1865:24, 29; Cooke 1972a:437–438, 449–450.
37. Lothrop 1937:4–6; de Herrera 1725:II:92, 96–97; de Espinosa 1864:488; Sauer 1966:271; Cooke 1976c:315.
38. Cooke 1972a:459.
39. Martyr 1912:I:309; Wafer 1903:146–147.
40. de Andagoya 1865:16–17; de Espinosa 1864:516–517; de las Casas 1876:IV:209; Fernández de Oviedo 1853:III:126–127, 129; de Herrera 1725:II:87, 134; Martyr 1912:I:284; Lothrop 1937:20–22.
41. de Espinosa 1864:497; Fernández de Oviedo 1950:141.
42. de Andagoya 1865:31; Lothrop 1937:61, 1954:229, 232; Stirling 1949a:385, 394.
43. de Andagoya 1865:14–16; de Espinosa 1864:505; Fernández de Oviedo 1853:III:125–126, 154–156, 1950:124–125, 128–129; Martyr 1912:I:219, 285; López de Gómara 1922:I:165; de Herrera 1725:II:100–101, 132–134; Wafer 1903:60–62; Lothrop 1937:7–29, 1950:131–132, 1954; Stone 1966:230–232.
44. de Herrera 1725:II:100.
45. Lothrop 1937:fig. 150.
46. Cooke 1976d:452.
47. Martyr 1912:I:219; de Herrera 1725:II:6.
48. Fernández de Oviedo 1950:116.
49. Fernández de Oviedo 1853:III:125–131, 138, 142, 1950:116–117; de Espinosa 1864:495; de Andagoya 1865:II–12, 30; Wafer 1903; Lothrop 1937:13–14, 22–24, 1948b:255; de Herrera 1726:III:18.
50. López de Gómara 1922:I:163; Fernández de Oviedo 1853:III:126, 138, 1950:122, 142; Wafer 1903:138–144.
51. Fernández de Oviedo 1853:III:129, 142; Lothrop 1937:26.
52. de Espinosa 1864:495.
53. Fernández de Oviedo 1950:129.
54. Fernández de Oviedo 1853:III:126, 138, 1950:123, 141–142; de Andàgoya 1865:xii, 11; Martyr 1912:I:404–405; Lothrop 1937:13–14, 22–23, 1948b:255; Cooke 1972a:I:459.
55. Martyr 1912:I:285; Fernández de Oviedo 1853:III:134; Lothrop 1937:22–23.
56. Bray 1974b:43; Plazas and Falchetti 1978:41–42.
57. de Herrera 1725:II:131; Bray 1974b:41–42; 1978:24–26; Fernández de Oviedo 1851:I:184–186, 1950:248–252.
58. Gordon 1957:42; Sauer 1966:227–229.

Fig. 34. Cast-gold pendant representing a curly-tailed animal, Guapiles, Linea Vieja region, Costa Rica. Height:3.1 cm. Length:5 cm. Weight:13 grams. No. 37. The pendant may have been traded from central Panama to Costa Rica. The metal is very thin, the product of well-controlled casting (Sonin, personal communication).

59. Martyr 1912:I:221.
60. Sauer 1966:276.
61. Bray 1974b:46, 1978:26.
62. Emmerich, personal communication; Bray 1974b:46–48.
63. Translated and quoted by Sauer 1966:276.
64. de Andagoya 1865:x; Sauer 1966:227.
65. Stone and Balser 1958:11.
66. Dade 1960:fig. 19a; Ichon 1975:59, 84; Torres de Arauz 1972a:47, 1972b:61–63; Cooke 1972a:I:425–429; 1976b:28; 1976d:458–459, personal communication.
67. Grossman 1972; Lothrop 1937:70.
68. Lothrop 1937:70; Root 1949:214; Lechtman 1971:3; Plazas and Falchetti 1978:32.
69. Bray 1978:39–40.
70. Wafer 1903:56–57; Lothrop 1937:75, 77, 1950:49–50; Plazas and Falchetti 1978:40; Stone and Balser 1958:13; Sauer 1966:229, 246, 276–277; Martyr 1912:I:221, 308–311; de Andagoya 1865:xi–xii, 10; de Herrera 1725:II:88.
71. Fernández de Oviedo 1851:I:186, 1950:252; Sauer 1966:244; Patterson 1971:290.
72. de Andagoya 1865:xi–xii, 10–11; Fernández de Oviedo 1851:I:183–189, 1950:251; Bray 1974b:41–42, 1978:24.
73. de Andagoya 1865:10.
74. Sonin, personal communication.
75. Plazas and Falchetti 1978:24–25.
76. Lothrop 1937:186–190.
77. Benzoni 1857:236; de Acosta 1880:I:227.
78. Lothrop 1937:73–81, 108.
79. Root 1949:222; Lothrop 1937:78–81.
80. Lothrop et al. 1957:62; Emmerich 1965:166; Plazas and Falchetti 1978:29, fig. 9.
81. Fernández de Oviedo 1855:IV:599; Martyr 1912:I:344; Lothrop 1937:78, 80; Stone and Balser 1958:13.
82. Lothrop 1937:80; Root 1949:214, 1961:251; Bray 1974a:34, 1978:27–28.
83. Lothrop 1937:77, 81; Root 1949:214, 1961:251; Bray 1974a:34, 1978:28; Plazas and Falchetti 1978:28.
84. Ralegh 1848:96.
85. Lothrop 1937:77, 81; Sonin, personal communication.
86. Lothrop 1950:52.
87. Bergsoe 1938:35–37; Root 1949:220–221, 1961:251–252; Lothrop and Bergsoe 1960:106–108; Lechtman 1971:2–4; Stone and Balser 1958:20, 21; Bray 1974a:37–38, 1978:37–38; Plazas and Falchetti 1978:37–38.
88. López de Gómara 1922:I:170.
89. Fernández de Oviedo 1851:I:189; see also 1950:253–254.
90. Bergsoe 1938:36; Root 1949:220; Lothrop and Bergsoe 1960:106–108; Plazas and Falchetti 1978:37–38.
91. Plazas and Falchetti 1978:29.
92. Lothrop 1937:80.
93. Plazas and Falchetti 1978:37–38.
94. Bergsoe 1938:9–12.
95. Sonin, personal communication.
96. Root 1949:211; Easby 1956:404, 406; Stone and Balser 1958:18.
97. Lothrop 1937:86 and fig. 269d.
98. Lothrop 1937:fig. 90; Stone and Balser 1958:19.
99. Lothrop 1937:87.
100. Bergsoe 1937:31; Lothrop 1937:84–85; Stone and Balser 1958:17.
101. Lothrop 1937:fig. 142.
102. Lothrop 1937:plate II, figs. 166–167, 182–186; Mason 1940, 1943:53; Stone and Balser 1958:19.
103. Bray 1974a:33–36, 1978:31–36; Plazas and Falchetti 1978:32–35; Stone and Balser 1958:15–17; Easby 1956:406–408.
104. Lothrop 1937:82; Easby 1956:408; Lothrop et al. 1957:31; McGimsey 1968:47.
105. Lothrop 1937:front plate 87, 186; Emmerich 1965:95–96.
106. Sonin; personal communication, Ralegh 1848:96; Benzoni 1857:250–251; Lothrop 1937:82, 1952:16–19; Root 1949:209–210; Easby 1956:409; Stone and Balser 1958:13–14, 23; Emmerich 1965:169; Bruhns 1972; Bright 1972; Bray 1974a:36, 1978:27–38, 118; Plazas and Falchetti 1978:30–31, 36–38; Lange 1978:112.
107. Lothrop 1956:38–40; Emmerich 1965:90–91.
108. Lothrop 1937, 1942; Mason 1940, 1941, 1942, 1943:50, 52–56.
    There have been other finds of gold objects associated with polychrome pottery (Mitchell 1962; Biese 1962:fig. 5a, 1966:fig. 1d; Doyle 1960; Dade 1960:19a; Ichon 1975:59; Cooke 1976d, 1976e), but the objects are either nondiagnostic in style or of styles that occur very rarely in central Panama, and thus they are not very useful for improving knowledge about the dating of goldwork styles.
109. Lothrop 1950:56–59; McGimsey 1968:50.
110. Cooke 1976d:458–459, personal communication.
111. For examples, see Lothrop 1937:184–185; Biese 1962:fig. 5a.
112. Cooke 1976d:476, fig. 12a.
113. Lothrop 1937: figs. 88 and 95.
114. Lothrop 1937:fig. 95.
115. Lothrop 1937:plate IIIf, figs. 147 and 148, 1952:95–97; Emmerich 1965:72, 97; McGimsey 1968:48–49.
116. Mason 1940; Lothrop 1937:figs. 160 and 175.
117. Lothrop 1937:fig. 150; Biese 1967:202.

118. Lothrop 1937:fig. 150; Biese 1967:208.
119. Biese 1967:207.
120. For rare exceptions, see Lothrop 1937:fig. 160a and Verrill and Verrill 1953:plate XI9.
121. Lothrop 1937:123.
122. Lothrop 1937:fig. 2.
123. Emmerich 1965:94-95.
124. Emmerich 1965:94-95.
125. Linares 1976, 1977:59-70.
126. Cooke 1978:11-12.
127. Bray 1974b:46-47.
128. Lothrop 1952:94-105; Stromsvik 1942:fig. 13c; Emmerich 1965:94, 116, 121; Pendergast 1970; Stone and Balser 1958, 1965; Balser 1966; Bray 1977.
129. Lothrop 1937:69-70; Emmerich 1965:72, 74, 78-79; Biese 1967:208; Torres de Arauz 1972b:63.
130. From a speech by the oldest son of a paramount chief in Darien, as told to Martyr (1912:I:220) by one of the Spanish explorers.
131. Biese 1967:203.
132. Sauer 1966:262.
133. Martyr 1912:I:301.
134. de Herrera 1725:II:95.
135. Fernández de Oviedo 1853:III:43.
136. Anderson 1911:189.
137. de Andagoya 1865:23; Sauer 1966:283-289; Torres de Arauz 1972b:90; Cooke 1976b:32.
138. Vasquez de Espinosa 1942:305-306.
139. Sauer 1966:275-276.
140. Martyr 1912:I:407.
141. Lothrop 1937:8; Emmerich 1965:92.
142. Sauer 1966; Plazas and Falchetti 1978:153.
143. Sauer 1966:244.
144. Lothrop 1948a:147; Cooke 1972a:I:447.
145. Cooke 1976b:32.
146. Emmerich 1965:xxi, 170.

REFERENCES

Anderson, C. L. G.
  1911   Old Panama and Castilla del Oro. Washington, D.C.: Press of the Sudwarth Company.
Balser, Carlos
  1966   Los objectos de oro de los estilos estranjeros de Costa Rica. Actas y Memorias del 36 Congreso Internacional de Americanistas, Barcelona, Madrid, Seville, 1964. Vol. 1, pp. 391-398. Sevilla.
Baudez, Claude S.
  1963   Cultural Development in Lower Central America. In Aboriginal Cultural Development in Latin America: An Interpretive Review. Betty J. Meggers and Clifford Evans, eds. Pp. 45-54. Smithsonian Miscellaneous Collections, Vol. 146, No. 1. Washington, D.C.:Smithsonian Institution.
Benzoni, Girolamo
  1857   History of the New World. W. H. Smyth, trans. and ed. London:Hakluyt Society.
Bergsoe, Paul
  1937   The Metallurgy and Technology of Gold and Platinum among the Pre-Columbian Indians. Ingeniorvidenskabelige Skrifter, No. A-44. Copenhagen.
  1938   The Gilding Process and the Metallurgy of Copper and Lead among the Pre-Columbian Indians. Ingeniorvidenskabelige Skrifter, No. A-46. Copenhagen.
Biese, Leo P.
  1962   La Arena de Quebra—A Mixed Cultural Site on the Azuero Peninsula. Panama Archaeologist 5(1):28-35.
  1964   The Prehistory of Panama Viejo, Panama. Bureau of American Ethnology Bulletin 191, Anthropological Papers, Nos. 150-168, pp. 1-51. Washington, D.C.: Smithsonian Institution.

Fig. 35. Cast-gold frog pendant, Parita, Herrera Province, Panama. Length:3.6 cm. Weight:7.5 grams. No. 35. Impressions on the inside of the pendant indicate that the model for casting was built up of small, square sheets of wax (Sonin, personal communication).

1967   The Gold of Parita. Archaeology 20(3):202–208.

1966   Rió Cativé Geometric Ware: A New Pottery Type from Panama. Ethnos 31(1–4):90–95.

Bray, Warwick

1974a   Gold Working in Ancient America. In El Dorado: The Gold of Ancient Colombia. Pp. 41–52. New York: Center for Inter-American Relations and the American Federation of the Arts.

1974b   The Organization of the Metal Trade. In El Dorado: The Gold of Ancient Colombia. Pp. 41–52. New York: Center for Inter-American Relations and the American Federation of the Arts.

1977   Maya Metalwork and Its External Connection. In Social Process in Maya Prehistory: Studies in Honor of Sir Eric Thompson. Norman Hammond, ed. Pp. 365–403. London: Academic Press.

1978   The Gold of El Dorado. London: Times Newspapers Limited on Behalf of The Gold of El Dorado Exhibition.

Bright, A. L.

1972   A Goldsmith's Blowpipe from Colombia. Man 7(2):311–313.

Bruhns, Karen Olsen

1972   Two Prehispanic Cire-Perdue Casting Molds from Colombia. Man 7(2):308–311.

Bull, Thelma E.

1958   Excavations at Venado Beach, Canal Zone. Panama Archaeologist 1:6–14.

1959   Preliminary Report on an Archaeological Site, District of Chamé, Province of Panama. Panama Archaeologist 2(1):91–137.

1961   An Urn Burial, Venado Beach, Canal Zone. Panama Archaeologist 4(1):42–47.

1965a   Report on Archaeological Investigations, Azuero Peninsula, Province of Herrera, Republic of Panama. Panama Archaeologist 6(1):31–64.

1965b   Site Report List—Republic of Panama. The Archaeological Society of Panama, Miscellaneous Publications in Isthmian Archaeology, No. 2. Canal Zone.

Cooke, Richard G.

1972a   The Archaeology of the Western Coclé Province of Panama. Unpublished Ph.D. dissertation. 2 vols. London: Institute of Archaeology.

1972b   Resumen de investigaciones arqueologicas en la provincia de Coclé, entre Diciembre de 1969 y Abril de 1971. In Actas del Simposium Nacional de Antropologia, Arqueologia y Etnohistoria de Panama, pp. 125–141. Universidad de Panama and Instituto Nacional de Cultura, Panama.

1976a   Panama: Region Central. Vinculos 2(1):122–140. San Jose, Costa Rica: Museo Nacional.

1976b   El hombre y la tierra en el Panama prehistorico. Revista Nacional de Cultura 2:17–38. Instituto Nacional de Cultura, Panama.

1976c   Una nueva mirada a la evolucion de la ceramica de las provincias centrales. Actas del IV Simposium Nacional de Antropologia, Arqueologia y Etnohistoria de Panama, pp. 309–365. Universidad de Panama and Instituto Nacional de Cultura, Panama.

1976d   Rescate arqueologico en el Caño (NA-20), Coclé, Panama. Actas del IV Simposium Nacional de Antropologia, Arqueologia y Etnohistoria de Panama, pp. 447–482. Universidad de Panama and Instituto Nacional de Cultura, Panama.

1976e   Informe sobre excavaciones en el Sitio CHO-3, Miraflores, Rio Bayano, Febrero, 1973. Actas del IV Simposium Nacional de Antropologia, Arqueologia y Etnohistoria, pp. 369–426. Universidad de Panama and Instituto Nacional de Cultura, Panama.

1977   Los Impactos de las comunidades agricolas sobre los ambientes del tropico estacional: algunos datos del Panama pre-Columbino. Actas del IV Congreso Internacional de Ecologia Tropical. Panama. In press.

1978   Maximizing a Valuable Resource: The White-tailed Deer in Prehistoric Central Panama. Paper presented at the 42nd Annual Meeting of the Society for American Archaeology, Tucson, Arizona.

1979   Polychrome Pottery from the "Central Region" of Panama at La Pitahaya (IS-3). In Adaptive Radiations in the New World Tropics. Olga Linares and Antony Ranere, eds. Peabody Museum Monographs, No. 5. Cambridge : Harvard University Press. In press.

Cooke, Richard G., and Marcella R. Camargo

1977   Coclé y su arqueologia; una breve historia critica. La Antigua 9:115–172. Universidad Santa Maria de la Antigua, Panama.

Dade, Phillip L.

1959   Tomb Burials in Southeastern Veraguas. Panama Archaeologist 2(1):16–34.

1960   Rancho Sancho de la Isla: A Site in Coclé Province, Panama, A Preliminary Report. Panama Archaeologist 3(1):66–87.

1961   The Provenience of Polychrome Pottery in Panama. Ethnos 26(4):172–197.

1970   Veraguas, Heartland of Panama's Pre-Colombian Art. Ethnos 35(1–4):16–39.

1972   Archaeology and Pre-Colombian Art in Panama. Ethnos 37(1–4):148–167.

de Acosta, Joseph

1880   The Natural and Moral History of the Indies. Edward Grimston, trans., and Clements R. Markham, ed. 2 vols. London: Hakluyt Society.

de Andagoya, Pascual

1865   Narrative of the Proceedings of Pedrarias Davila in the Provinces of Tierra Firme or Castilla del Oro, and of the Discovery of the South Sea and the Coasts of Peru and Nicaragua. Clements Markham, trans. and ed. London: Hakluyt Society.

de Espinosa, Gaspar

1864   Relacion hecha por Gaspar de Espinosa, Alcalde Mayor de Castilla del Oro, dada a Pedrarias de Avila, Lugar Teniente General de aquellas Provincias, de todo lo que sucedio en la entrada que hizo en ellas, de order de Pedrarias. In Collecion de Documentos Ineditos . . . del Real Archivo de Indias. Joachim F. Pacheco et al., eds. Tomo 11. Pp. 467–522. Madrid: Imprenta Espanola.

1873   Relacion e Proceso quel licenciado Gaspar Despinosa, Alcalde Mayor, hizo en el viaje que por mandado del muy magnifico Senor Pedrarias de Avila, Teniente general en estos Reynos de Castilla del Oro por sus Altezas, que desde esta Cibdad de Panama a las Provincias de Paris e Nata, e a las otras Provincias Comarcanas. In Documentos eneditos relativos al desumbrimiento, conquista y organizacion de las antiguas posesiones espanolas de America y Oceania sacados de los archivos del Reino y muy especialmente del de Indias. Tomo 20. Pp. 5–119. Madrid: Imprenta del Hospicio.

de Herrera, Antonio

1725–1726

    The General History of the Vast Continent and Islands of America, commonly call'd The West-Indies. John Stevens, trans. 6 vols. London: Jerome Batley.

REFERENCES

de las Casas, Bartolomé
  1875-1876
        Historia de las Indias. 5 vols. Madrid: Imprenta de Miguel Ginesta.
Doyle, Gerald A.
  1960   Metal and Pottery Associations. Panama Archaeologist 3(1):47-51.
Easby, Dudley T.
  1956   Ancient American Goldsmiths. Natural History 65(8):401-409.
Elliot, D. H.
  1965   Panama's Parita Pyramids. Panama Archaeologist 6(1):66-67.
Emmerich, André
  1965   Sweat of the Sun and Tears of the Moon: Gold and Silver in Pre-Colombian Art. Seattle: University of Washington Press.
Fernández de Oviedo y Valdes, Gonzalo
  1851-1855
        Historia general y natural de las Indias. 4 vols. Madrid: Imprenta de la Real Academia de la Historia.
  1950   Sumario de la natural historia de las Indias. Mexico City: Fondo de Cultura Economica.
Fried, Morton H.
  1960   On the Evolution of Social Stratification and the State. In Culture in History: Essays in Honor of Paul Radin. Stanley Diamond, ed. Pp.
            713-731. New York: Colombia University Press.
  1967   The Evolution of Political Society: An Essay in Political Anthropology. New York: Random House.
  1978   The State, The Chicken, and The Egg; or, What Came First? In Origins of the State: The Anthropology of Political Evolution. Ronald
            Cohen and Elman R. Service, eds. Pp. 35-47. Philadelphia: ISHI Publications.
Gordon, Leroy B.
  1957   Human Geography and Ecology in the Sinu Country of Colombia. Ibero-Americana, No. 39. Berkeley: University of California Press.
Grossman, Joel
  1972   An Ancient Gold Worker's Tool Kit. Archaeology 25(4):270-275.
Haberland, Wolfgang
  1978   Lower Central America. In Chronologies in New World Archaeology. R. E. Taylor and Clement W. Meighan, eds. Pp. 395-430. New York:
            Academic Press.
Helms, Mary W.
  1976   Competition, Power and Succession to Office in Pre-Colombian Panama. In Frontier Adaptations in Lower Central America. Mary W.
            Helms and Franklin O. Loveland, eds. Pp. 25-36. Philadelphia: ISHI Publications.
Ichon, Alain
  1975   Tipos de sepultura precolombina en el sur de la peninsula de Azuero. Publicacion especial de la Direccion Nacional de Patrimonio
            Historico, Instituto Nacional de Cultura. La Editora de La Nacion, Panama.
Kubler, George
  1962   The Art and Architecture of Ancient America: The Mexican, Maya. and Andean Peoples. Baltimore: Penguin Books.
Ladd, John
  1957   A Stratigraphic Trench at Sitio Conte, Panama. American Antiquity 22(3):265-271.
Lange, Frederick W.
  1978   Coastal Settlement in Northwestern Costa Rica. In Prehistoric Coastal Adaptations: The Economy and Ecology of Maritime Middle
            America. Barbara L. Stark and Barbara Voorhies, eds. Pp. 101-119. New York: Academic Press.
  1964   Archaeological Investigations in the Parita and Santa Maria Zones of Panama. Bureau of American Ethnology Bulletin 193. Washington,
            D.C.: Smithsonian Institution.
Lechtman, Heather N.
  1971   Ancient Methods of Gilding Silver: Examples from the Old and New Worlds. In Science and Archaeology. Robert H. Brill, ed. Pp. 2-30.
            Cambridge: MIT Press.
Linares, Olga
  1968   Cultural Chronology of the Gulf of Chiriqui, Panama. Smithsonian Institution Contributions to Anthropology, Vol. 8. Washington, D.C.:
            Smithsonian Institution.
  1976   Animals no comestibles son temibles. Revista Nacional de Cultura No. 2, pp. 5-16. Instituto Nacional de Cultura, Panama.
  1977   Ecology and the Arts in Ancient Panama: On the Development of Social Rank and Symbolism in the Central Provinces. Studies in
            Pre-Colombian Art and Archaeology, No. 17. Washington, D.C.: Dumbarton Oaks, Trustees for Harvard University.
Linné, Sigvald
  1929   Darien in the Past. Goteborgs Kungl. Vetenskaps-och, Vitterhets-Samhalles Handlingar, Fermte Foljden, Ser. A, Bd. 1, No. 3. Goteborg:
            Elanders Boktryckeri Aktiebolag.

Fig. 36. Cast-gold bell with bird on top, Parita, Herrera Province, Panama. Height:3.6 cm. Weight:25.5
grams. No. 42. The clapper of the bell is copper.

López de Gómara, Francisco
1922   Historia general de las Indias. 2 vols. Madrid: Calpe.
Lothrop, Eleanor
1948   Throw Me a Bone. Whittlesey House. New York: McGraw-Hill.
Lothrop, Samuel K.
1934   Archaeological Investigation in the Province of Coclé, Panama. American Journal of Archaeology 38(2):207–211.
1937   Coclé: An Archaeological Study of Central Panama. Part I. Historical Background. Memoirs of the Peabody Museum of Archaeology and Ethnology, Vol. VII, Part I. Cambridge, Mass.: Peabody Museum, Harvard University.
1942   Coclé: An Archaeological Study of Central Panama. Part II. Pottery of the Sitio Conte and Other Archaeological Sites. Memoirs of the Peabody Museum of Archaeology and Ethnology, Vol. VIII. Cambridge, Mass.: Peabody Museum, Harvard University.
1948a   The Archaeology of Panama. In Handbook of South American Indians, Julian Steward, ed. Vol 4, pp. 143–168. Bureau of American Ethnology Bulletin 43. Washington, D.C.: Smithsonian Institution.
1948b   The Tribes West and South of the Panama Canal. In Handbook of South American Indians. Julian Steward, ed. Vol. 4, pp. 253–256. Bureau of American Ethnology Bulletin 43. Washington, D.C.: Smithsonian Institution.
1950   Archaeology of Southern Veraguas, Panama. Memoirs of the Peabody Museum of Archaeology and Ethnology. Vol. 9, No. 3. Cambridge, Mass.: Peabody Museum, Harvard University.
1952   Metals from the Cenote of Sacrifice, Chichén Itzá, Yucatan. Memoirs of the Peabody Museum of Archaeology and Ethnology, Vol. 10, No. 2. Cambridge, Mass.: Peabody Museum, Harvard University.
1954   Suicide, Sacrifice and Mutilations in Burials at Venado Beach, Panama. American Antiquity 19(3):226–234.
1956   Jewelry from the Panama Canal Zone. Archaeology 9(1):34–40.
1959a   A Re-Appraisal of Isthmian Archaeology. Amerikanistische Miszellen, Mitteilungen aus dem Museum für Völkerkinde in Hamburg. Vol. 25, pp. 85–91.
1959b   The Archaeological Picture in Southern Central America. Actas del 33 Congreso Nacional de Americanistas, San Jose, July 20–27, 1958. Vol. I, pp. 166–172. San Jose, Costa Rica: Lehman.
1960   C-14 Dates for Venado Beach, Canal Zone. Panama Archaeologist 3(1):96.
1966   Archaeology of Lower Central America. In Handbook of Middle American Indians. Gordon F. Ekholm and Gordon R. Willey, eds. Vol. 4, pp. 180–208. Austin: University of Texas Press.
Lothrop, Samuel K., and Paul Bergsoe
1960   Aboriginal Gilding in Panama. American Antiquity 26(1):106–108.
Lothrop, Samuel K., W. F. Foshag, and Joy Mahler
1957   Pre-Colombian Art: The Robert Woods Bliss Collection. New York: Phaidon Press, Garden City Books.
McGimsey, Charles R., III
1959   A Survey of Archaeologically Known Burial Practices in Panama. Actas del 33 Congreso Internacional de Americanistas, San Jose, July 20–27, 1958, Vol. II, pp. 247–256. San Jose, Costa Rica: Lehman.
1968   A Provisional Dichotomization of Regional Styles in Panamanian Goldwork. Actas y memorias del 37 Congreso Internacional de Americanistas, 1966. Vol. IV, pp. 45–55. Buenos Aires.
Mahler, Joy
1961   Grave Associations and Ceramics in Veraquas, Panama. In Essays in Pre-Colombian Art and Archaeology, Samuel K. Lothrop and others. Pp. 218–228. Cambridge: Harvard University Press.
Martyr D'Anghera, Peter
1912   De Orbo Novo: The Eight Decades of Peter Martyr D'Anghera. Francis Augustus MacNutt, trans. and ed. 2 Vols. New York: G. P. Putnam's Sons.
Mason, J. Alden
1940   Ivory and Resin Figurines from Coclé. University Museum Bulletin 8(4):13–21.
1941   Gold from the Grave. Scientific American 165(5):261–263.
1942   New Excavations at the Sitio Conte, Panama. Proceedings of the 8th American Scientific Congress, Washington, D.C., May 10–18, 1940. Vol. 2, pp. 103–107.
1943   The American Collections of the University Museum. University Museum Bulletin 10(1–2):49–56.
Mitchell, Russel H.
1962   A Pre-Colombian Burial in Panama. Archaeology 15(4):227–232.
Mitchell, Russel H., and John Acker
1961   A Pottery Collection from Parita. Panama Archaeologist 4(1):4–30.
Patterson, Clair C.
1971   Native Copper, Silver and Gold Accessible to Early Metallurgists. American Antiquity 36(3):286–321.
Pendergast, D. M.
1970   Tumbaga Object from the Early Classic Period, Found at Altun Ha, British Honduras (Belize). Science 168(3927):116–118.
Plazas de Nieto, Clemencia, and Ana-Maria Falchetti de Saenz
1978   El Dorado, Colombian Gold. Australian Art Exhibitions Corporation Limited.
Ralegh, Walter
1848   The Discovery of the Large, Rich and Beautiful Empire of Guiana, with a Relation of the Great and Golden City of Manoa (which the Spaniards call El Dorado), etc., performed in the year 1596. Robert H. Schomburgk, ed. London: Hakluyt Society.
Ranere, Anthony J., and Pat Hansell
1978   Early Subsistence Patterns along the Pacific Coast of Central Panama. In Prehistoric Coastal Adaptations: The Economy and Ecology of Maritime Middle America. Barbara L. Stark and Barbara Voorhies, eds. Pp. 43–59. New York: Academic Press.
Root, W. C.
1949   Metallurgy. In Handbook of South American Indians. Julian Steward, ed. Vol. 5, pp. 205–225. Bureau of American Ethnology Bulletin 143. Washington, D.C.: Smithsonian Institution.

REFERENCES

1961   Pre-Colombian Metalwork of Colombia and Its Neighbors. *In* Essays in Pre-Colombian Art and Archaeology. Samuel K. Lothrop and others. Pp. 242–257. Cambridge, Mass.: Harvard University Press.

Sander, Dan, and Russell H. Mitchell

1960   Report on Fabric and Figurine, Venado Beach, Canal Zone, Panama. Archaeologist 3(1):52–53.

Sander, Dan, Russel H. Mitchell, and P. G. Turner

1958   Report on Venado Beach Excavations, Canal Zone, Panama. Archaeologist 1(1):26–28.

Sauer, Carl Ortwin

1966   The Early Spanish Main. Berkeley: University of California Press.

Stirling, Matthew W.

1949a   Explaining the Past in Panama. National Geographic Magazine 95(3):373–399.

1949b   The Importance of Sitio Conte. American Anthropologist 51:514–517.

1950   Exploring Ancient Panama by Helicopter. National Geographic Magazine 97(2):227–246.

Stone, Doris

1966   Synthesis of Lower Central American Ethnohistory. Handbook of Middle American Indians. Gordon F. Ekholm and Gordon R. Willey, eds. Vol. 4, pp. 209–233. Austin: University of Texas Press.

Stone, Doris, and Carlos Balser

1958   The Aboriginal Metalwork in the Isthmian Region of America. San Jose, Costa Rica: Museo Nacional.

1965   Incised Slate Disks from the Atlantic Watershed of Costa Rica. American Antiquity 30(3):310–329.

Stromsvik, G.

1942   Substela Caches and Stela Foundations at Copan and Quirigua. Carnegie Institution of Washington, Contributions to American Archaeology and History, Vol. 7, no. 37, Publication 528. Cambridge, Mass.: Carnegie Institution of Washington.

Torres de Arauz, Reina

1972a   Arte Precolombino de Panama. Instituto Nacional de Cultura y Deportes, Direccion de Patrimonio Historico, Panama. Ciudad de Panama: La Editora de la Nacion.

1972b   Nata Prehispanico. Centro de Investigaciones Antropologicas, Publicacion Especial No. 3. Panama City: Universidad de Panama. Arte Pre-Colombino de Panama. Panama City: Instituto Nacional de Cultura y Deportes.

Vasquez de Espinosa, Antonio

1942   Compendium and Description of the West Indies. Charles Upson Clark, trans. Smithsonian Miscellaneous Collections, Vol. 102. Washington, D.C.: Smithsonian Institution.

Verrill, A. Hyatt

1927a   Excavations in Coclé Province, Panama. Indian Notes 4(1):47–61.

1927b   The Pompeii of Ancient America: A Vast Settlement Destroyed Centuries Before Christ. The World's Work 53(3):279–288.

1928   A Mystery of the Vanished Past in Panama. Newly Discovered Relics of a Prehistoric Civilization Destroyed by Earthquake or Volcanic Eruption. Illustrated London News, Oct. 13. London.

1929   Uncovering an Ancient Pompeii in America. The Sunday Star, Sept. 8. Washington, D.C.

1942   Old Civilizations of the New World. New York: The New Home Library.

Verrill, A. Hyatt, and Ruth Verrill

1953   America's Ancient Civilizations. New York: G. P. Putnam's Sons.

Wafer, Lionel

1903   A New Voyage and Description of the Isthmus of America by Lionel Wafer. Reprinted from the original edition of 1699. George Parker Winship, ed. Cleveland: The Burrows Brothers Company.

Wassen, S. Henry

1960   A Find of Coclé-style Pottery in a Single Veraguas Grave, Panama. Etnografiska Museet, Goteborg Arstryck for 1957–1958, pp. 62–81.

ACKNOWLEDGMENTS

There are many people to be thanked for their contributions to this paper. Robert Sonin, the consultant on goldworking technology, was extremely helpful, spending many hours examining the Coclé gold collection under the microscope. The consultant on Panamanian archaeology, Richard Cooke, was also most helpful and furnished bibliographic references and unpublished information. His extensive works on the subject greatly facilitated the preparation of the paper and his criticisms cleared up some of its errors. André Emmerich provided some valuable unpublished information about Coclé gold, and Julie Jones gave the benefit of her opinion in the choice of some of the artifacts for the exhibit. Nancy Barton and Alexandra Roosevelt greatly improved the paper by their editorial comments. Brenda Holland and Mary Jane Lenz helped in many phases of the work, as did Isabel Morales, Susan Dublin, Tim Kugelman, and Susan Mareska. The staff of the Library of the Museum of the American Indian and the American Museum of Natural History greatly facilitated my search for literature.

Fig. 37. Double crab pendant of cast gold, Panama. Length: 4.9 cm. Weight: 21.5 grams. No. 29. The pendant is decorated with a hammered gold dangler, and each crab has a hole in the back for a pearl or stone inlay. A similar ornament was found in grave 5 at Sitio Conte, Coclé Province, Panama (Lothrop 1937:fig. 48b).

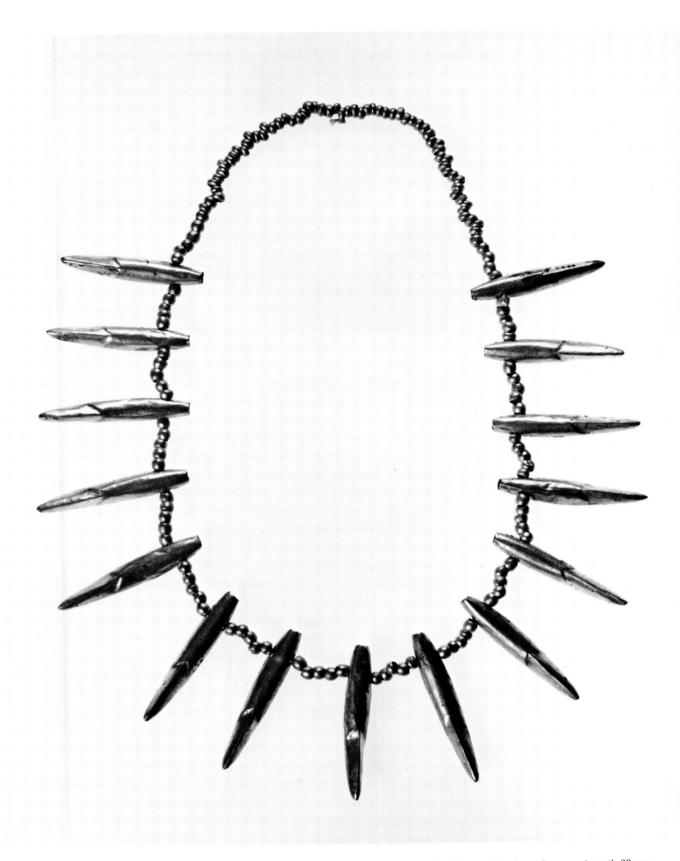

Fig. 38. Necklace of embossed beads and pendants in the shape of animal teeth (restrung), Parita, Herrera Province, Panama. Length:28 cm. Weight:46 grams. No. 23.

tHe BASKETMAKER

THE POMOANS OF CALIFORNIA

SALLY MCLENDON AND BRENDA SHEARS HOLLAND

Fig. 1. Title page. Twined mush cooking pot with horizontal-band design, made by Mary Benson, Central Pomo. Height:12 cm. Diameter:18 cm. No. 44.

Fig. 2. Mary Benson, Central Pomo, coiling a basket, probably photographed in 1904 at the Louisiana Purchase Exposition in St. Louis.

When Americans began arriving in California in the 1840s, they found native populations that had developed the exploitation of the plants in their environment to a striking degree. Clothing, housing, and the technology used in acquiring most nonplant protein all ingeniously utilized native plant fibers, to the near exclusion of animal products such as skin and bone. The diet, too, was heavily biased toward plant materials, in particular, highly nutritious nuts such as acorns, pine nuts, buckeyes, and mesquite beans. These could be harvested in large quantities during a few weeks at predictably recurring seasons and stored for use throughout the rest of the year, providing most of the advantages of agriculture with much less human effort and destruction to the environment.

The inventiveness with which plant resources were shaped to human cultural purposes in California found its ultimate expression in the extensive, elaborate, and varied utilization of plant fibers in basketry. Basketry products were central and indispensable in the cultures of all Californian groups, many of which developed the craft of basket manufacture beyond the requirements of successful utilitarian function. For many such groups, if not for all, baskets were a medium for the expression of talent and artistic sensibility, prestige and pride. They were an ever-present source of aesthetic pleasure and visual enrichment in the context of everyday life. In short, basketry was an art form in which color of materials, shape, design, texture, and fineness of weave were manipulated for ends that were purely aesthetic as well as practical (fig. 1).

Non-Indian Americans have only begun to appreciate the environmental logic and success of the California Indians' adaptation to their environment, but apparently their manipulation of resources for aesthetic ends in basketry was more easily recognized. By the beginning of the 1890s, collecting American Indian baskets had become a passionate pursuit for many Americans, and by the turn of the century American Indian baskets had become requisite for many fashionable decors (fig. 4). Dealers emerged to cater to this appetite, as did authorities to establish standards. (Frequently, the two roles were represented by a single individual.) The result was that by 1900 the production of baskets provided a major source of cash income for many Native Americans of California, and the production of baskets for a commercial market quickly came to take precedence over all previous motivations for basketmaking.

Most northern Californian native peoples made baskets of largely similar shape, design, and function; however, the new collectors and authorities, including professional anthropologists, identified certain groups as excelling at the craft. Among these, the various groups that have come to be known in the anthropological literature as "Pomo" dazzled all authorities with their range of techniques; the fineness of their weave; the range, subtlety, and beauty of their designs; and their sumptuous and unique use of brilliantly colored feathers, beads, and iridescent abalone-shell pendants.

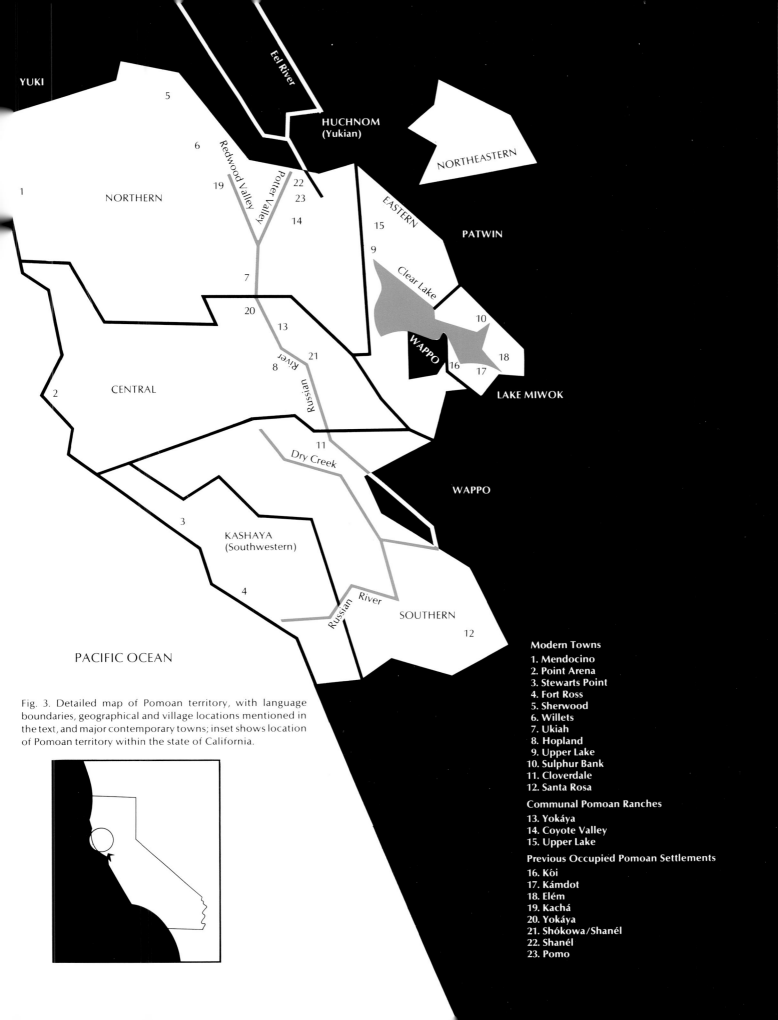

YUKI

Eel River

HUCHNOM
(Yukian)

NORTHEASTERN

5

6

Redwood Valley

Potter Valley

19

22

23

14

EASTERN

15

PATWIN

1

NORTHERN

9

Clear Lake

7

20

13

21

8

Russian River

CENTRAL

2

11

Dry Creek

WAPPO

10

18

16

17

LAKE MIWOK

WAPPO

3

KASHAYA
(Southwestern)

4

Russian River

SOUTHERN

12

PACIFIC OCEAN

Fig. 3. Detailed map of Pomoan territory, with language boundaries, geographical and village locations mentioned in the text, and major contemporary towns; inset shows location of Pomoan territory within the state of California.

Modern Towns

1. Mendocino
2. Point Arena
3. Stewarts Point
4. Fort Ross
5. Sherwood
6. Willets
7. Ukiah
8. Hopland
9. Upper Lake
10. Sulphur Bank
11. Cloverdale
12. Santa Rosa

Communal Pomoan Ranches

13. Yokáya
14. Coyote Valley
15. Upper Lake

Previous Occupied Pomoan Settlements

16. Kói
17. Kámdot
18. Elém
19. Kachá
20. Yokáya
21. Shókowa/Shanél
22. Shanél
23. Pomo

Diversity Of The "Pomo"

Pomo baskets are not, and were not in the past, made by a single tribe of Native Americans. Rather, what are called Pomo baskets were produced by members of some seventy-two autonomous groups, living roughly a hundred miles north of San Francisco in the coast range of mountains (fig. 3). They spoke seven distinct but related languages, six of which had a number of dialects. These seven languages were assigned confusingly similar names by the anthropologist Barrett,[1] according to their relative geographical location: Northern Pomo, Central Pomo, Southern Pomo, Southwestern Pomo (now called Kasháya), Northwestern Pomo, Eastern Pomo, and Southeastern Pomo (fig. 3).

The speakers of these seven languages did not perceive themselves as constituting a homogeneous group. Nor did they perceive themselves as having more in common with one another than they did with the various other groups located adjacent to them who spoke unrelated languages and were assigned completely different names (such as Wappo, Yuki, Lake Miwok). The baskets produced by these other groups were often very similar to those produced by the nearest Pomoan groups, so that distinguishing a Lake Miwok basket from, say, a Pomo basket produced by the nearest Pomoan group is frequently very difficult. The earliest comprehensive collections of Pomoan baskets give provenience in terms of individual autonomous groups.[2] Examination of these precisely provenienced collections reveals that there were subtle differences in design, technique, and preferred shapes for a given function from one autonomous Pomoan group to the other. Thus, what are called Pomo baskets represent an areal type, rather than the homogeneous product of a single group.

The term "Pomo" was applied to these groups by anthropologists in the last quarter of the nineteenth century and was later adopted by basket collectors, dealers, and the federal government. It is an anglicization of the name of the permanent village of one of the autonomous Pomoan groups, pʰoˑmoˑ—"magnesite-hole-at"—in southern Potter Valley on the east fork of the Russian River.[3]

Annual Cycle

There are essentially two seasons in this part of California: a cool, rainy season (during which snow falls in the mountains), from November to May; and a long, hot, dry season, from May through October. For most of the Pomoan groups, the subsistence cycle has not been described in detail, but apparently it was finely adapted to the special characteristics of the environment in which each group lived.[4]

Evidently, all the groups spent most of the rainy season in the permanent villages, the men spending most of their time in the ceremonial house, even sleeping there, and the women and children living in the dwelling houses. Waterfowl were hunted and some small mammals trapped or shot for food, but it was mainly the food stored during the dry season that was consumed. Toward the end of the rainy season, most groups seem to have caught large quantities of fish during the spring spawning runs, and these were processed for storing. During the dry season, foods were collected as they became ripe; sometimes a portion of the village would move off to camp temporarily near the plants or fish being harvested; sometimes there would be daily foraging trips from the village. In either case, it seems that most groups never left the permanent village completely empty. (Indeed, it would be difficult to see how they could have, given the amount of food that was stored and the extent of wealth that ideally was accumulated.) Deer were hunted at any time of the year, but their hunting required considerable ritual preparation. It appears that deer meat was not dried and stored aboriginally but, rather, was obligatorily shared among the social groups in the village.

Nature Of The Variation
Among The Various Pomoan Groups

These various Pomoan groups shared no single homogeneous culture, but differed in details of social organization, kinship, and ritual. The Northern Pomo community of Kachá in Redwood Valley had a single chief, who was elected,[5] whereas the Central Pomo community of Yokáya on the Russian River had a head chief and three subchiefs,[6] the right to the chieftainship passing from a man to his sister's son. The Central Pomo community of Shókowa seems to have had the most complex political organization of all, for, according to Stewart, before the arrival of Europeans they were governed by twenty chiefs.[7] There were two main chiefs, a war captain, seven speaking assembly-house chiefs, and one or more ordinary assembly-house chiefs for each ceremonial assembly house. Only the war captain was elected. All others were chiefs by virtue of inheritance, the incumbent chief picking his successor from among his kinsmen.

Apparently, the population size of these communities also varied considerably. The Northern Pomo community of Kachá had a population of approximately 125, according to Kniffen, whereas the Central Pomo community of Yokáya had, according to Stewart, a population of 500 to 1,000.[9] The Central Pomo community of Shókowa had 1,500 residents, according to Jeff Joaquin, who had been born about 1859 and whose father had been a member of this group.[10]

In some communities, important sources of food, such as large manzanita trees, acorn trees, and good fishing sites were privately owned by individual families (as among the Kachá, Yokáya, Shókowa, and the three Southeastern Pomo–speaking communities of Kói, Elém, and Kámdot). In other communities all land and sources of food were held communally (as among the five Eastern Pomo–speaking communities and the Northern Pomo–speaking communities of Sherwood Valley).

The various Pomoan groups inhabited three distinct environments, with which differences in house type and subsistence base were correlated. Moving from east to west, the zones are: 1) the lake zone surrounding Clear Lake; 2) the valley zone of the Russian River and Eel River drainages; and 3) the coast-redwood zone of the Pacific Coast north of Fort Ross.

On the coast the usual dwelling was a fairly small, single-family conical structure of redwood slabs leaned together against a centerpole.[11] Along the Russian River houses were larger, dome-shaped or oblong multifamily dwellings of willow poles lashed and thatched with native grasses resembling a "large, flattish haystack."[12] In the Southern Pomo–speaking area, Powers observed an immense, L-shaped multifamily dwelling. In the lake area, houses were round or elliptical multifamily dwellings, thatched with a variety of native rush growing at the edge of the lake, which locally is called *tule.*[13]

The various Pomoan groups are usually referred to as hunters and gatherers by anthropologists. Contemporary hunters and gatherers, such as the Bushmen of Africa, have been observed to have extremely low population densities—less than one person per square mile, according to Lee and DeVore.[14] Some of the Pomoan groups, however, have been estimated to have population densities as high as 16.67 persons per square mile (for the Kuhlanapo group of Eastern Pomo speakers living at Clear Lake),[15] but averaging 2 or 3 to 7 or 8 persons per square mile.[16] This great density among nonagriculturalists no doubt reflects the utilization of two major subsistence resources—fish and acorns—both of which could be harvested in copious quantities in a brief period of time (fish during the spring spawning runs, acorns in the fall) and stored for use throughout the year. The possibility of harvesting a year's supply of food in a few weeks made possible a more sedentary life style, the accumulation of reserves, and the development of wealth, presumably also freeing time for elaborating the aesthetic dimension of basket production.

These distinct groups did have in common a number of features. They all lived in sizeable, permanent villages that were mutually linked by marriages, trade, and reciprocal participation in each other's ceremonials. They all drew their subsistence from fishing, gathering, and hunting, although the precise techniques as well as the major foodstuffs they utilized differed somewhat according to which of the three types of environment they lived in. In addition, they all shared a common expertise in, and similar technology for, the making of the various types of basketry, which were so central to aboriginal life in all of northern California; and, finally, all decorated baskets were made by women.

Fig. 4. Typical parlor around turn of the century, probably Grace Nicholson's house.
"It is a fad nowadays to have a number of Indian baskets strewn around the parlor, and the demand for them at present is quite pronounced" (Wilcomb cited by Frye 1977).

Training In Basketmaking

The manufacture of a fine basket was and is a time-consuming process for any basketmaker but particularly for a Pomoan basketmaker. It begins with the collection of the appropriate materials and is constructed with advance knowledge of its intended function, shape, and design. Many basketmakers observe special taboos and rituals in the process of gathering materials and constructing the basket.

The actual techniques for the acquisition and preparation of materials, the construction of the baskets, and the basic design elements are learned by example. When questioned, basketmakers invariably say that they learned their craft by watching their mothers, who spent a great deal of time making baskets. They remember being interested in the process and actively seeking to learn how to weave. Apparently, the mother would provide the observant and curious child with scraps of materials and would let the child practice while watching her at work; she would perhaps give assistance if the child experienced some difficulty. Possibly as a result of this, superior basketmakers commonly have mothers who are superior basketmakers; this expertise tends to be associated with successive generations of kinswomen. For example, the remarkable weaver Mary Benson (fig. 2) was the daughter of an equally famous weaver, Sarah Knight (fig. 5).

Unfortunately, there are no detailed studies of the techniques by which mastery of fiber manipulation, design elements, and the principles of design construction were passed from mother to child. Mastery of the syntax of combining the basic design elements into what appear to be endlessly different compositions seems to have been achieved purely through observation of one's mother's production of such compositions over a period of years, and it was and is unconscious and intuitive. All basketmakers of talent agree, however, that one must not only have in mind from the outset precisely how the finished basket will look but also preserve this mental conception over the several months or years that may be required to finish a truly superb and complex basket.

Fig. 5. Sarah Knight, Central Pomo and mother of Mary Benson, weaving a twined basket.
"... on the 20th of June we lost the old lady (mother-in-law). . . . Mary was very much shocked. . . . We have few baskets now. if you want them. Grace II have them sent down. We have three tiny ones and three large ones. Three small ones is marys work the others we received as Presents when the old lady died" (William Benson to Grace Nicholson, July 14, 1913, Museum of the American Indian Archives).

History Of Contact And Its Effects

The earliest description of a Pomoan-like basket is from Drake's expedition, which stopped on the northern California coast in 1579, in the vicinity of Point Reyes. One account of the expedition's experiences describes baskets made "of Rushes like a deep boat, and so well wrought as to hold Water. They hang pieces of Pearl shells, and sometimes Links of these Chains on the Brims, to signify they were only used in the Worship of their Gods; they are wrought with matted down of red Feathers into various Forms."[17] It is not at all certain that the Indians contacted by Drake were members of any of the Pomoan groups, but it sounds very much as if Drake saw one of the supremely valuable Pomoan ceremonial baskets, which were woven so that the exterior surface was entirely covered with glowing red woodpecker crest feathers.

During the nineteenth century the various Pomoan groups came into permanent contact with various representatives of European society. In 1811 the first Russian settlement in California was established in Kasháya Pomo territory, at what is now Fort Ross, and the Kasháya were prevailed upon to settle there and work for the Russians. In 1817 the Spanish established a mission at San Rafael, to which Kasháya and Southern Pomo–speaking groups were removed. By 1823, when California had become a province of Mexico, a mission was established at Sonoma, which also drew on various Pomoan groups for labor and for converts. In 1827 an attempt was made to found a twenty-second mission at Santa Rosa, on the site of a large Southern Pomo–speaking village, to which other Southern Pomo–speaking groups were moved. Between 1834 and 1836 the Mexican government secularized the missions, and Mexican ranchers began running cattle in the valleys along the Russian River and around Clear Lake on large land grants acquired from the Mexican government. They usually pressured the local Pomoan groups to relocate near the ranch house and to provide young men to work as *vaqueros*. The grazing cattle significantly altered the food-gathering possibilities of the environment for the Pomoan groups.

Fig. 6. William Benson's coiled "po" basket, Central Pomo. *A*, bottom view; *B*, side view. This basket took four years to complete and has an unusual start of magnesite. Height:6 cm. Diameter:12 cm. No. 49.

"no Grace the Po basket hasent grode much sense the warm weather. at present I am plowing Hops for the Ranch. (Indians)" (William Benson to Grace Nicholson, April 14, 1915, Museum of the American Indian Archives).

"I have mary helping me on the basket . . . the basket is growing but it cannot be rushed. it lack about 15 rounds and it takes three to four days to the round the stitches are now going up the 67 mark and you know if we rush it we might spoile it. so its best to work on it as we are working" (William Benson to Grace Nicholson, February 3, 1917, Museum of the American Indian Archives).

Beginning in the 1830s, epidemics of European diseases are reported, including a smallpox epidemic in 1837 that spread from the Russian settlement on the Coast, among the Kasháya, through the Southern Pomo, both northward along the Russian River and eastward to Sonoma and then north to Clear Lake. It is estimated to have killed at least a quarter of the aboriginal population.

By the 1850s California had become an American territory and American homesteaders were eagerly laying claim to the most agriculturally promising portions of the Pomoan territory, continuing the significant changes in the environment and increasingly restricting the hunting and gathering areas to which the various Pomoan groups were permitted access. European-introduced diseases continued to reduce the size of the original populations, and by 1872 the various Pomoan groups apparently were considerably troubled by the experience of contact with Western society and allowed themselves to be swept up by a Messianic movement, called the "1870 Ghost Dance" by anthropologists.[18] All the Pomoan groups gathered at Clear Lake for upward of two years and waited for the world to end. Shortly after the movement subsided and people returned to their former locations, a remarkable new development occurred: several of the former autonomous groups (which previously had been related to a degree by ties of marriage and exchange) banded together. They pooled their proceeds from agricultural labor and organized new communities on land bought back from the white settlers. This was done by Central Pomo-speaking groups at the Yokáya *rancheria* in 1881, by Northern Pomo-speaking groups in Coyote Valley in 1878, and by Eastern Pomo- and Northern Pomo-speaking groups at Upper Lake also in 1878, and probably elsewhere by other groups.[19] These communities proved very successful and their residents prospered. They continued their former hunting and gathering as much as possible. Agricultural labor, particularly harvesting crops such as hops or string beans, provided cash for taxes, coffins, and other new necessities that were available in the white towns that had sprung up. Women discovered that their traditional crafts had a cash value, and they began to manufacture baskets specifically for sale. By the 1890s there was a brisk business carried on by professional basket buyers, who made semiannual trips into northern California to purchase baskets.

Fig. 7. Miniature Pomoan baskets. Diameters:0.5 cm. to 6.5 cm. *A*, no. 51; *B*, no. 52; *C*, no. 54; *D*, no. 52; *E*, no. 57; *F*, no. 56; *G*, no. 50; *H*, no. 51; *I*, no. 55; *J*, no. 53. See artifact listing for complete details.

Collectors, Dealers, And The Commercial Market

The development of a commercial market for baskets and their collection as art objects subtly influenced the craft. The showy, feathered ceremonial baskets were particularly sought, as were both miniatures and gigantic curiosities. Manufactured items of metal and ceramic replaced most basket use in daily life, and gradually the more utilitarian and less strikingly decorated and designed baskets of everyday life ceased to be made.

Dr. John Hudson, living in the town of Ukiah in the area formerly controlled by Central Pomo-speaking groups, began assembling a large and representative collection of Pomoan baskets in 1888, with detailed proveniences and considerable information about function and use. Hudson's wife, Grace Carpenter Hudson, a successful and admired painter at the turn of the century, had been born of pioneer stock in Potter Valley and grew up with considerable knowledge of the traditional life style and language of the various Pomoan groups near her family home. Through her, Hudson was introduced to the topic that would subsequently become the passion of his life, eventually taking him completely away from the practice of medicine. In 1893 he published "Pomo Basket Makers" in the *Overland Monthly* (a journal founded by Bret Harte in 1867 to do for California what the *New Yorker* and *New York* magazine now do for New York). During the summer of 1893 he introduced the anthropologist H. W. Henshaw of the Smithsonian Institution to the various Pomoan groups living in the vicinity of Ukiah and helped him to buy baskets and take photographs. In 1899, after considerable negotiation, Hudson sold his collection to the Smithsonian Institution, starting something of a competition among other important museums of the country for similarly comprehensive collections. A fellow resident of Ukiah, Carl Purdy, who raised and sold plants, also traded in baskets and assembled an important collection for the American Museum of Natural History in New York.

The collections that Hudson and Purdy assembled (perhaps together with the one assembled by Charles P. Wilcomb) are the closest we have to type collections of Pomoan basketry. They tended, however, to focus on baskets produced by members of Pomoan groups living in the vicinity of Ukiah (i.e., individuals from Central Pomo-, Northern Pomo-, and Eastern Pomo-speaking groups). Thus their collections, marvelous though they are, do not accurately reflect the total range of baskets produced by Pomoan language-speaking groups; and current conceptions as to the nature of Pomoan basketry characterize primarily the baskets produced by Central Pomo-, Northern Pomo-, and Eastern Pomo-speaking groups.

Although there were still many Pomoan basketmakers in the 1890s, Hudson claimed that the quality of technique and design characteristic of these groups before contact with white civilization had suffered a decline as baskets came to be manufactured purely as sources of income. At the end of the nineteenth century he felt that truly superb baskets were still produced in only three communities: the self-owned communities at Upper Lake, in Coyote Valley, and that of the Yokáya group, seven miles south of the contemporary town of Ukiah. He proposed that the best baskets were made by members of this last group, saying: "Among them [the Yokáya] are a few women who cultivate the ancient arts and whose productions are superb, worthy of the choicest selections."[20] We know who some of these superb Yokáya basketmakers were from the evidence of the photographs that the anthropologist Henshaw took of basketmakers at the Yokáya community in 1893,[21] from the photograph collection of Robert Lee, of Ukiah, and from the Benson-Nicholson correspondence.[22] They included Joseppa Dick (called by another collector, "the queen of the weavers among the Pomo of Mendocino),"[23] Mary Pinto, Eliza Coons, Sarah Knight and her daughter Mary Benson.

Although these women's products are an important component in all major collections of Pomoan baskets in this country, we know very little about most of them.

At present, we know most about Mary Benson, because the Museum of the American Indian fortunately possesses a collection of sixty-four baskets manufactured by her and her husband, William Benson, for the basket dealer Grace Nicholson, as well as the Benson correspondence with Nicholson between 1903 and 1932.

Fig. 8. Coiled ceremonial cup with red woodpecker crests, Pomoan, collected about 1867 by Judge Nathan Bijur on his way to negotiate the Alaska Purchase. Height: 7 cm. Diameter: 15 cm. No. 19.

Mary Benson was probably born in the early 1870s, during a decade of upheaval and change for the various Pomoan groups, beginning with the millenarian 1870 Ghost Dance movement and its expectation of the end of the world, and closing with the successful communal purchase of a community site in 1881 by the Yokáya community. She must have grown up in a still largely traditional, Central Pomo–speaking world, which the community was able to maintain on the land they purchased. At the turn of the century, they still had both an above-ground ceremonial house and a traditional, semisubterranean sweat house and ceremonial house. Mary Benson and her husband spoke Central Pomo by preference all their married lives, and her deep attachment to the environs of her childhood are suggested in a comment her husband made to Nicholson in 1905 when the two were discussing the possibility of their purchasing land to the south: "It would be alright as far as I am concerned but mary you know is hard to move from this valley."[24] It is not known when she married William Benson, an Eastern Pomo speaker who had been born at Clear Lake, but they were already married when the correspondence with Nicholson began in 1903, and they remained married until Mary Benson's death on June 4, 1930.

In 1904 Hudson took both William and Mary Benson to the Louisiana Purchase Exposition in St. Louis, where they demonstrated Pomoan basketmaking and sold their wares. (Although men did not normally make decorated baskets, William Benson made superb ones [figs. 6a and b].) Both won prizes. Shortly before, the Bensons had been contacted by one of the most interesting of the basket buyers who sprang up after the turn of the century, Grace Nicholson, the orphaned and penniless daughter of a prominent Philadelphia family, who sought and found her fortune in the West. Coming to California around the turn of the century, she discovered the basket trade when she sold some baskets she had bought to the anthropologist C. Hart Merriam. She seems to have revolutionized the business, turning what for others was a profitable hobby or sideline into a profession. She went on collecting trips throughout the West and supplemented Native American crafts with Oriental art.

Grace Nicholson seems to have been fiercely competitive and very early on began to seek exclusive access to the Bensons' production, which she finally assured herself by guaranteeing them a certain sum each year (five hundred dollars a year, she indicates in one letter),[25] to free them from other work so that they could devote more time to basketmaking.

Fig. 9. Three twined baskets made by Mary Benson, typical spiral design of the Central Pomo. Heights: 9 cm. to 21 cm. Diameters: 12 cm. to 36 cm. Nos. 40, 41, and 42. Even though the same design elements are being incorporated into an overall design composition, there are subtle differences in the execution of the design elements. Their relative sizes and their shapes introduce a sense of variation from one basket to the next. The largest basket is one of Mary's earliest. Note how size and fineness of weave decreased over the years.

Like the other collectors, Grace Nicholson was interested in authenticity and encouraged the use of traditional materials, techniques, and designs. She urged the Bensons to use only aboriginally native materials and to make the baskets as fine as possible. (Collectors of Pomoan baskets, in fact, were constantly counting the number of stitches to the inch in a basket—the finer the basket the greater the number of stitches.) As a result, over the years of their association, one can see Mary Benson's baskets decreasing in size while increasing in fineness of stitch (fig. 9).

The basket collection assembled by Judge Nathan Bijur about 1867, while he was in California on his way to negotiate the Alaska Purchase, provides an interesting source of comparison. His collection, formed before a commercial market had developed, illustrates the exuberance and subtle delicacy with which new materials such as glass trade beads were initially incorporated into traditional baskets (color plate 10*b* and *i*; nos. 27 and 29). The efforts of turn of the century collectors to form collections representative of basketry before contact with Europeans—and hence free from all traces of contact—also severely restricted the scope for innovation and creativity. The design compositions of Mary Benson's baskets have a certain austere beauty as compared to those in the Bijur collection. Mary Benson was clearly producing art objects—museum material and no longer the stuff of everyday life.

The Role Of Basketry In Traditional Pomoan Life

Basketry was required for the Pomoan subsistence system. The technology of fish and acorn acquisition made extensive, almost exclusive, use of basketry. Fish were caught in a variety of basketry traps (each designed to capitalize on peculiarities of the spawning behavior of a species or on water conditions at the time of spawning). They were transported in baskets to the dwellings, where they were stored after being dried. Acorns were collected, transported, and stored in baskets until needed (fig. 10); then they were ground to flour in basket mortars placed on mortar rocks, sieved in basketry sieves, cooked in baskets (fig. 1, no. 5),[26] and eaten from baskets (fig. 15).

Many different wild grass seeds were also harvested, using a basketry seedbeater and a finely woven burden basket (fig. 11). The seeds were then winnowed on a basketry tray, stored in basketry seed bins (fig. 13), parched on basketry platters (color plate 10a), ground in the basket mortar, sifted with basketry sifters (no. 8), cooked in baskets, and eaten from baskets. Seasonal foods such as grasshoppers and army worms were gathered in baskets and parched on basketry trays. Kelp and shellfish were collected in baskets and the shellfish were then boiled in baskets. Honey and pine sugar were collected and served in baskets, as were berries and a variety of wild fruits, including wild cherries, wild grapes, and manzanita fruit. Field mice, ground squirrels, quail, dove, and other game birds, as well as rabbits were caught in basketry traps. Water was kept in watertight baskets of an especially strong weave (no.

20) and drunk from basketry cups (fig. 8).

Baskets and basketry products were not, however, limited to subsistence uses. They played an important role at every stage of the life cycle. Newborn babies were washed in particularly beautiful, flaring, coiled baskets, which were saved and given to the child when he or she had grown up (fig. 17). Babies were placed in basketry carriers at birth, and until around the age of two they spent most of their waking hours watching the world from a securely immobilized, upright position, propped against a tree or rock or on their mother's back. Brilliantly colored, miniature feather baskets or abalone-shell pendants or, in the spring, fresh flowers were often hung from the bent hoop at the top of the carrier to serve as aboriginal creative playthings. Until the age of five or six, children continued to be transported on the backs of their mothers or grandmothers, standing in burden baskets, the bottoms of which had been suitably padded with a soft, flexible material.

Miniature mortar baskets, burden baskets, and baby carriers (figs. 12, 30, and 36a) were made as toys for little girls (educational toys and child-sized learning materials evidently being a very old idea). Girls at puberty were isolated in a small structure attached to their house, and during this period they used a fine, flaring, coiled basket (similar in shape to the basket in which they had been washed as babies) for washing. This basket, too, was saved throughout the girl's childbearing years and used only during her menses (fig. 17).

Fig. 10. Spaced lattice-twined acorn storage basket, Pomoan. Height:34 cm. Diameter:56 cm. No. 6.

Marriages were formalized somewhat differently by different Pomoan groups, but apparently they always involved the use of baskets as both gifts and containers (figs. 16, 18, and 33). For most if not all Pomoan groups, marriages seem to have involved both feasts and a public exchange between the two families united by marriage of the two staple foods that were the ritual foods *par excellence*: acorn mush and pinole (a porridge made from a mixture of parched wild seeds). These foods were given in the most perfectly made and extravagantly beautiful baskets. Beautiful and well-made baskets were also used to serve the various foods consumed during the feast. In most groups, the bride's family seems to have given the groom's family gifts of such fine baskets. Among the Eastern Pomo–speaking groups of the lake zone, it was the glowing baskets covered with red woodpecker crests (no. 30)—called by collectors "sun baskets"—that were ideally given; but among Central Pomo–speaking groups of the Russian River valley it would seem that this was not necessarily the case, since an unfeathered though beautiful basket in the museum collection (fig. 33) was specifically described as made as "the wedding kind used in marriage ceremonials."[27]

All but the Northern Pomo–speaking groups of Sherwood Valley cremated their dead, and baskets figured prominently in the expressions of grief preceding and during the cremation. According to Loeb, the body was left in the house for three or four days, during which time people came in to pile on the body gifts of robes, blankets, beads, and fine baskets, particularly the jewel–like feather baskets for which the Pomoan groups are so famous (color plate 10).[28] (The family of the deceased was expected subsequently to provide reciprocal gifts of equal value.) The deceased was cremated together with his possessions, which always included a number of baskets. The mourners encircled the funeral pyre during the cremation and expressed their grief by adding still more objects of value to the fire, usually baskets or native clamshell and/or magnesite beads.

The religious systems of the various groups are poorly understood and described, but evidently ceremonials often involved the use of ritual foods: acorn meal or the seed meal from which pinole was made. These were sprinkled ceremonially, shaped into balls and thrown, or consumed as mush and pinole. In addition, all ceremonials seem to have ended with a grand feast for all participants—onlookers as well as those performing. Several sources mention that in addition to its use as a wedding present, the most valued red-woodpecker-crest-covered basket was used as a container for the sacred balls of meal during ceremonials.[29]

Baskets were also used to store ceremonial regalia in the semisubterranean ceremonial house and to store valuables as well as food products in dwellings. Shamans are said to have used the boat-shaped baskets characteristic of the Pomoan groups for the storage of their ritual paraphernalia (fig. 34).

Even the basketry materials themselves and the water necessary to keep the roots suitably moist in weaving were stored in baskets during the production period.

Although the timing of most occasions for which baskets would be used was fairly predictable, a death, of course, could occur when one least expected it, so Pomoan families found it desirable to have constantly on hand a good quantity of fine baskets, including ones decorated with feathers, which thus constituted a form of wealth.

Fig. 12. Miniature Pomoan mortar basket and stone. *A*, twined mortar basket. Height:7 cm. Diameter:23 cm. No. 15; *B*, mortar stone, Height:4 cm. Width:21 cm. No. 16. The mortar basket may have been made for a child.

Fig. 13. Twined Pomoan seed bin or granary. Height:32 cm. Diameter:45 cm. No. 7. Note "dau" (break in pattern) on left side. The "dau," according to Hudson (1899), means "door" and allows a spirit to enter the basket and inspect the work; however, Purdy relates a myth which suggests that "spirits inhabited the baskets, and that they needed the dau, or door, to escape through when the basket was destroyed" (1903:321).

Fig. 11. "Gathering Seeds." Pomoan woman with a burden basket and a seedbeater. Photograph by Edward S. Curtis, probably taken in the early 1920s in the vicinity of Yokáya.

Fig. 14. Twined mush bowl made by Mary Benson, Central Pomo. Height: 12 cm. Diameter: 17 cm. No. 45. The zigzag is mainly an Eastern Pomo design element, which was used occasionally by some Central Pomo basketmakers.

Fig. 15. Central Pomo woman pounding acorns in mortar stone and basketry hopper, Yokáya, California. The various twined baskets on the ground are used in food gathering and preparation.

Fig. 16. Coiled wedding basket made by Mary Benson, Central Pomo, in 1909. Height:11 cm. Diameter:36 cm. No. 38.

Fig. 17. Coiled puberty or baby-washing basket, with clamshell beads and black quail topknots, probably Central Pomo, possibly made by Mary Benson. Height:19 cm. Diameter:30 cm. No. 23.

Fig. 18. Twined wedding basket decorated with black quail topknots, clamshell beads, and glass beads; probably Northern Pomo, probably collected before 1900. Height:21 cm. Diameter:35 cm. No. 37.

Fig. 19. Close-up view of twined basket edge. No. 44. "Twine baskets are the most ancient of all baskets. There are some forms of twine baskets that no modern basketmaker knows how to make" (Elsie Allen 1972).

Techniques Employed In The Construction Of Pomoan Baskets

There are two distinct types of baskets—sewn, or coiled, and woven—and the Pomoan groups made both. Sewn, or coiled, baskets are built on a coiled foundation linked together by a sewing fiber. An awl is used to pierce a hole in the coil through which the sewing fiber is passed. Woven baskets are built on a vertical foundation (warp) with horizontal fibers (weft) woven between the warp rods.

In weaving baskets, Pomoan basketmakers use the technique of plain weft weaving, as well as variations of the six basic techniques of twining listed below.[30] (Twining is a form of weaving in which two or more fibers twist in a spiral around each other as they pass between the warps.) Both men and women twine; the men's ware, however, is limited to openwork items such as fish traps, which they particularly need for the work they do (no. 11). When either men or women make basketry items of this nature, the wefts are twisted up to the right. This is in sharp contrast to the decorated baskets made only by women in which the twining direction is down to the right.

It is not unusual for a Pomoan basket to be constructed in more than one weave. Pomoan work is unique in this respect. Using several twining weaves in one basket to obtain specific results, either aesthetic or functional, seems, in fact, to be a classic Pomoan basketry trait.

Fig. 20. Bowl-shaped basket made by Mary Benson, Central Pomo, in three-strand braiding. Height:12 cm. Diameter:18 cm. No. 43. It is unusual for an entire basket to be woven with this technique. *"About the shuwitgu [three-strand braiding] I could not build it for the prise you said ($25). you know how long it took me to make the one I made for you. so I would not think of builleding one for no less than $50 you know Grace, my time is worth something besides my material"* (Mary Benson to Grace Nicholson, February 29, 1908, Museum of the American Indian Archives).

Fig. 21. Plain weft weaving.

Plain weft weaving (commonly referred to in the basketry literature as "wickerwork") consists of one weft element alternating over and under one or more warp elements. Only one type of basketry implement, the seedbeater (fig. 21; no. 12), is woven with this technique.

Fig. 22. Plain weft twining, pitch down to right.

Plain weft twining ("plain twining" or "simple twining," also frequently called "bamtush" by collectors, from a Northern Pomo term) consists of two weft elements twisting around one or more warp elements. This process is repeated on the same warp rods in the next round, so that the weft pattern lines up vertically along the warp. This technique seems to be used most often in mush bowls, cooking pots, burden baskets, and trays (figs. 22 and 13).

Fig. 23. Alternate pairs twining.

Alternate pairs twining ("diagonal twining" or "twill twining," also called "chuset" by collectors, from a Northern Pomo term) consists of two weft elements twisting around two warp elements. On each successive round a different pair of warp rods are embraced by the weft strands. Therefore, the weft pattern lines up diagonally. An odd number of warps are needed for this technique (fig. 23). It is often used for mush bowls (fig. 14) and burden baskets.

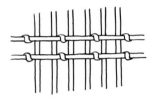

Fig. 24. Full turn twining, interior view.

Full turn twining ("wrapped twining" or "bird cage twining," also called "lit" by collectors, from a Northern Pomo term) is usually used in combination with alternate pairs twining to execute the elaborate spiral designs made by the Central Pomo (fig. 9). On rare occasions it is combined with plain weft twining to create horizontal-band designs (color plate 10a). In this technique, the light-colored weft strand runs along the basket's interior. The dark-colored weft runs along the basket's exterior and is wrapped and twisted around the inside weft through the spaces between the warps. This results in an exterior color pattern that cannot be seen on the inside of the basket (fig. 24). The exterior surface can appear to be alternate pairs twining (as in the design of fig. 14) or plain twining (color plate 10a), depending upon how this technique is executed.

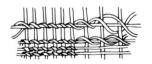

Fig. 25. Lattice twining.

Lattice twining (called "ti" or "tee" by collectors, from the Northern Pomo term *t'i*) consists of three weft elements, one of which is rigid. The two flexible strands twist around both the rigid weft and the warp (fig. 25). When this technique is spaced on the warp, an openwork vessel such as a sifter or storage basket results (fig. 10). An openwork storage basket allows air to circulate around its contents. When compactly twined, this technique strengthens a basket and adds to its water-holding properties. Lattice twining is also used to reinforce the bottom or sides of mortar baskets or winnowing trays (color plate 10a).

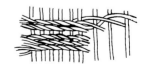

Fig. 26. Three-strand twining.

Three-strand twining is commonly used to strengthen or decorate a basket (fig. 26). As the three weft strands twine in a spiral around the warps, each passes over two warp rods and behind one. As a result, the outside of the basket looks as though a twisted cord had been laid around the basket; the inside is identical to that of plain twining. This technique is often used as the last row of twining in a basket.

119

Fig. 27. Three-strand braiding.

Three-strand braiding is a variation of three-strand twining and has been considered to be identical in final appearance.[31] The difference in execution is that the weft elements are both twined and interlaced as they pass around the warp (figs. 20 and 27). However, this technique is most often used at the bottom of a basket,[32] for it seems to securely lash the warp elements and to be an ideal base for warps. When used on the main body, it may also serve to stabilize a basket and tightly bind the finished edge to help prevent unraveling.

Twined baskets are usually finished by cutting off the elements about a quarter inch above the last row of twining (fig. 19). This unique finish seems to be diagnostic of Pomo twined baskets. However, the rims of some baskets, such as mortar and burden baskets, are usually reinforced with bound hoops of willow or oak.

In addition to seedbeaters woven of plain weft weaving and the various baskets that are twined, Pomoan women produce superb coiled baskets. The following two techniques are used almost exclusively: *one-rod coiling* (figs. 16 and 28) (called "tsai" by collectors, from the Northern Pomo term 'cay) and *three-rod coiling* (called "shibu" by collectors, from the Northern Pomo term *šibu*) (see figs. 17 and 29). The main difference between the finished products of these two techniques is that in one-rod coiling the vessel walls are smoother. A distinct advantage of three-rod coiling over all other basketry techniques, at least for the Pomoans, is that it lends itself to the addition of feathers as decorative elements.

Coiled baskets are coiled to the basketmaker's left. Depending upon shape and size, they are begun on a tight spiral of the foundation itself or around a knot of weft fibers. Barrett claimed in 1908 that an interesting variation had recently appeared: sometimes a clamshell bead provided the start for a coiled basket.[33] However, the Bijur collection in the Museum of the American Indian, which was probably formed about 1867, includes an example of such a bead start (no. 31). Perhaps beads always formed a possible starting point for baskets of a ceremonial nature. This technique may have given William Benson his novel idea of beginning a basket with a magnesite base (fig. 6). A coiled basket is finished by tapering the end of the foundation to fit as smoothly as possible onto the preceding round.

A "basketry" baby carrier used by the Pomoans is constructed in a different fashion than those described above. Vertical willow rods are reinforced with a rigid weft and lashed together with twine (fig. 30).

Fig. 28. One-rod coiling, cross-section and detail of No. 38.

Fig. 29. Three-rod coiling, cross-section and detail of No. 23.

Fig. 30. Miniature Pomoan baby carrier, possibly child's toy. Height:15 cm. Diameter:10 cm. No. 17.

Basketry Materials And Their Acquisition

Several types of natural materials are ingeniously combined in Pomoan baskets, each having a specific aesthetic and/or structural property. In terms of basketmaking properties, each of these materials grows best in certain environments and usually has the most desirable characteristics only if collected at certain times of the year and if properly prepared. In fact, for each type of material there are distinct methods of preparation and storage.

Unfortunately, the actual collection and processing of these natural materials have not been thoroughly investigated. Only one suitably detailed study exists—that by David Peri and Scott M. Patterson (1976) of the collection and processing of the roots of a *Carex*, or sedge, species (*Carex barbarae* or *Carex mendocinensis*). Their study superbly documents the care, skill, and knowledge that goes into the acquisition of materials. In addition to *Carex*, two other materials were used for the light-colored horizontal fibers of twined baskets: 1) the roots of certain conifers, ideally the digger pine (*Pinus sabiniana*); or 2) splittings from the bark of willow (Hudson specifies the gray-leaf willow, *Salix sessifolia hindsiana*). The *Carex* species was used for the light-colored wrapping fiber of coiled baskets.[34]

The darker-colored materials with which designs were usually woven were either the reddish-colored strips of the bark of redbud shoots (*Cercis occidentalis*) or the split roots of the bulrush (*Scirpus pacificus*), which were dyed black or dark brown with several techniques. Occasionally among some groups, the split roots of the bracken fern (*Pterium aquilinum*) were dyed and used for design fibers. Twined baskets were predominantly made with design fibers of redbud, while coiled baskets show dyed bulrush and occasionally bracken.

Rods were prepared from the shoots and branches of willow for the warp of twined baskets and for the foundation of coiled baskets. According to Hudson it was specifically the gray-leaf willow that was used.[35] They were harvested in early spring, immediately scraped or peeled to the woody tissue, and bound in a sheaf for summer seasoning.

It is not possible to make a basket impulsively. The different materials all have to be collected at the appropriate time of the year and held until all the materials to be used are assembled. However, supplemental materials can often be acquired out of season, for basketry materials were, and still are, sold by basketmakers to one another for fixed prices.

At the time of actual basket construction, materials are soaked in water to keep them pliable. As they are needed, fibers are shaved to the desired fineness then either coiled or twined into the desired basket.

A basketmaker's tool kit of approximately 150 years ago probably would have included a basket in which to soak the materials, an obsidian knife with which to shape the fibers, and a bone awl made from a deer fibula (fig. 31). By the 1870s the tool kit had become virtually what is still in use today: a pan of water, a piece of broken glass or a bit of broken knife, a good pair of scissors or a single-edge razor blade, and a steel awl set in a wooden handle (fig. 31).

Fig. 31. Tools used in Pomoan basketmaking: bone awl. Length: 13 cm. No. 35; steel awl. Length: 8 cm. No. 36.

Design

Although a plain basket is quicker and easier to produce and equally adequate to utilitarian functions, virtually all Pomoan baskets made by women were woven with designs in either black or dark, shiny, reddish brown fibers. The designs were often quite elaborate, and if the basket was intended for ceremonial functions (including serving food at feasts), a third dimension of design was added by incorporating native clamshell beads (*Saxidomus nuttallii*), abalone pendants (*Haliotis*), and a variety of feathers in patterned ways. It seems clear that baskets served important decorative and symbolic functions in addition to their utilitarian ones and that they constituted a major source of aesthetic and intellectual stimulation in the traditional environment.

Design Elements And Design Compositions

Baskets are woven with a total design conception in mind, but basketmakers perceive this totality as composed of a number of design elements. Each of these component design elements has its own name, which frequently differs from one autonomous group to the next, and they are quite finite in number. Hudson claimed to have identified after ten years of research a total of eighty to eighty-five named design elements.[36] Barrett found a total of fifty-four, not all of which were used by all members of the Northern Pomo–, Central Pomo–, or Eastern Pomo–speaking autonomous groups that he consulted: Northern Pomo speakers recognized and named thirty-five design elements, Central Pomo speakers thirty-two, and Eastern Pomo speakers twenty-five, of which an even smaller number were in common use.[37] In each basket, two or more design elements are creatively combined by the basketmaker into larger design compositions which do not have names but can be labeled descriptively by their makers.[38] The two-part structure of basketry design means that while baskets often look very similar, there appear to be no truly identical baskets produced. This remains the case even though there is a relatively small number of named design elements in current use in any given Pomoan group. The design elements constitute, in fact, a sort of finite lexicon; and the basketmaker's art can be compared to a syntax that permits the lexicon to be endlessly combined into distinctive structures. The design compositions of the four baskets in figure 32, for example, all utilize the same diamond-shaped design element. This design element was called "turtle" or "turtle neck" by Eastern Pomo and Southeastern Pomo speakers,[39] and "turtle back" by Northern Pomo speakers.[40] The size of the design element, its placement on the surface of the basket, and its combination with other design elements are all manipulated to produce considerable variation.

Fig. 32. Four Pomoan baskets illustrating different uses of same or similar design elements. *A*, twined mush bowl made by Mary Benson. Height:16 cm. Diameter:25 cm. No. 2; *B*, coiled basket with black quail topknots, red woodpecker crests, and clamshell beads. Height:7 cm. Diameter:20 cm. No. 3; *C*, coiled basket with redbud design fibers. Height:11 cm. Diameter:25 cm. No. 4; *D*, coiled basket made by Mary Benson. Height:9 cm. Diameter:25 cm. No. 1.

Fig. 33. Coiled wedding basket made by Mary Benson, Central Pomo, completed in 1922, decorated with clamshell beads. *A*, bottom view; *B*, side view. Height: 18 cm. Diameter: 34 cm. No. 39. This is an unusual shape for a Pomo basket.

"This kind of basket is used in marriage ceremonials and its very hily praised. mother or sister of the man receves this gife and its giving by the mother or sister bride. the dising is called part arrow head roughened with fan back desing. the arrow head desing means the children of young marred capel, wished to be good hunters and the fan back desing means, wishing the children never to be meet with accident and good health" (William Benson to Grace Nicholson, February 24, 1922, Museum of the American Indian Archives).

Design Symbolism

The design elements themselves strike non-Indian Americans as being basically geometric shapes, but the names collected for most of these designs refer to objects and phenomena familiarly found in the environments of the various Pomoan groups. According to Hudson they represent animals and objects that figure in the mythology and cosmology of the various groups.[41] Thus, Hudson says that the "turtle/turtleback" design element of figure 32 symbolizes the "turtlebacks which were seen floating on the waves" of Clear Lake at Creation.[42] Students of Pomoan basketry have long disagreed about the degree to which design elements have such symbolic significance. However, explications of the intended symbolic content of a basket's design have occasionally been collected from the maker. The Museum of the American Indian is fortunate in possessing such a basket and its design interpretation (fig 33).

The Two Types Of Design Compositions

Apparently design elements were incorporated into two major types of design compositions. One type involved an overall pattern of repetitions of one or more design elements covering the entire surface of the basket. This overall pattern would be enclosed by a circle of design at the bottom and the top of the basket (figs. 9, 17, 33, and 34). These enclosing designs can be called *initial* and *finishing designs*. The finishing design is characterized by the least variation. With only an occasional exception, it consists of a ring of alternating blocks of dark and light materials, woven just at the rim (fig. 14). The initial design could be a ring of alternating dark and light blocks identical to the finishing design, or it could be any of several design elements arranged in a circle (see figs. 33a and 34a for two possible initial designs). The initial design is particularly interesting, because it is almost never visible when the basket is placed on a surface (as it normally is). Its presence suggests that basket designs were composed with the whole basket in mind, as seen from the bottom, rather than solely in terms of the walls of the basket, which would be visible in use (figs. 33b and 34b).[43]

The other major type of design composition involves successive horizontal bands of designs, which are distributed at regular intervals over the surface of the basket. These begin as quite simple, thin, and delicate designs, and they become wider and more complex toward the upper third of the basket. This type of design composition is uniquely associated with twined baskets (fig. 1).

The Association Of Design Elements
With Specific Autonomous Groups

Hudson proposed that each of the various Pomoan groups had a characteristic design element, which enabled members of other groups to determine where a basket had been made.[44] Thus Hudson found the design called ci·yóci·yò, "zigzag" (or xá·tʰi·yòtʰi·yò, "waves on the lake" in Eastern Pomo) to be characteristic of the Eastern Pomo-speaking groups living around the northwestern side of Clear Lake (fig. 14); whereas arrowpoints were emblematic of the Kachá of Redwood Valley. Unfortunately, it appears he did not leave a complete inventory of the design elements emblematic of each group, and thus it is difficult to evaluate the accuracy of his hypothesis. However, the Purdy and Briggs collections of the American Museum of Natural History and the collection formed by Hudson around the same period of time, which is in the Smithsonian, all provide information as to the group origin of each basket collected in terms of the self-designations used by the Indians themselves. An examination of the basketry designs in these collections reveals a number of pervasive patterns in those baskets having overall design patterns. The zigzag design element does, in fact, occur predominantly on baskets produced by members of the Eastern Pomo-speaking groups living around the northwestern end of Clear Lake, although there are also one or two examples of this design element to be found on baskets attributed to the Central Pomo-speaking Yokáya group, now living a few miles south of Ukiah. Censuses taken around 1900 show at least twenty Eastern Pomo speakers residing with this latter group, and Hudson specifically mentions that the Yokáya used yet another Eastern Pomo design element, since "they are close kin of the Lake tribes."[45] It is thus likely that the baskets from Yokáya which show the overall zigzag pattern reflect the presence of Eastern Pomo speakers in the Yokáya community.

The Purdy, Briggs, and Hudson collections reveal that the arrowpoint design element (fig. 8) occurs alone in an overall pattern, not just on baskets from Kachá, which was Northern Pomo speaking, but on all baskets coming from Northern Pomo-speaking groups.

In addition, elaborate diagonal overall design compositions based on more than one design element are predominantly attributed to Central Pomo-speaking groups (Yokáya, Shanél, or Hopland) (see fig. 9), as are the delicate compositions of latticelike elements (see fig. 33b).

There seems in fact to have been a strong interrelationship between a basket's shape, size, function, design, the materials utilized in its manufacture, and the specific Pomoan group to which its maker belonged, but the details of this interrelationship have been little studied. Thus tray-shaped parching and winnowing baskets are predominantly twined, but a few coiled ones have been collected that consistently have Northern Pomo-speaking communities given as their source. Baskets for cooking and serving acorn

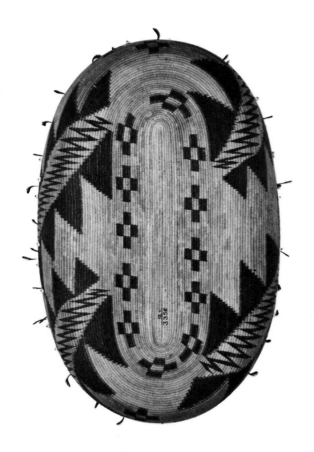

Fig. 34. Coiled oval ceremonial or gift basket, decorated with black quail topknots, clamshell beads, and blue glass beads, Pomoan. A, bottom view; B, side view. Height: 14 cm. Length: 60 cm. Width: 36 cm. No. 22. Baskets of this shape were often used for storing ritual paraphernalia.

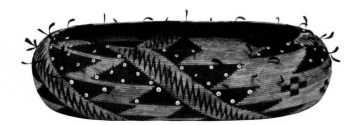

mush and pinole are predominantly twined, but a few coiled ones have been collected, again from Northern Pomo–speaking groups. Diagonal overall design compositions, alternate pairs twining, and the use of redbud and sedge are predominantly associated with cooking and serving vessels. Diagonal overall designs, alternate pairs twining, and the use of redbud and pine root are associated with burden baskets produced by Central Pomo–speaking communities, but none are associated with traylike parching and winnowing baskets, mortar baskets, or cups. Cups are consistently coiled and flat bottomed.

Use Of Feathers And Beads As Design Constituents

Pomoan basketmakers are particularly and justly famous for their incorporation of feathers and beads into baskets as they are made. This adds quite remarkable dimensions of movement, texture, and color to the basket. Apparently, such baskets always had a ceremonial function. Only feathers from certain parts of certain birds were used, and, interestingly, all the birds figure in myths related by the various Pomoan groups. The brilliant red crests, or topknots, of the acorn woodpecker (*Melanerpes formiocivorus*), the curving black topknots of the California valley quail (*Lophortyx californicus*), the iridescent green head and neck feathers of the male mallard duck (*Anas platyrhynchos*), the pale yellow feathers from the breast of the meadowlark (*Sturnella neglecta*), and the orange body feathers of the Bullock's oriole (*Icterus galbula*) were among those primarily used.

After contact with Western society, basketmakers experimented with blue feathers of the bluebird (*Sialia mexicana*) and the California jay (*Cyanocitta cristata*), the reddish brown breast feathers of the robin (*Turdus migratorius*), and the dark brown feathers of the varied thrush (*Ixoreus naevius*). Barrett says that the red shoulder patches of the redwing blackbird (*Agelaius phoeniceus*) are sometimes used, as well as black feathers from this bird, and, rarely, the black head feathers of the brant (*Branta nigricans*).[46]

Twined baskets were decorated either with clamshell beads or quail topknots, or a combination of the two. In coiled baskets the entire surface might be covered with feathers, either woodpecker feathers exclusively, or a mixture of several types worked into designs. Totally feathered baskets usually had a handle of beads and a ring of clamshell beads at the rim, often interspersed with quail topknots and with dangling pendants of abalone shells (fig. 35). These baskets were made to be seen from below, in movement, probably with the intention that firelight would highlight the colors.

Coiled baskets might also have tufts of woodpecker crests woven in at regularly distributed intervals on the light-colored sewing elements, contrasting with the darker woven patterns (fig. 8). Woodpecker crests were used alone or in combination with scattered quail topknots or with scattered quail topknots and clamshell beads, producing subtly beautiful effects. After

contact with Western society, the Pomoan groups sometimes added very fine trade beads to combinations of woodpecker crests, quail topknots, and clamshell beads; and some basketmakers began to experiment with creative uses of trade beads (no. 26), while others made baskets that were entirely beaded (no. 27).

Pomoan Basketry Today

A few basketmakers continue to weave today and, according to David Peri, in the last five years there has been an upsurge of basket production and interest in basketmaking among Pomoan basketmakers. In 1978 eighty-four weavers were identified in Mendocino, Lake, and Sonoma counties and the Sacramento Valley.[47] Most of these artisans are of Pomoan descent and weave in the "Pomo" style. From November 1977 to October 1978, economic benefits totaling approximately $100,000 were realized from the sale and exchange of finished baskets and sedge coils and from fees for teaching and demonstrating basketmaking.[48]

The local interest in basketmaking has spread to a much wider audience, especially through the media of print and film. Women such as Elsie Allen of Cloverdale and Mollie Jackson of Ukiah have been featured in books on basketry;[49] and films illustrating the techniques of making Pomoan baskets are available through the University of California Media Center. Access to the necessary materials is a problem. Sedge beds at Dry Creek are some of the few remaining sources of root material used in the Pomoan basketry produced today. They will soon be inundated when Dry Creek is dammed. It is hoped that experiments currently underway will result in the transplanting of these sedge beds to other sections in the Dry Creek area.[50] The success of this project is vital for the survival of the craft—coupled, of course, with knowledgeable artisans to practice it.

Fig. 35. Coiled basket fully feathered, with clamshell beads and pendants of glass beads and abalone, Pomoan, made before 1906. Height:65 cm. Diameter:16 cm. No. 32.

NOTES

1. Barrett 1908.

2. The John Hudson collection at the Smithsonian Institution was collected from 1888 through 1899. The Carl Purdy collection at the American Museum of Natural History was collected prior to 1900. The Charles P. Wilcomb collection at the California State Indian Museum was collected from about 1890 through 1905.

3. See McLendon and Oswalt 1978. Magnesite is a claylike mineral used to make beads that are highly valued among the Pomoan groups.

4. See McLendon and Lowy 1978:308–310 for details of the subsistence cycle of Eastern Pomo-speaking groups.

5. Kniffen 1939:375.

6. Stewart 1943:35.

7. Stewart 1943:46.

8. Kniffen 1939:375.

9. Stewart 1943:43.

10. Stewart 1943:45.

11. Barrett 1916.

12. Powers 1877:163.

13. Powers 1877:175.

14. Lee and DeVore 1968:11.

15. Kunkel 1962:263.

16. Kunkel 1962:275, 331, 376.

17. Barrett 1908:33.

18. This was the first millenarian movement to spread from Paiute charismatic leaders to Native American populations that were agonizing under the disintegrative effects of contact with Europeans. The Plains 1890 Ghost Dance was the second such movement. It also started among the Paiute but spread east rather than west.

19. Unfortunately, most of the other Northern Pomo-speaking groups were forced to move to Round Valley reservation outside of Pomoan territory about this time.

20. Hudson 1899:2.

21. Smithsonian Institution Archives.

22. Museum of the American Indian Archives.

23. Briggs, letter to Clark Wissler, March 1931, American Museum of Natural History Archives.

24. Benson, letter to Grace Nicholson, September 26, 1905, Museum of the American Indian Archives.

25. Nicholson, letter to the Bensons, June 17, 1931, Museum of the American Indian Archives.

26. Cooking was done by placing hot rocks into the baskets containing meal and liquid, and stirring them with a wooden paddle until the food, usually acorn mush, reached the desired temperature.

27. Benson, letter to Grace Nicholson, February 24, 1922, Museum of the American Indian Archives.

28. Loeb 1926:286–291.

29. Barrett 1952:54; Hudson 1899.

30. The terminology used for basketry weaving techniques is mainly from *The Primary Structures of Fabrics* (Emery 1966).

31. Barrett 1908:147; Mason 1902. However, in decorated baskets twined by Pomoan women, three-strand braiding seems to be consistently twined up to the right. This is in contrast to the other twining techniques which are twined down to the right.

32. Mason 1901:118.

33. Barrett 1908:159.

34. Occasionally splittings from hazel (*Corylus rostratus*) and willow saplings were used as wrapping fibers in coiled baskets and warp rods in both coiled and twined baskets.

35. Hudson n.d.a.

36. Hudson n.d.b.

37. Barrett 1908:254–255.

38. Barrett 1908.

39. Purdy 1902:35; Barrett 1908:226.

40. Hudson n.d.b; Barrett 1908:226.

41. Hudson n.d.b.

42. Hudson n.d.b.

43. When feathers and/or clamshell beads are incorporated, the finishing design seems to be absent as frequently as it is present. Otherwise the finishing design is always present in the basket collections examined, except for miniature baskets and five baskets in the Hudson collection of the Smithsonian. These are all coiled baskets with flaring rims, and all except one were produced in Northern Pomo-speaking villages. These five baskets are strikingly similar in shape and design composition to the Yuki baskets studied by Isabel Kelly (1930). The Yukis lived just to the north of the Northern Pomo.

44. Hudson n.d.b.

45. Hudson n.d.a.

46. Barrett 1908:143.

47. The figure of eighty-four includes seven men and consists of those people who know how to weave but may not be actively producing baskets. The number of weavers in each area is as follows: Sonoma 31; Mendocino, 21; Lake, 28; Sacramento Valley, 4.

48. David Peri, personal communication.

49. Allen 1972; Newman 1974.

50. David Peri, personal communication.

REFERENCES

Allen, Elsie
   1972   Pomo Basketmaking: A Supreme Art for the Weaver. Healdsburg, California: Naturegraph Publishers.
American Museum of Natural History Archives
   1901 and 1931
             Briggs Collection Accession Papers.
Barrett, S. A.
   1908   Pomo Indian Basketry. University of California Publications in American Archeology and Ethnology, Vol. 7, No. 3. Pp. 134–308. Berkeley: University of California Press.
   1916   Pomo Buildings. In Holmes Anniversary Volume: Anthropological Essays Presented to William Henry Holmes in Honor of his 70th Birthday. Pp. 1–17. Washington, D.C.: J. W. Bryan Press.
   1917   Ceremonies of the Pomo Indians. University of California Publications in American Archeology and Ethnology, Vol. 12, No. 30. Pp. 397–441. Berkeley: University of California Press.
   1952   Material Aspects of Pomo Culture: Part One. Bulletin of the Public Museum of the City of Milwaukee. Vol. 20.
Curtis, Edward S.
   1924   The Pomos. In The North American Indian: Being a Series of Volumes Picturing and Describing the Indians of the United States and Alaska. Frederick W. Hodge, ed. Vol. 14. Pp. 55–70. Norwood, Mass.: Plimpton Press. (Reprinted. New York: Johnson Reprint, 1970.)
Emery, Irene
   1966   The Primary Structures of Fabric. New York: The Spiral Press; Washington, D.C.: The Textile Museum.
Frye, Melinda Young
   1977   Pioneers in American Museums: Charles P. Wilcomb, Museum News May/June:55–60. Published by the Oakland Public Museum.
Gifford, Edward W.
   1967   Ethnographic Notes on the Southwestern Pomo. University of California Anthropological Records 25:1–47.
Henshaw, H. W.
   1893   Pomo Indian Photographs. Smithsonian Institution Archives.
Hudson, J. W.
   1893   Pomo Basket Makers. Overland Monthly, 2nd series, 21:561–578.
   1899   Catalog accompanying Hudson collection purchased by Smithsonian, Smithsonian Archives.
   n.d.a.   Ethnographic notes. Smithsonian Archives.
   n.d.b.   Correspondence with Otis T. Mason, 1896–1903, Smithsonian Archives.
Kelly, Isabelle
   1930   Yuki Basketry. University of California Publications in American Archeology and Ethnology, Vol. 24, No. 9. Pp. 421–444. Berkeley: University of California Press.
Kniffen, Fred B.
   1939   Pomo Geography. University of California Publications in American Archeology and Ethnology, Vol. 36, No. 6. Pp. 353–400. Berkeley: University of California Press.
Kroeber, A. L.
   1909   California Basketry and the Pomo. American Anthropologist 11:233–249. (Reprinted in The California Indians. R. F. Heizer and M. A. Whipple, eds. Pp. 251–263. Berkeley: University of California Press, 1951).

Fig. 36. Twined burden baskets, Pomoan. A, overall spiral design. Height:30 cm. Diameter:32 cm. No. 14; B, horizontal-band design. Height:49 cm. Diameter:60 cm. No. 13.

REFERENCES

Kunkel, Peter H.
1962   Yokuts and Pomo Political Institutions: A Comparative Study. Ph.D. Dissertation, University of California, Los Angeles.
Lee, Richard B. and Irven DeVore
1968   Problems in the Study of Hunters and Gatherers. *In* Man the Hunter. Lee and DeVore, eds. Chicago: Aldine Publishing Company.
Loeb, Edwin M.
1926   Pomo Folkways. University of California Publications in American Archeology and Ethnology, Vol. 19, No. 2. Pp. 149-405. Berkeley: University of California Press.
Mason, Otis T.
1901   The Technic of Aboriginal American Basketry. American Anthropologist 3:109-128.
1902   Aboriginal American Basketry: Studies in a Textile Art without Machinery. *In* Annual Report of the Smithsonian Institution. Pp. 171-548. Washington, D.C.: Smithsonian Institution.
McLendon, Sally and Robert L. Oswalt
1978   Pomo: Introduction *In* Handbook of North American Indians. William Sturtevant, general ed. Vol. 8. California. Robert Heizer, ed. Pp. 274-288. Washington, D.C.: Smithsonian Institution.
McLendon, Sally and Michael J. Lowy
1978   Eastern Pomo and Southeastern. *In* Handbook of North American Indians. William Sturtevant, general ed. Vol. 8. California. Robert Heizer, ed. Pp. 306-323. Washington, D.C.: Smithsonian Institution.
Museum of the American Indian Archives
1903-1930
        Correspondence between Mary and William Benson and Grace Nicholson.
n.d.   Grace Nicholson's Catalog.
Newman, Sandra Corrie
1974   Indian Basket Weaving. Flagstaff, Arizona: Northland Press.
Peri, David W. and Scott M. Patterson
1976   The Basket Is In The Roots, That's Where It Begins. Journal of California Anthropology 3:17-32.
Powers, Stephen
1877   Tribes of California. Contributions to North American Ethnology 3. Washington, D.C.: U.S. Geographical and Geological Survey of the Rocky Mountain Region.
Purdy, Carl
1902   Pomo Indian Baskets and Their Makers. Los Angeles: Out West Co. Press (Reprinted. Ukiah, Calif.: Mendocino County Historical Society,. n.d.).
Stewart, Omer C.
1943   Notes on Pomo Ethnogeography. University of California Publications in American Archeology and Ethnology, Vol. 40, No. 2. Pp. 29-62. Berkeley: University of California Press.

ACKNOWLEDGMENTS

We wish to extend our special thanks to David Peri, Sonoma State University, and Bruce Bernstein, California State Indian Museum, Sacramento, for their counsel and encouragement and especially for sharing information from their own research. We also wish to express our gratitude to Stanley Freed, American Museum of Natural History, for providing us with the opportunity to study the Purdy and Briggs collections of Pomoan basketry; and the National Museum of Natural History, Smithsonian Institution, for providing access to the Hudson collection of Pomoan basketry. In addition, we are grateful to Sandra Harner for her counsel regarding basketry techniques.

Fig. 37. Polly Holmes, Southeastern Pomo basketmaker, holding "story" basket, No. 34. Photograph collected by Sally McLendon.

Fig. 38. Coiled "story" basket made by Polly Holmes, Southeastern Pomo, decorated with clamshell beads and black quail topknots. Height:20 cm. Length:77 cm. Width:59 cm. No. 34. This basket may be commemorative of a special event.

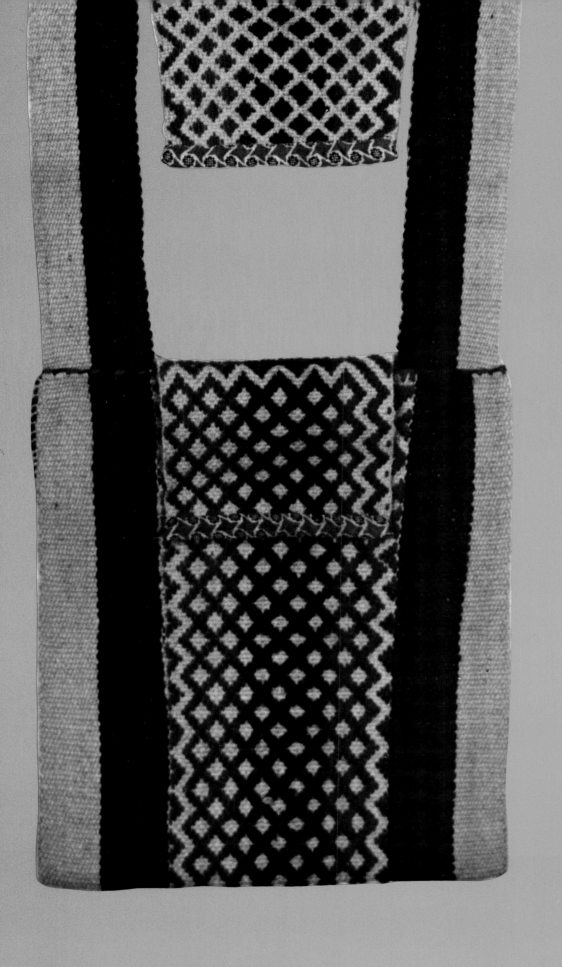

GINA LACZKO

the WEAVER
THE ARAUCANIANS OF CHILE

GINA LACZKO

The Araucanian-speaking peoples of Chile have traditionally occupied the area between the Rio Choapa in Coquimbo Province and the Gulf of Corcovado, Chiloe Province—a distance of about eight hundred miles in central Chile (figs. 1 and 2). This linguistic group is made up of the Mapuche (numerically the largest), the Huilliche, the Cunco, the Chono, Chilotes, Picunche, and Pehuenche, as well as several other smaller divisions. Although they are nearly always linked in the literature, these peoples never really formed a political unit; at best, they were occasionally a loose confederation, especially before contact with the Europeans. Their name, *Araucanian*, was given them by the soldier-poet Ercilla, who wrote an epic poem in Spanish about his military experience, fighting them in colonial Chile. Impressed with their formidable skills in battle, Ercilla returned from Chile and wrote *L'Arucana*.[1] Although the title was meant to imply a location ("muddy water," from the Araucanian *rau*—"clay" + *co*—"water"), it has come to define all those speaking the Araucanian language. They themselves do not use the name, nor do they accept the label "Indian," which to them has come to be a degrading term; rather, they refer to themselves as *Mapuche*, or "people of the land" (*mapu*—"land" + *che*—"people").

Further distinctions are based upon where a Mapuche lives: thus, a Mapuche from the north is designated a *Picunche* (*picun*—"north" + *che*); from the south, *Huilliche* (*huilli*—"south" + *che*); from the east, *Puelche* (*puel*—"east" + *che*). In other cases, Mapuche are distinguished by an important natural resource, like the *Pehuenche* (*puhuene*—a pine tree, *Araucaria araucana*, which has seeds that once formed a staple of the diet + *che*). Historians and anthropologists have come to use these terms to refer to separate groups of people, but to the Mapuche no such definite divisions have ever existed. In their world there are only two divisions—those who are Mapuche and those who are not.[2]

Fig. 1. A view of Mapuche land in southern Chile.
"The climate where these people live resembles somewhat that of Puget Sound, and is beautiful, although disagreeably windy during part of the year. Houses of the aboriginal type are still to be found. The material culture is quite rich. The Indians, for instance, weave blankets with beautiful and intricate native designs. Weapons and even household utensils of primitive type are still abundantly to be seen" (Bullock 1921:496).

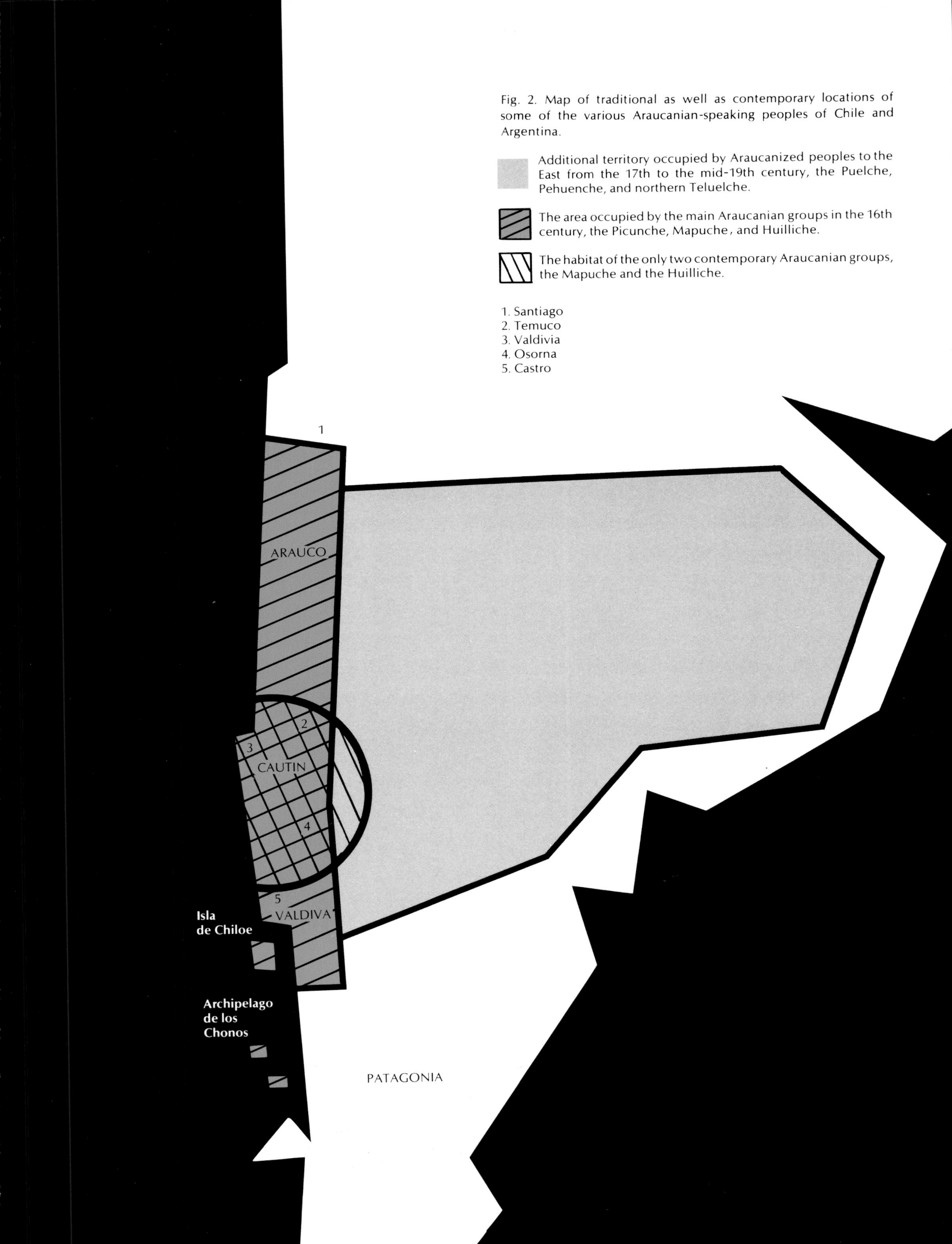

Fig. 2. Map of traditional as well as contemporary locations of some of the various Araucanian-speaking peoples of Chile and Argentina.

Additional territory occupied by Araucanized peoples to the East from the 17th to the mid-19th century, the Puelche, Pehuenche, and northern Teluelche.

The area occupied by the main Araucanian groups in the 16th century, the Picunche, Mapuche, and Huilliche.

The habitat of the only two contemporary Araucanian groups, the Mapuche and the Huilliche.

1. Santiago
2. Temuco
3. Valdivia
4. Osorna
5. Castro

1

ARAUCO

2

3

CAUTIN

4

5

VALDIVA

Isla de Chiloe

Archipelago de los Chonos

PATAGONIA

Fig. 3. A traditional *ruca* (home) near Temuco, Chile.
"We were back at the ruca, impressed by the cleanliness of everything and everybody, as we had been with every Araucanian household and person we had seen anywhere. Whether we came upon a family unexpectedly or not, always all was clean" (Hilger 1966:121).

Fig. 4. The *ruca* or home of an Araucanian *machi* (shaman or medicine woman) near Temuco, Chile. Her *rewe,* a carved pole that marks her profession, can be seen on the right surrounded by poles and twigs from sacred trees.

Origins And History

It is now generally believed that the Araucanian-speaking peoples were themselves intrusive into Chile. Entering the area through southern Andean mountain passes, they drove a wedge between existing indigenous groups. They intermarried and were so successful in adopting the material culture characteristic of the native peoples that their own origins became obscured; apparently the only tradition they retained was military skill and fierceness.

The territory occupied by the Araucanians is often described as having a pleasant Mediterranean climate. The summers are cool and dry, but the winters are very wet, rainfall totaling between eighty and one hundred inches. As a result, visitors and traders are usually forced to restrict their activities to the summer months, for roads normally are impassable in the winter. The wet season also afforded a seasonal break to the three-hundred-year war of resistance the Araucanians waged against the Spanish.

Snow and freezing temperatures are rare and are usually restricted to the higher altitudes. Until recently, the central valley of Chile was heavily wooded, and this Araucanian territory is still thought to be the best farmland in all of the country. The people have always been farmers, raising maize, potatoes, beans, squash, chile peppers, quinoa, oca, and, today, wheat. In earlier times they were virtual vegetarians, since warfare with the Spanish supplanted hunting as the men's occupation. Guinea pigs and llamas were kept, but llamas were slaughtered only for religious festivals. All the farm work was done by women, and the fields were scattered in a variety of locations for fear of losing the crops to the Spanish. Since the 1860s when reservations were established, however, the men have taken over much of the farm work, the women tending only the small kitchen gardens.

Outside of warfare, Araucanian sociopolitical organization barely exists. Families, either nuclear or extended, live in their own *ruca* ("house"). There were never, and still are not, any Araucanian towns. Some *ruca* are clustered in groups of three or four, while others stand alone, just within sight of another *ruca*. The lack of any settlement organization has been a distressing problem to the Spanish and the Chilean government in turn, as well as to the anthropologist. Mischa Titiev noted: "There are no streets, no central plazas, no stores or public buildings, in short, nothing that suggests the spatial arrangement of a village or town."[3] Each family's *ruca* is so private that no one may approach it without a formal invitation, and there are no direct paths from one *ruca* to another.

Before the initiation of the first reservation system in the 1860s, there were no formal leaders. Lineage heads (the Araucanians are patrilineal) were merely spokesmen for their kinsmen, and dissent was common; even today, a direct command can be avoided simply by moving to another *ruca*. When the Chileans attempted to place the Araucanians on the reservations, they created as many "chiefs" as there were allotments —about three thousand—and these leaders (called *caciques* by the Spanish) wielded considerable power and became wealthy through tribute. With the new reservation system that was initiated in the 1880s, however, this changed, although there remain *caciques* today, and it is traditional to ask their permission to farm a section of land on the reservation.

Religious ceremonies and beliefs are equally unstructured. There is a belief in a supreme god who is good and spirits who are bad, as well as a tradition of ancestor worship. The most important ceremony is the *ñillatun*, a fertility rite that combines features of curing and divination practices, hockey games, assembly customs, *machi* ("shaman") lore, and purification of the field to prevent contamination of the ancestors from the forces of evil. There is no particular season during which the festivals are held, nor is there any particular cycle. Again, it is Titiev who laments the "lack of regularity in the ritual calendar," as well as the problem even of determining "the names or characteristics of the deities or spirits to whom the prayers are addressed."[4] Faron[5] believes that much of the confusion arises because the *ñillatun* is a ceremony that changes with the needs of the Araucanians and thus it is held in any time of stress so that the people can present their needs to their ancestors and their gods. Usually lasting two days, the religious ceremony consists of prayer, dancing, music, and the ritual sacrifice of an animal, usually a sheep.

The *machi*, or shaman, is the religious practitioner who is present in the Araucanian community every day. Personifying what the Araucanian feels are the forces of "good," the *machi* is primarily a curer, possessed with supernatural power that allows him or her to fight off the forces of "evil." The *machi* carries a drum, called a *kultrun*, a special drumstick, and a gourd rattle when curing a patient. The *machi's ruca* is marked with a *rewe*, or carved pole (fig. 4).

Before the reservations were initiated Araucanian life was markedly different when any local population was at war. After successfully halting the spread of the Inca Empire in the fifteenth century, the Araucanians waged a highly successful three-hundred-year war with the Spanish. This extraordinary and unique military history has been the subject of nearly all of the studies made of these people. Altough apparently they engaged in many feuds among themselves, when faced with the Europeans they utilized a fairly complex military system, dividing Araucanian territory into three districts, called *butanmapos*, each administered by three officials: the *Toqui-Guilman* ("commander"), the *Guinca-Guilman* ("field commander"), and the *Pelqui-Guilman* ("diplomatic courrier"). Over them all was the *Toque-General*, who could unite under his command any or all of the *butanmapos*, his directive taking precedence over the war effort of any local *Toqui*. The success of this organization, as well as the fierceness and determination of the Araucanian warriors, became legendary, and the stories of their cannibalism, cruelty in battle, and vindictive treatment of captives were widespread. Few if any of the early historians attempted to look behind this behavior for its origin and cause. Fewer still were willing to see the Araucanians in any other context but war.[6]

Before 1900 the only nonmilitary glimpses reported of the Araucanians were from adventurers, ship-wrecked sailors, and deserters, who found generous hospitality and refuge freely offered them by the Mapuche.[7] From these accounts it is possible to reconstruct a culture in which the private image and the public face of the people were completely opposed. Although the men were almost totally occupied by war, there is good evidence to suggest that they played an important part in child care and at least seasonally helped with the agricultural work. The women were neither slaves nor unduly oppressed, although they did undertake nearly all the work required to furnish the needs of day-to-day living: gathering of foodstuffs, the cultivation of crops, most shamanistic and curing activity, all food preparation, early child training and care, and the manufacture of garments, baskets, and pottery. It is no wonder that most women were grateful that their husbands were polygamous (the practice of taking more than one wife); although the Spaniards were scandalized, the women generally admitted that they looked forward to the additional wives (who were traditionally the first wife's younger sisters), so that they would have someone with whom to share the work. Each wife had her own hearth, her own section of the *ruca* (house), (figs. 3 and 4), her own bed, and her own loom.

History Of Weaving

The history of Araucanian weaving is somewhat obscure, since archaeological evidence for textiles is lacking in this wet climate. It seems probable that the women were weavers even before contact with the Inca. Latcham[8] suggests that the material used originally for weaving was vegetal fiber from plants and the inner bark of trees, especially *Bromelia landbecki*; this practice still persists in the traditional manufacture of ropes, baskets, carrying bags, cords, and fish lines. Later, contact with the Inca Empire probably resulted in the availability of the hair of the llama and alpaca, two domesticated animals whose hair was used extensively for weaving for a very long time in Peru. The northern Mapuche, or Picunche as they were designated, who were allied with the Inca, had a greater supply of this animal hair than did the central or southern peoples, who remained remote and hostile to northern intervention and innovation. It was therefore possible that Araucanian weaving did not become an important craft until the advent of the Spanish, who brought with them sheep.

Fig. 5. Wood spindle, clay whorl, and partially spun wool yarn, Mapuche, Puerto Dominquez (Laguna de Budi), Imperial, Cautin, Chile. Length: 47.5 cm. No. 33.

Training And Technology

All Mapuche women were, and still are, expected to be good weavers. Training begins quite young, with both boys and girls of about ten years of age learning to prepare and spin wool; and men, when they have the time, often help with the spinning and plying of yarn. But the actual weaving of the textile itself is exclusively the work of the older girls and women. Training is through observation: girls watch their mothers as well as other women in the area, in order to learn the technique. Much knowledge is freely shared, some patterns, for example, being known to all Mapuche women. But each family is said to have "professional secrets," special designs that are shared only among a woman and her daughters. Some weavers, called *vaqueanas*, are considered master weavers and are greatly respected. They alone attempt the most complicated pieces, like the *trarihue* ("belt"), *lama* ("saddle blanket"), and the more ornate ponchos. When it is rumored that one of these *vaqueanas* is ready to set up her loom, all the girls of the district come to watch her work, and some will even serve an apprenticeship under such an important weaver.[9]

The process involved in making any woven textile is long and complicated. Several days before a family intends to shear its sheep, the wool is given a washing while it is still on the animal: the women pour a decoction of canelo leaves (*Drimys winteri*) over the animal, and the men work it into the wool. This serves as a first cleaning. When a woman is ready to undertake a project, she selects the amount of sheared wool required and again washes it: it is first plunged into hot water and then rushed to a cold stream nearby. This process causes the wool to shrink. After carefully being pulled apart to thoroughly remove all dirt and foreign particles, the wool is hung on the family's fence to dry in the sun and wind. The women and children prepare the wool for spinning without the help of any specific tools; the fibers are untangled and made parallel by gently combing them with the fingers. The more parallel the fibers are as they go into the yarn, the stronger, neater, and more even will be the yarn that is spun. Soft wads of these straightened fibers are prepared for spinning, by being pulled into elongated wads that can be wound about the spinner's forearm and wrist (fig. 6).

Fig. 6. Two Mapuche girls from the vicinity of Temuco, Chile; the girl on the right is preparing the wool for spinning, and the one on the left is spinning.
"It is a common sight to see several little girls from six to ten or twelve years of age out in the fields all day looking after the sheep. Sometimes they have a large hank of yarn and a spindle and you may see them assiduously spinning, aptly giving the spindle a turn now and again and rolling up the thread in a ball" (Wilson 1924).

"She pulled the wool into elongated wads, wound loosely around her arm, and then fastened an end of it to the end of the yarn on the spindle on the ground, letting it lean against her, twisted the wad of wool that extended between it and her arm, lifted the spindle, and gave it a twist in midair. This spun the yarn. Since she wanted very finely spun yarn, she twirled the spindle three times in midair" (Hilger 1957:377).

The Araucanian spindle is of simple construction: it is a wood spindle with a clay whorl that gives balance, steadiness, and momentum to the whirling motion (fig. 5). Spinning (*feun*) can be done while standing or walking, although the yarn produced is necessarily thick, since it must be strong enough to support the weight of the spindle. The preferred attitude for the spinner is to be seated, usually on a low bench. Yarn spun in this way can be as fine as the weaver desires, since the spindle in this case rests on the ground and is not supported by the yarns (figs. 6, 7, and 8). Although one early account[10] laments the tediousness and slowness of this process, the women apparently do not mind the task; in fact, they describe the movement of the spindle as *pitroifeun* ("dancing"). Young girls, out to mind the family sheep, often take wool and spindles along with them to the pastures. But the favorite time to spin is after the evening meal, when the family sits together and discusses the day's events.

Fig. 7. Woman seated on a low bench, spinning, near Temuco, Chile.
The Araucanians describe the movement of the spindle as *pitroifeun*, "dancing."

Wool is spun into four grades. *Feu* is the finest grade, used for the weaving of shawls and dresses. The second finest grade is *huini*. The third grade, *trapemfeu*, is composed of two or more strands piled together. The coarsest grade is *piulo* used, among other ways, to bind warp yarns for a type of resist dyeing known as *ikat* and to lash together the bars of a loom. After the wool is spun into yarn, it is wound into balls for storage until enough is made to complete the proposed textile.[11]

It is the yarn, not the unspun wool, that is dyed, and there appears to be only one exception to this routine: Joseph[12] suggests that if a poncho is to be of a single color, it is dyed after it is woven. Normally, however, when the colors for the proposed weaving are decided upon, the woman rewinds the yarn into skeins of about an arm's length; these are composed of varying quantities depending upon the amount of yarn that is required in a particular color, as well as the size of the dye pot.

Originally, dyes were made from natural vegetal material (see color plate 7 for skeins dyed in this way) and minerals. Today, commercial dyes are used for two reasons: first, the natural materials are becoming harder to find as the environment changes with the advance of "civilization,"[13] and, second, the women say that the tourists like the brighter, aniline colors and that the naturally dyed, darker colors (which they prefer) "are difficult to sell."[14] Dyeing is usually done in a store-bought iron kettle, except for black, which is always dyed in a pottery *olla* ("water jar"), "for black dyed in a kettle fades the next day. A woman who does not have an *olla* usually weaves her *kepam* ("dress") from the wool of black sheep."[15] The yarn is boiled with the dye concoction for varying lengths of time, depending upon the strength of the color desired. Natural dyes are set—that is, the colors are rendered more or less permanent—with just putrid urine or with urine and earth of a "specific quality" as mordant.[16] Commercial dyes are usually set with alum. Mothers are assisted in this process by their daughters, because, as one said, "That is the way she learns; that is how I learned—by helping my mother dye."[17]

Among those Araucanians living in Argentina, the wool is also bleached, in order to make it white —"whiter than white, a color known as *lüu*."[18] The desired amount of yarn is wound onto a leaf or small stick and then buried in a white clay known as *mallo* for about two months; wool so treated will not take any other coloring. There is some evidence to suggest[19] that in earlier years Araucanians purchased red trade cloth (identified as red ferret or Manchester cloth), which they unraveled, respun, and wove into garments for its color before a satisfactory red dye was available —aniline or coal-tar dyes not being discovered until the 1850s.

Araucanian textiles fall into several categories: clothing, horse equipment, and other utilitarian pieces, as well as "tourist items." These categories in turn determine the kind of loom that is used, its size, the method of warping (preparing the loom for weaving by lining up the initial yarns on which to weave), as well as the designs to be incorporated. In addition, the skill of the weaver also sets limitations, only the *vaqueana* attempting the most complicated textiles and designs. Further, except for those pieces offered for sale outside the Mapuche community, all textiles are made to measure. Each piece of clothing, whether poncho, dress, or shawl, is made to fit the individual who is to wear it; even sleeping blankets (*pontros*) are made to the size of the user. These measurements are taken by using a piece of yarn and tying knots at the appropriate points.

The *Kepam* And *Iculla* ("Dress" And "Shawl")

Probably the plainest category of weaving is the woman's dress, called *kepam*, or (now), *chamal* (nos. 8 and 9). (Originally the term *chamal* referred to any rectangular piece of textile intended for clothing, the woman's *chamal* being a *kepam*, or wraparound dress, and the man's *chamal* being a *chiripa*, or breechclout. But since most men wear Western-style trousers today, *chamal* has come to mean *kepam*.) The dress is essentially a rectangular length of cloth that is wrapped around the body and reaches nearly to the ankles. It is held in place at the waist by a belt, or *trarihue*, and is fastened over one or both shoulders, depending upon whether the woman has a nursing infant. Originally the fastening or pin was a cactus spine,[20] but today it is typically just a safety pin; for dress occasions, elaborate and traditional and (today) inherited silver ornaments are used. Some women add a Western-style white cotton blouse to the outfit, as well as a cotton apron; both are made from purchased fabric and both are handsewn, since no Mapuche can afford a sewing machine (figs. 6, 10, and 11). Dresses have no designs incorporated into them, and they are typically black (no. 8); a very few are a blue grey shade (*plomo*), dyed with earth found along the Pacific Coast (no. 9).

Shawls (*iculla*) (nos. 10, 11, and 12) are frequently added to the outfit. Old-style shawls are black, with four finished edges (figs. 8 and 13); newer style shawls, which are possibly based on purchased models and are markedly more rectangular than the old-style *iculla*, are often plaid (fig. 6) or show a banding in a second color (figs. 11, 14, and 15) and have fringe. For dress occasions, the *iculla* is fastened with an elaborate silver breast ornament (fig. 14) or sometimes a silver pin with a round head, either globular or flat (fig. 16). All women own silver jewelry, regardless of their social status (a woman's status is usually based on her fertility), and today such pieces are considered heirlooms. The wearing of both traditional silver jewelry and old-style clothing is a matter of pride among Mapuche women; those who do so are "pointed out by other women as being dressed in the 'real Mapuche way of old times'."[21] Faron,[22] who did field work among the Chilean Mapuche, notes that although women may wear purchased Western clothing for everyday work, they still wear traditional clothing for festivals and whenever they venture off Mapuche land and into local Chilean towns. He sees such traditional clothing functioning as symbols of Mapuche distinctiveness and as an indication of continuing indigenous social integration. In Argentina, not as many women have or even make the *kepam* or the *iculla*; Hilger[23] quotes a sixty-year-old woman: "It is a great pity that all this had to end. I wore a *kepam* until the soldiers came and chased us from place to place. It was impossible in those days for women to set up their looms long enough to weave. We had to buy ticking then to make clothing. Anyway, the Whites wanted us to do away with our own way of doing things, and that included our way of dressing."

Fig. 8. Three women in traditional clothing. The two seated women are spinning. Mapuche, Temuco, Chile.

". . . but their earrings or rather ear-plates, are the most remarkable of all their decorations; they are of thin silver, shaped like the blade of a garden-hoe, and not less than about one-half the usual size of one, covering the greater part of the face; that part which would correspond with the ring for the handle, being large enough to receive the ear, upon which it is suspended " (Gardiner 1841:179).

The Araucanian Loom

The loom on which the *kepam* and *iculla* are woven is an elementary form (figs. 9, 10, and 12), since it is really little more than an adjustable, rectangular wooden frame. The four principal members are lashed to each other at right angles with leather thongs, strips of fabric, strong yarn, or even vines. The desired finished size of the piece to be woven determines their placement. The tall, upright poles that rest on the floor and lean up against a wall are called by a term that may be translated, "with both feet on the ground."[24] Both these poles, as well as the two horizontal beams, are made of wood that does not easily splinter, usually *rauli* (*Nothofagus procera*).[25]

To warp the loom the women often work in pairs. First, the loom is positioned horizontally, about twenty

Fig. 9. Traditionally dressed women and a man standing with a loom.

This photograph is obviously posed; women never weave standing, and the lack of shedding apparatus and most weaving tools suggests that this textile is completed. This photograph, taken near Temuco, Chile, was published in 1927 in an article by Looser, who wrote one of the first papers on Araucanian weaving; it is a companion photograph to Fig. 8.

inches from the ground. The warp yarns are then continuously wrapped around what are the upper and lower beams (when the loom is in position) in a pattern that looks like a figure eight when viewed from the side. Just above and below the crossing point of the "eight," rods are inserted, the *rañiñelhue* ("dueña," or "guardian of the half or middle"). Next, the weaver, who for plain weave[26] needs two sheds[27] to control the alternate warps, lashes the yarns of what will be the lower shed to the heddle bar;[28] the heddle ends rest on secondary uprights lashed to the original frame. To control the alternate shed, a shed rod[29] is apparently inserted between the warps in exactly the same position as the lower *rañiñelhue*, only the shed rod is not lashed to the loom frame. Although Joseph[30] states specifically that it is the *rañiñelhue* that are used, and no shed rod is employed at any time, all available photographs of Araucanian weaving in progress distinctly show the weavers using a shed rod, with both *rañiñelhue* removed once the loom is set upright. Further, Joseph[31] illustrates and describes the warping of the loom only for a fringed-finished textile, for which it is not necessary to weave to the edge of each warp loop.[32] If a four-selvedge textile is desired, as in the black *iculla* (shawl) or *kepam* (dress), it is necessary to tie rather than wrap the warp loops to the upper and lower loom bars: in this case the first weft[33] is extra strong and is called a *heading cord*. The heading cord is lashed to the loom bar with a strong cord or yarn using spiral motion. Figures 9 and 10 show heading cords in use; figure 10 shows both a heddle and a shed rod. All these preparations completed, the loom is then set upright and the weaving can begin.

Women usually sit or kneel on the floor while weaving (fig. 10). Weaving always proceeds from the bottom up; as the work progresses out of the weaver's reach, a second rod is placed adjacent to the lower beam, and the completed textile is wrapped around both of them; the upper cross piece is then lowered. At some point, the entire loom is turned and work is begun at the other end. As the area between the woven sections narrows, a needle is used to insert the final weft yarns. Usually the weave is so skillfully accomplished that it is not possible to easily detect where the work has been completed (fig. 18). In the case of the *lama* ("under-saddle blanket") the area where the work is finished has become conventionalized and is easily seen: the pattern is suspended in favor of a horizontal band of stripes, actually a plain weave without patterning (fig. 21). Thus, the *lama* loom must be turned when the work is about half completed; for other textiles, the weavers often wait until the work is nearly completed before they reverse their looms.[34] Thus, the simple construction of the loom belies the skill required of any Araucanian woman: "The Araucanian weaver pursues her task with infinite patience, interrupting it only for the daily household chores. To produce a skillfully woven fabric on an Araucanian loom calls for endurance, physical strength, and deftness, qualities which the women of this sturdy, tough, and much-tried race possess to a high degree."[35]

Macuñ ("Poncho")
Probably the most striking pieces woven by the Araucanians are men's ponchos. Even the earliest adventurers in the area found them extraordinary, and nearly every account mentions these garments. One traveler noted: "They possess the art of weaving, for which they were famous before they were visited by the Europeans; indeed, I have seen some of their woolen ponchos, which for fineness of thread, evenness of weaving, durability and brilliancy of color and elegancy of pattern, are superior to anything of the kind I have ever beheld."[36] The reference to "brilliancy of color" may be somewhat puzzling when the ponchos of today are considered (color plate 7); but from these first chroniclers it appears that a rather brilliant blue green or turquoise color was widely used in earlier times for both men's and women's garments. It is unfortunate that there is no mention of the source for the color, for turquoise is a very difficult shade to achieve with natural dyes. It is possible that the source was either copper or the *pallo* earth used today to achieve a blue grey. The turquoise color apparently marked an individual as belonging to a low social class, while higher status individuals wore ponchos and *kepams* of white, red, or dark blue.[37] Since about the middle of the nineteenth century, however, turquoise was apparently abandoned as a widely used color for clothing, and the ranking or status element in women's clothing seems to have disappeared altogether. Men's ponchos, however, are still ranked according to the skill required in the weaving of them. Only the wealthiest of men can afford certain classes of these garments, and to own and wear a poncho of an intricate pattern is a definite indication of a man's position in the community.

Fig. 10. A weaver from the vicinity of Temuco, Chile. This woman is just finishing an ikat-dyed poncho. The completed part of the textile is wound on the lower loom bar and a second beam; the warp loops are bound on the upper loom bar by a yarn that lashes the heading cord to the loom bar.

Both *poncho* and *macuñ* are Araucanian terms for the same garment, according to Falkener,[38] who lived among the Puelche in the 1730s; the former term was adopted into the Spanish and English vocabularies, while *macuñ* is now the preferred term among the Araucanians themselves. The form of the garment itself, however, has apparently remained unchanged for centuries: it is a rectangle of fabric with a slit in the center so that it can be put over the head. It allows for totally free movement of the arms, for work, combat, and riding on horseback; in addition, the Araucanian examples are virtually waterproof and offer excellent protection against the wind. The Spaniards quickly saw the value of such a garment, and both the men and women adopted it almost immediately. Thus, Mapuche ponchos were greatly in demand, and they quickly became an accepted medium for trade. The accounts between 1758 and 1826 note that Araucanian ponchos were valued at from four dollars for a plain poncho to one hundred fifty or two hundred dollars for one of a more complicated pattern, an enormous sum for the time. They also state that a wife's duty to her husband included the weaving of one extra poncho a year for trading purposes, making a man with many wives a very wealthy man. Demand for ponchos was so great that European manufacturers tried to imitate them (unsuccessfully, since the Europeans used elaborate floral designs); other schemes were fostered by "an ingenious Swiss assisted by a skillful mechanic," who set up a cloth manufactory in Santiago, and by some Spaniards who tried in the cities to set up workshops which employed Araucanian weavers making garments to order.[39] Ponchos were traded for cattle and horses, as well as for a variety of other European goods; and even among the Araucanians they could be used as a part of the bride price and were considered legitimate spoils of war. Eventually they became such an important commodity that seasonal fairs and trade circuits were established and a precise and formalized method of trading was employed, heavily punctuated with courteous behavior.[40]

Unfortunately, descriptions of how these ponchos actually looked are not clear enough to tell whether contemporary classifications are in any way equivalent. The categories are quite clear for those made in the recent past. The term *macuñ* (no. 7) is used to designate the simplest kind of poncho of a uniform color with no decoration. A poncho with any decoration whatsoever is called *macuñ nequer*, a category that embraces four distinct types. (All four types of *macuñ nequer* are illustrated in color plate 7.)

The least complicated of these four consists of stripes, either in an all-over pattern or isolated and running in three bands down the garment (fig. 17), called *macuñ huirican* (nos. 4, 5, and 6).

The second type of decorated poncho is *macuñ nimin* (no. 3), in which elaborate, complementary-warp patterned bands are worked into the field of the poncho as decoration.[41] The designs consist of either stylized figures or geometric shapes and are similar to motifs used on *trarihues*, or belts.

The third type of decorated poncho is the *macuñ trarican* (no. 2). These ponchos are decorated with a dyed pattern, using what is known as the *ikat* technique. Ikat is a process for the resist dyeing of the yarn intended for weaving; those parts that are to remain undyed are protected by binding them with a material that will prevent the dye from penetrating. Araucanians use other yarn (spun to the coarsest grade, *piulo*) or the white clay *pallo* (already noted for its use in permanently bleaching yarn) to achieve this reserve. Since it is the warp yarns that are used for the Araucanian ikat, the woman must set up and warp her loom, work out the pattern and bind off the appropriate threads to be reserved, carefully remove the warp from the loom, and dye it. The dyed yarn must then be put back on the loom in the identical order, so that the design remains intact. Finally, the warp must be unwrapped and cleaned of the clay resist; then the actual weaving can begin. Figure 10 shows a woman just finishing such a textile; figure 19 shows a man wearing a poncho with ikat bands; in color plate 7, the ponchos on the left show ikat dyeing.

Fig. 11. *Machi* (shaman), *left,* and her young apprentice, both in traditional clothing, Mapuche, Chile.
Both women are carrying a *kultrun* (shallow drum), which is beaten almost continuously in some ceremonies, to help induce a trance state; the drumstick is a specially made one that symbolizes the shaman's power (Faron 1968:73).

Ikat is distinctive and easy to recognize (fig. 18): "Textiles patterned acording to the ikat method may be recognized by the fact that the colors bleed or merge into each other in the direction of the threads which have been dyed by this process. It is this circumstance which imparts to the fabrics the peculiar softness of design which constitutes their principal charm. This typical appearance of ikat fabrics is due to the dye penetrating slightly below the edges of the resist. It is, moreover, impossible to prevent the threads from moving out of position when they are being stretched on the loom or during the actual process of weaving, and this displacement also results in blurring."[42]

These second and third types of decorated ponchos—trarican and nimin—were attempted only by master weavers and could be afforded only by the relatively wealthy. They would be worn only on dress occasions, and they comprised only about two percent of all the ponchos in use.[43]

The fourth type of decorated poncho (no. 1) is so rare that apparently it has no specific name. It combines the features of both the trarican and nimin macuñ, so that complementary-warp patterned bands alternate with ikat panels. Joseph[44] notes that such a garment existed when he did his field work but that few women were skilled enough to do such work.

Hilger[45] makes a point of stating that she did not see any ikat dyeing when she was in Chile in the late 1940s. Some people who have worked among the Mapuche in the early 1970s state that they had no knowledge of any such complicated and elaborate ponchos; the standard pieces offered for sale had plain or tweedlike backgrounds (achieved by the use of warp yarns made of strands of two different colors plied together) and three areas of simple stripes, much like the poncho shown in figure 17. In the 1970s, ikat had become almost unknown and no ponchos with beltlike bands were ever seen, although some belts were noted. Women's clothing had never been seen offered for sale by any recent visitors.[46]

Trarihue And *Lama*
("Belt" And "Under-Saddle Blanket")

The two types of Araucanian textiles that require the most skill on the part of the weaver are the *trarihue* (nos. 13, 14, 15, 16, 17, 18, 19, 20, 21, 22, 23, and 24), or belt, and the *lama* (nos. 25, 26, and 27), or blanket that is put under the saddle. Both of these are ornamented with a variety of complicated design motifs, and they employ one of several weaving techniques. Only a *vaqueana*, a master weaver, would think of attempting either of these pieces: "A woman that has mastered the technique of weaving these belts may claim the title of 'master' and is highly respected. When at work, she is regularly surrounded by eager pupils and curious onlookers."[47]

Since belts are worn wrapped around the waist at least twice, are used by young and old, men and women, and are again made to order, they can vary in length from about six to ten feet. Preparing a warp of this length by the usual method used to warp the loom

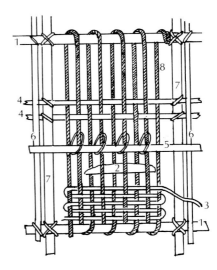

1. Colohe, "breast beam"
2. Nerehue, "weaving sword"
3. Tihuchúe, "weft"
4. Rañiñelhue, "guardian of the half"
5. Tonon, "heddle"
6. Param-tononhue, "rest for heddle"
7. Huicha-huichahúe, "with both feet on ground"
8. Huitral, "warp"

Fig. 12. Diagram of the Araucanian loom, taken from Joseph (1929). In this illustration, Joseph indicates that the weaver permanently fastens the *rañiñelhue* to the loom frame. Photographs of weavers do not show these pieces in position while the work is in progress; rather, they show the women utilizing a moveable shed-rod instead. Joseph's illustration also shows the warp loops passing around the loom bars, rather than the use of the heading cord.

Fig. 13. A young Araucanian woman from the Temuco vicinity, Chile.

"From every ruca [house] footpaths lead in several directions—one always leads to the source of water supply. A woman on foot carries light weight things, maybe vegetables and ears of grain or herbs, in either a basket or a wilal, a netted carrying bag; occasionally she carries things in her apron. Heavy loads, such as bark or pieces of wood used in dyeing, she carries on her back in a wilal suspended by a headband; bundles of grain, either in her arms or on her head". (Hilger 1957:192–193)

Fig. 14. Araucanian woman from the Temuco vicinity, Chile, wearing traditional dress and jewelry.

"Araucanians are hospitable among themselves and toward strangers. Willingness to help can be relied on. . . . Praising an individual's intelligence is the finest compliment that can be paid an Araucanian; he is deeply hurt by expressions of disdain for his intelligence. Patience is an accomplishment, especially on the part of women" (Hilger 1966:xviii).

for broad fabrics—for a *kepam* or poncho—is frequently difficult and cumbersome, and often the women employ a different working method.

First, four round stakes are driven into the ground in a straight line, until each stands at a height of about twenty inches. The first three stakes are about sixteen inches apart, and the fourth is six feet or so from the last one in line. Most of the techniques used for belts involve two sets of warp of contrasting color, which exchange position to form the design; therefore, these two colors of warp are wound alternately on the stakes. For the actual weaving process, the warp is taken off the posts and transferred to the loom; the unwoven warp yarns are wound on the upper horizontal beam and are gradually unwound as the completed section of the belt is wound on the lower beam.[48] Some belts are warp-faced plain weave (no. 24); others, especially those showing recognizable human and animal figures, are warp-faced double cloth[49] (nos. 18, 21). But the majority of belts (at least in the museum collections) are woven in the technique of complementary warp with three-span floats in alternating alignment[50] (nos. 14, 15, 16, 17, 19, 20, 22, and 23); the decorative bands in the *macuñ nimin* are woven with the same technique (no. 3).

The designs employed in the ornamentation of belts are among the most complicated motifs that an Araucanian weaver knows (fig. 24). Many writers have speculated that these were originally derived from Inca weavers, either during the expansion of the Inca Empire in the fifteenth century or by imitation of the *yanacona* weavers, who were Inca slaves brought by the Spanish into the Araucanian territory.[51] The argument is a difficult one to prove, since known Inca designs are not at all similar to modern Araucanian ones.[52] It is probable that certain designs simply grew out of the techniques and materials: even-armed crosses, diamonds, stripes, steps, and "Greek key" designs are found almost universally as weaving patterns in cultures around the world. What is more certain is that Araucanian weavers appear to attach no religious or symbolic significance to any of their designs. The women pride themselves on the fact that no one works from a sketch or set pattern; and some women go so far as to state that no two weavers ever use the same designs. Observations do not support this last belief, since certain designs (figs. 23, 25, and 26) are quite common, although each example may vary in proportion or minor detail: "I saw the patterns my mother wove and I remembered them. From them and others I saw I worked out my own. We carried the patterns in our mind. No woman would think of copying patterns. Every woman thinks out her own and then dyes her yarn accordingly."[53] There does appear to be the notion that some patterns are much harder to conceive and execute than others. The Argentinian Mapuche weavers told Hilger[54] that there are some designs which all women know and use, with only slight variations. They are considered ordinary and have specific names, such as "crawling worms" and "tail-feathers-of-a-bird." "We make these when we are tired; they take no thinking. Every woman knows them."

The *lama* (nos. 25, 26, and 27), or under-saddle blanket, also requires a great deal of skill on the part of the weaver. Coming from the Araucanian word *lami*—or *dami*, "mat"—the *lama* has several uses: formerly it was placed under the wood-frame saddle to protect the horse's back, or it was thrown over a stool as a covering. Now *lamas* are sold in pairs as "throws," preferably for either side of a bed. Several weaving techniques are used: the least common is a simple gauze weave,[55] a crossed-warp technique (no. 26). More common is a supplementary-warp patterned weave[56] (fig. 21) or complementary-warp weave (no. 25). *Lamas* of these last two techniques were still being made in great quantities during the period 1972–1973.[57] Larger blankets, bed-cover size, were also made in the same manner, especially for sale.

Fig. 15. Elderly Mapuche woman from the Temuco vicinity, Chile.
"Older women generally wear more traditional styles of clothing" including the *"untailored type of heavy woolen dress,"* a *"belt that encircles the figure twice and is looped at the left side,"* an apron, and *"when the weather is cool a shawl is draped over the shoulders."* Most go barefoot (Titiev 1951:31).

Choapino ("Pile Saddle Blanket")

Probably the most popular tourist weaving is the *choapino* (nos. 28 and 29). A pile blanket, originally woven only in black or white, it was used over the wood-frame saddle. Often the horseman used a number of *lamas* and *choapinos* to pad his horse and prevent chafing; and the blankets doubled as bedding at night. But one traveler noted that while several saddle blankets made for an easy seat and a relatively comfortable ride, the mount was made so wide by the numerous blankets "that the lower limbs of the riders often became permanently bent out by it."[58] Photographs from the early part of this century show women setting off for market on saddles piled so high with blankets that the riders were obliged to perch cross-legged on top. For the tourist, however, the *choapinos*, woven in brilliant, aniline colors, serve as small throw rugs and chair covers.

The weaving of these pieces is done on the basic loom used for all fabrics. The warp and the weft are of single-color, strong yarn; often the weft is composed of paired yarns. All sources that describe the making of the *choapino*[59] state that tufts of precut yarn are wrapped on the warp yarns, in-between rows of regular weft, as illustrated in figure 20. The "knot" (actually a weft-wrapping technique) is the same structurally as the "Ghiordes knot" used in the Near East for making carpets,[60] but the visual effect of the finished product is instead similar to that of a Scandinavian rya rug (no. 28).

In contrast to this technique, at least one *choapino* (no. 29) in the Museum collection is made in another way: the yarn forming the tufts is passed around the weft as well as the warp, suggesting a postweaving embellishment. This process is not usually described in the literature on Araucanian weaving.

Since it is the "knots," and not the warp or the weft yarns, that create the design, the weaver must plan out the design in a different manner than she does in her other weaving. It is enough to simply count the yarns and divide them into sections when working out any geometric shapes that are parallel or perpendicular to the warp or weft; thus, designs like stripes, squares, rectangles, and crosses are easy to produce. More complicated are diamond and triangle shapes, or curved-line designs of humans or animals, for in these cases the count changes with each pass of the weft.[61]

Once the "knotted" pattern is completed, the pile is trimmed to an overall even length. Often either end is decorated with an extralong fringe, called "rain," which is the same color as the foundation into which it is worked. *Choapinos* are expensive for the weaver to make: aniline dyes are increasingly costly; two kilos of wool are required (approximately the amount from the shearing of two sheep); and, if well made, they take two to three weeks to complete. But they are much in demand and can most easily be sold outright or bartered for commodities in Chilean stores.

Kutama ("Saddle Bag")

The other item frequently offered for sale is the double-bag saddle bag (nos. 30, 31, and 32). These are woven all in one piece, again using the broad-fabric loom. The pouches are formed by either end of the weaving, but the central section is composed of three discontinuous wefts. Thus the two straps and both flaps when completed form three parallel units, with woven slits dividing them. The center unit is then cut crosswise in the middle, bound off in cloth or yarn, and folded down to form flaps for the pockets[62] (fig. 22). Saddle bags are most often made of brilliantly colored yarn. The designs and techniques vary: some are plain, while others are fancier, using a complementary-warp (no. 32), supplemetary-warp pattern (no. 31), or alternating float-weave technique (no. 30). As in other textiles, the skill of the individual weaver determines the technique that is chosen, as well as the intricacy of the design motifs.

Fig. 16. Young girl in traditional clothing and jewelry; her belt shows a design typical of supplementary warp–patterned weaving.

"Girls formerly wore clothes like those of adult women. Usually the mother wove a kepam to fit the girl. 'I recall my mother taking my measurements for one she was getting ready to weave for me: I had only one; she had made that one out of the less worn-out part of an old one of hers'" (Hilger 1957:224).

The Araucanians Today

It should be noted that the major part of the Museum of the American Indian–Heye Foundation collections in Araucanian weaving was accessioned in 1930 and was probably made not long before that date. Collected by Samuel K. Lothrop, an archaeologist working in the area, the collection has excellent provenience information but little ethnographic data since Lothrop was not studying the Araucanian peoples as a contemporary population. The balance of the collection was acquired by George Heye himself (the museum's founder), mostly through purchases in Europe, and those pieces are poorly provenienced.

The weaving information has been taken from anthropologists who worked among the Mapuche in central Chile in the 1920s, 1940s, and 1950s. These peoples demonstrate far more cultural homogeneity than do the geographically more extensive Araucanian populations of the 1700s and 1800s; in fact, many of the Araucanians visited by the early chroniclers are now extinct, others have been absorbed by Chilean or Argentinean society, and some groups have ceased to have an independent tradition and have become more like the central Chilean Mapuche (whom *we* call "Mapuche").

This reduction of diversity began with the inauguration of the present *reducciones* ("reservations") in 1884. Since that time, the territory that the Araucanians were permitted to occupy has shrunk drastically, while the population has remained relatively stable. Their shrinking land base has resulted in a concentration of indigenous peoples around the Chilean town of Temuco and a much closer proximity between families. Added to this, government policy centered on "development" and "progress," and Mapuche lands were thought to be underproductive; there was also the belief that the Mapuche had somehow been awarded the best agricultural land in Chile. Thus there was enormous pressure for the Araucanians to acculturate and give up their land. This shrinking land base created a great deal of stress on traditional life styles and political organization.

With the election of Salvador Allende as president in September 1970, reservation life began to marginally improve for the Mapuche. Land reform, an official policy of Allende's presidency, was initiated, breaking up the large land holdings and increasing the allotments to smaller landowners. The Mapuche greatly benefitted from this policy. In addition, the government did much to try to remove from the social attitude the stigma of being Mapuche: "I want to tell you that the race that defended itself with heroism, from the initial beginnings of our history, has been losing its lands, has been forgotten. . . . I want to tell you that it is a national obligation, it is an imperative of our conscience, not to forget what Chile owes to the Araucanian nation and race, origin and base for what we now are."[63]

Allende set up cooperatives for the sale of Mapuche craftwork, which paid the weavers fair prices for their

Fig. 17. Mapuche man wearing a *macuñ huirican*, the simplest of the decorated poncho.

"They wear a garment called a poncho which serves not only for a cloak but for a saddle covering, also a bag during the day and a bed at night; it is about four or five feet square, with a slit in the center for the head and hanging down all around the body, and upon the whole is a comfortable garment" (Prince a/k/a "Will the Rover" 1851:21).

Fig. 18. Detail of ikat-dyed poncho, *macuñ trarican*, Mapuche, Temuco, Cautin, Chile. No. 2. The characteristic "bleed" of the ikat is easily seen in this detail; the fringe, made from warp yarns, also shows ikat patterning. The selvedge on this poncho is also remarkable. It appears to be the result of the use of multiple bobbins of weft, five on each side of the fabric. In each passage of weft through the fabric, one bobbin from each side is used, passing in opposite directions. The weft yarns on each side interlace with each other between passages through the warp.

Fig. 19. Elderly woman and a man, both in traditional costume. The man is wearing a poncho with ikat-dyed bands.

"Most married men wear a moustache and are proud of it. Often they let it grow past the corners of the mouth. . . . Formerly men cut their hair shoulder length; they did not wish to appear like women. Most men today have their hair cut short as Chilean men do. An occasional one wears his long. . . . 'I noticed while visiting south of here that Mapuche men who were pointed out to me as having been best able to defend their rights against the Chilean Government were those who still wore braids'" (Hilger 1957:59).

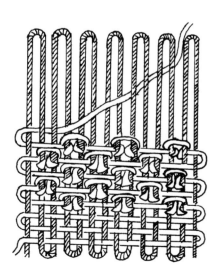

Fig. 20. Diagram illustrating the manufacture of the *choapino*. In this illustration, first published by Joseph (1929), the "Ghiordes knot" is alternated with the weft. Close examination of textiles in the Museum of the American Indian—Heye Foundation collections reveals that not all *choapinos* are woven in this manner.

work, not "trading-post prices."[64] There was a system set up for the even distribution of the raw materials, so that anyone who wanted to weave might have the opportunity to do so. Wool, for example, was not for personal use. All wool was turned into a central agency for redistribution, and each weaver could apply as often as twice a week for an allotment. No one could receive extra wool, but all who applied got an allotment equal to everyone else's. The Mapuche recognized the philosophy behind the even-handed policy and apparently cooperated fully with the program. Women wove ponchos, throws resembling both the *lama* and *choapino,* and larger blankets. Husbands were usually the salesmen, stopping at friendly Chilean houses to offer merchandise for sale on the way to the stores in town. Most important, the Allende government made it "patriotic" to own some Mapuche weavings or to wear a handmade poncho.

The overthrow and death of Salvador Allende by the military junta in September 1973 was a disaster for the Mapuche. All the land reform was immediately reversed and most cooperatives were closed. Mapuches who had vaguely complained of not having as much wool for weaving as they wanted now found that they had little or none at all. The official policy of the government became one of rapid and forced assimilation; the "patriotic" history that was emphasized became the Spanish and colonial one, not that of the Araucanians.

The present situation of the Mapuche is a bleak one. Although the current Mapuche population totals about one million people, or about ten percent of the population of Chile, official Pinochet government policy is devoted to "reforms" that would result in "the loss of Mapuche customs and traditions."[65] With unemployment on the *reducciones* running as high as eighty percent, and Mapuche students excluded from state educational institutions,[66] it becomes difficult to predict how many of the Araucanian people will be able to survive such severe repression. But at least one writer suggests that their culture will again become one of resistance and will therefore survive: "The Araucanian people, and especially the Mapuche, have experienced many defeats, but they were never completely put down or destroyed."[67] One can only hope the prediction is an accurate one.

Fig. 21. Detail of *lama* (under-saddle blanket), Mapuche, Temuco, Cautin, Chile. No. 27.
This close-up shows clearly how supplementary warps float on a plain-weave ground to create the pattern. The bands occur in the center of the textile and were probably woven last, after the loom had been turned.

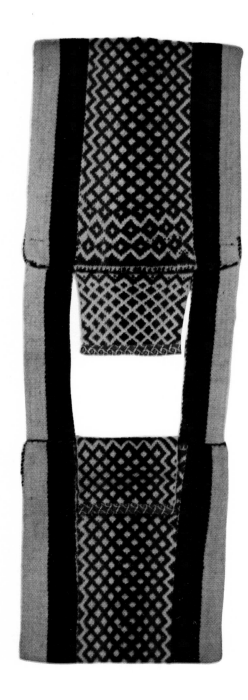

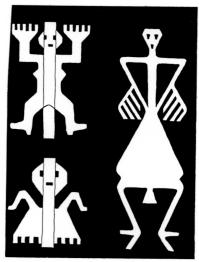

Fig. 23. Some common motifs used by Araucanian weavers.

Fig. 22. Set of *kutama* (saddle bags), Mapuche, Quepe, Temuco, Cautin, Chile. Dimensions: 10.5 cm. × 91 cm., when flat. No. 31. *Kutama*, saddle bags, are woven of one length of fabric. The ends are folded up and stitched to form the pockets at either end. The center sections are woven with three discontinuous wefts, the outer pieces forming the straps; the central portion is cut in half, bound off (in this case in a commercial cotton cloth), and folded down to form the flaps over the pockets.

Fig. 24. Three *trarihue* (belts). *A*, Mapuche, Quepe, Temuco, Cautin, Chile. Length:292 cm. including fringe, Width:7.5 cm. No. 16; *B*, Mapuche, Huentelulen, Canete, Arauco, Chile. Length:261 cm. including fringe, Width:5 cm. No. 13; *C*, Mapuche, Collico (Carahue), Imperial, Cautin, Chile. Length:243 cm. including fringe, Width:6 cm. No. 20.

The belts on the extreme left and right are ornamented with the same motif; the variations on this popular design led to subtle differences in its interpretation, and for that reason many weavers claim that no two women use the same design. The belt on the left demonstrates how the alternating alignment of the warps results in the design appearing in a dark color on one side of the weaving, while in white on the opposite face. The belt in the center was once used by a *cacique*, or Araucanian leader; the design is one that is typical for the technique, supplementary warp-patterned weaving. Fig. 16 shows a young girl wearing a similar *trarihue*.

Fig. 25. A popular weaving motif.

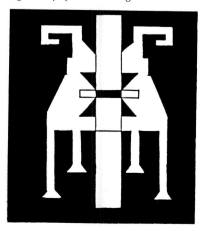

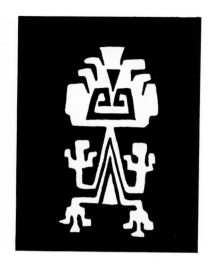

Fig. 26. Some common motifs used by Araucanian weavers.

ACKNOWLEDGMENTS

I would like to express my thanks to a number of people who either contributed directly to this study or whose critical comments proved valuable: to Ann Pollard Rowe of the Textile Museum, Washington, D.C., whose advice, comments, and instruction are enormously appreciated; to G. Lynette Miller, Museum of the American Indian–Heye Foundation Registrar, whose expertise in weaving was of great support to me in this study; to Susan Dublin, who translated numerous articles from the Spanish for me; and finally to a number of people contacted through Amnesty International, the United Nations Human Rights Committee, and several other agencies, who generously helped me to understand the current situation of the Mapuche, but who, for fear of political retaliation, must remain anonymous.

1. Ercilla wrote the nine-volume epic poem *L'Arucana* during the years 1569–1589; one translation into English, with detailed analysis, was published by Lancaster and Manchester 1945.
2. Hilger 1957; Pocock 1967.
3. Titiev 1951:25.
4. Titiev 1951:128–129.
5. Faron 1968.
6. Ellis 1956; Pocock 1967.
7. See, for example, Gardiner 1841; Prince 1851; Smith 1855.
8. Latcham 1909, Latcham and Oyarzun 1934.
9. Joseph 1929; Hilger 1957; Hilger and Mondloch 1969.
10. Stevenson 1825–1829.
11. Joseph 1929; Hilger and Mondloch 1969.
12. Joseph 1929.
13. Millan 1934.
14. Hilger 1957:230.
15. Hilger 1957:228.
16. Hilger 1957:230.
17. Hilger 1957:231.
18. Hilger 1957:378.
19. Stevenson 1825–1829; Gardiner 1841.
20. Stevenson 1825–1829.
21. Hilger 1957:225.
22. Faron 1961, 1968.
23. Hilger 1957:376.
24. Klein 1961:13.
25. Hilger and Mondloch 1969.
26. A warp-faced textile is one in which the warps are much more closely spaced than the wefts so that the weft does not show on either surface of the fabric but rather passes between two layers of warps. The simplest of the warp-faced weaves is warp-faced plain weave in which the weft passes over-one and under-one warp in each passage, reversing the over-under order from one passage to the next so that the interlacing order of the warp is also 1/1 (Rowe 1977:13).
27. The shed is the space between the warp yarns through which the weft is passed.
28. The heddle bar or rod is used to control one of the weaving sheds. For a plain weave, the weaver passes a cord alternately around the heddle bar and every other warp thread; thus when the heddle rod is pulled toward the weaver those warps are separated from the others, and the weft may be passed between them.
29. A shed rod is used to control the other of the two sheds for plain weave. Usually it is a smooth, round stick which is inserted under the warps which are not controlled by the heddle rod. Thus, the shed rod appears to be "inside" the warps, while the heddle rod is attached to the face of the weaving.
30. Joseph 1929.
31. Joseph 1929.
32. When the Araucanian loom is prepared, the weaver can wrap the continuous warp by looping the warp yarn over the top, and then around the bottom loom bar in a figure eight pattern. The passage of the warp over or under the loom bar creates open loops. If the finished weaving is to be fringed, these loops are what create the fringe. If, however, it is necessary to weave a textile with four finished edges, or four selvedges, another method must be used. The loops of the warp must pass around a heavy yarn or cord called a heading cord, which is in turn lashed to the loom bar. The use of a heading cord allows the textile to be woven all the way to the edge of the warp loops.
33. The weft is the set of yarns inserted over and under the warp yarns in the actual weaving process. In the finished textile they are transverse.
34. Joseph 1929; Hilger and Mondloch 1969.
35. Joseph 1929, translated in Klein 1961:13.
36. Miers 1826:459; for other examples see Frezier 1716: Ulloa and Ulloa 1758; Schmidtmeyer 1824.
37. Molina 1808; Stevenson 1825–1829; Miers 1826; Lancaster and Manchester 1945.
38. Falkener 1935, reprint.
39. Ulloa and Ulloa 1758; Molina 1808; Schmidtmeyer 1824; Miers 1826; Stevenson 1825–1829; Smith 1855.
40. See Ulloa and Ulloa 1758:280–282, 285–286 for a detailed account.
41. For complete explanations of weaving terms, see Rowe 1977.
42. Bühler 1942:1604.
43. Lothrop 1930.
44. Joseph 1929.
45. Hilger 1957.
46. Kalke, personal communication.

47. Klein 1961:16.
48. Joseph 1929; Klein 1961.
49. Warp-faced double cloth is a textile in which two complete layers have been woven simultaneously. The two sets of warps are contrasting colors and they exchange faces to create the pattern; the weft is a single continuous yarn which spirals around the front and back face. Except at points of color exchange the two layers are separate.
50. Complementary-warp weaves are defined by Rowe as weaves in which two sets of warps, usually of contrasting colors, are co-equal in the fabric. Both interlace in the same basic order, but opposite to each other. One of the two complementary sets can be made to dominate one face of the textile by floating all the yarns of the set on one face of the fabric, while the other set floats on the opposite face. In Araucanian measuring the complementary warp weave involves a three-span interlacing order of over three, under one, producing three-span floats (Rowe 1977:67).
51. Looser 1927; Latcham and Oyarzun 1934.
52. Rowe 1977.
53. Hilger 1957:378.
54. Hilger 1957:378.
55. Simple gauze is a crossed-warp technique. "In this structure, warps are drawn out of their normal parallel alignment, one (or more) warps crossing over its neighbor(s). This cross is held in place by a passage of the weft. The warps then recross to their original position" (Rowe 1977:99).
56. Supplementary-warp patterned weavings employ a second set of warps, usually of a contrasting color, to create a pattern on a complete ground fabric. The supplementary set of yarns are warped along with the warp for the ground weave. In Araucanian weaving the paired-warp ground is usually a plain weave, and the supplementary warps float on one face to form the pattern and float on the back between the pattern areas (Rowe 1977:34).
57. Kalke, personal communication.
58. Schmidtmeyer 1824:302.
59. Joseph 1929; Hilger 1957; Klein 1961.
60. Allen 1938; Klein 1961.
61. Joseph 1929.
62. Allen 1938.
63. From a speech by Salvador Allende quoted in Morris 1973:177.
64. Kalke, personal communication.
65. Ad Hoc Working Group, United Nations 1978.
66. Ad Hoc Working Group, United Nations 1978.
67. Berdichewsky 1975:32.

Fig. 27. Two common designs, thought to be easy to weave, used in Araucanian textiles: above, "tail-feathers-of-a bird"; below, "crawling worms."

Fig. 28. The interior of an Araucanian *ruca* (house). The older woman seated on the floor is working at the loom that clearly shows the use of the heading cord, heddle bar, and shed rod. Careful examination of this photograph shows that this weaver has already turned her loom, the completed textile being wrapped around the two bars at the top of the loom. The balls of dyed yarn used as weft are on the floor next to the weaver; unspun wool is seen in the basket behind the young girl. Both women are wearing plaid *iculla* (shawls).

REFERENCES

Ad Hoc Working Group for the General Assembly of the United Nations
   1978   Situation of Human Rights in Chile. Section E.
Allen, Helen L.
   1938   A Weaver Travelling in Chile. The Weaver 3(4):22-25.
Berdichewsky, Bernardo
   1975   The Araucanian Indian in Chile. Copenhagen: International Work Group for Indigenous Affairs, IWGIA Document 20.
Buhler, A.
   1942   Origin and Extent of the Ikat Technique. CIBA Review 44:1604-1611.
Bullock, S. D.
   1921   Report of the Meeting of December 14, 1921. American Anthropologist 23(n.s.):496-497.
Ellis, H. L.
   1956   The Indian Policy of the Republic of Chile. Unpublished Ph.D. Dissertation, Columbia University. Ann Arbor: University Microfilms No. 16, 278.
Falkner, Thomas
   1935   A Description of Patagonia and Adjoining Parts of South America. Reprint. Chicago: Armann and Armann.
Faron, Louis C.
   1961   Mapuche Social Structure. Urbana: The University of Illinois Press.
   1968   The Mapuche Indians of Chile. New York: Holt, Rinehart and Winston.
Frezier, M.
   1716   Relation du Voyage de la mer du Sud aux cotes du Chily et du Perou fait pendant les annees 1712, 1713, et 1714. Paris: Chez Nyon.
Gardiner, Capt. Allen F.
   1841   A Visit to the Indians on the Frontiers of Chile. London: Seely and Burnside.
Hilger, M. Inez
   1957   Araucanian Child Life and Its Cultural Background. Smithsonian Miscellaneous Collections. Volume 133. Washington, D.C.:Smithsonian Institution.
   1966   Nuernun Namku: An Araucanian Indian of the Andes Remembers the Past. Norman: University of Oklahoma Press.
Hilger, M. Inez, and Margaret Mondloch
   1969   The Araucanian Weaver. In Chile, Boletin: Museo de Historia Natural, Santiago de Chile 30:291-298.
Joseph, Hno. Claude
   1929   Los tejidos araucanos. Revista Universitaria XIII (10):978. Organo de la Universidad Catolica de Chile.
Kalke, Rev. David
   1979   Personal communication. Rev. Kalke was living on or near Mapuche land before, during, and after the military junta overthrew the Allende government in 1973. He was contacted through the generosity of Amnesty International.
Klein, O.
   1961   Textile Arts of the Araucanians. CIBA Review 1961(6):2-25.
Lancaster, Charles M. and Paul T. Manchester
   1945   The Araucaniad. Nashville: Vanderbilt University.
Latcham, Richard E.
   1909   Ethnology of the Araucanos. Journal of the Royal Anthropological Institute of Great Britain and Ireland 39:334-370.
Latcham, Richard E., and A. Oyarzun
   1934   Araucanian Art I: Textiles and Pottery. Bulletin of the Pan-American Union (English edition series) 68:352-362.
Looser, G. Walter
   1927   Araucanian Textiles. Bulletin of the Pan-American Union (English edition series) 61:357-366.
Lothrop, Samuel K.
   1930   Notes on Indian Textiles of Central Chile. Indian Notes, Museum of the American Indian—Heye Foundation 7(3):324-335.
Miers, John
   1826   Travels in Chile and LaPlata. 2 vols. London: Baldwin, Cradock and Joy.
Millan, Maria D.
   1934   Tejidos araucanos del neuquen. International Congress of Americanists Twenty-fifth LaPlata 1932, Actas y trabajos cientificos t.I:215-222.
Molina, Juan I.
   1808   The Geographical, Natural and Civil History of Chile. Middleton, Connecticut: R. Alsop.
Morris, David J.
   1973   We Must Make Haste—Slowly. New York: Random House.
Pocock, H. R. S.
   1967   The Conquest of Chile. New York: Stein and Day.
Prince, George [Will the Rover]
   1851   Rambles in Chili. Thomaston, Maine: D. J. Starrett.
Rowe, Ann Pollard
   1977   Warp-Patterned Weaves of the Andes. Washington, D.C.: The Textile Museum.
Schmidtmeyer, Peter
   1824   Travels into Chile over the Andes in the Years 1820 and 1821. London: Longman, Hurst, Rees, Orme, Brown and Green.
Smith, E. R.
   1855   The Araucanians. New York: Harper & Bros.
Stevenson, W. B.
   1825-29
          A Historical and Descriptive Narrative of 20 Years Residence in South America in three volumes. London: Hurst, Robinson.
Titiev, Mischa
   1951   Araucanian Culture in Transition. Ann Arbor: Museum of Anthropology, University of Michigan, Occasional Contributions 15.
Ulloa, Don George Juan, and Don Antonio de Ulloa
   1758   A Voyage to South America. London: Davis and Reynolds.
Wilson, Rev. W.
   1924   Family Life amongst the Araucanians. The South Pacific Mail, 23, October 1924, Valpariso, Chile.

Fig. 29. Araucanian woman from the Temuco vicinity, Chile. She is wearing a traditional old-style *iculla* (shawl), as well as a silver breast ornament, earrings, and a headband. Her apron is from commercial cloth.

Fig. 30. Elderly Araucanian couple from central Chile. The woman is wearing the traditional *kepam*, *iculla*, and *trarihue*. Her earrings of silver are not unusual (see quote with fig. 8). The man is wearing the old-style *chiripa* (breechclout), a man's *chamal*, and what appears to be a *macuñ huirican* (poncho with stripes). The women in the background are all wearing the *kepam* and *iculla*, and the woman on the left shows a silver *topo*, or shawl pin.

the POTTER

PRE-COLUMBIAN CULTURES OF THE SOUTHEASTERN UNITED STATES

KATHERINE KIMBALL

Fig. 1. (Title Page) Water bottle, Moundville, Hale Co., Alabama. Height:17.1 cm. Diameter:17.8 cm. No. 48. C. B. Moore (1907:351) wrote of this Moundville bottle, "a broad-mouthed water bottle (as were so many of the vessels found at Moundville) has for decoration an eagle's [falcon's] head and the open hand and eye, alternating each four times."

The pottery made by native peoples of the Southeast is all but unequaled by any other aboriginal ceramic tradition of the United States. Imaginative in design and innovative in technique of manufacture, the potters of Southeastern prehistory were accomplished artisans, who knew nothing of the potter's wheel.

The potter's art reveals even more than a thorough understanding and control of the clay medium. Something of the social system of which the potter was a part finds expression in his or her work. Thus, through close examination of the pottery, the particular set of socially defined constraints and traditions within which each artisan worked becomes more apparent. The adoption of innovations and outside influences can also be detected in the pottery of the Southeast.

Within the groundwork style thus at least partially defined for the artisan, the Southeastern potter created a vessel with specific purposes in mind, be they the everyday chores of cooking, serving, and storing or the periodic observance of ritual. Among the Southeastern societies we often find a clear dichotomy in terms of design between the pottery made for the sacred realm and the vessels made for secular purposes. To better understand this dichotomy, we shall investigate the development and technology of the craft and explore the religious, economic, and sociopolitical aspects of pottery in prehistoric societies of the Southeastern United States.

Fig. 2. An Alabama shell midden under excavation by the WPA, Bush Creek Island, Lauderdale Co., Florida.

1. Nacoochee Mound, White Co., Georgia
2. Cartersville, Bartow Co., Georgia
3. Moundville, Hale Co., Alabama
4. Durand's Bend, Alabama River, Dallas Co., Alabama
5. Ossabaw Island, Bryan Co., Georgia
6. Carney's Bluff, Clarke Co., Alabama
7. Fullmores Landing, Chattahoochee River, Houston Co., Alabama
8. Shoemake Landing, Chattahoochee River, Early Co., Georgia
9. Hardnut Landing, Flint River, Decatur Co., Georgia
10. Kerr's Landing, Flint River, Decatur Co., Georgia
11. Walton's Camp, Santa Rosa Sound, Santa Rosa Co., Florida
12. Pippen's Lake, Walton Co., Florida
13. Hogtown Bayou, Choctawahatchee Bay, Walton Co., Florida
14. Jolly Bay, Walton Co., Florida

15. Alligator Bayou, St. Andrew's Bay, Washington Co., Florida
16. Point Washington, Choctawahatchee Bay, Washington Co., Florida
17. Burnt Mill Creek. St. Andrew's Bay, Washington Co., Florida
18. Aspalaga, Apalachicola River, Gadsden Co., Florida
19. Bristol, Apalachicola River, Liberty Co., Florida
20. Pierce Mound, Apalachicola River, Franklin Co., Florida
21. Alligator Harbor, Franklin Co., Florida
22. Panacea Springs, Wakulla Co., Florida
23. Mound Field, Apalachee Bay, Wakulla Co., Florida
24. Warrior River, Taylor Co., Florida
25. Horseshoe Point, Lafayette Co., Florida
26. Fowler's Landing, Levy Co., Florida
27. Mount Royal, Putnam Co., Florida
28. Thursby Mound, Volusia Co., Florida

Fig. 3. Map of the southeastern United States showing archaeological sites.

The Setting

The boundaries of what are now the states of Louisiana, Mississippi, Alabama, Florida, Georgia, and Tennessee delineate the Southeast. It is a region interconnected by a network of rivers, their tributaries, and coastal shoreline. The climate is temperate and the land is rich in plant and animal resources. Even as cultivated plants increased in importance, wild foods continued to contribute a significant portion to the diet of these Southeastern peoples, up to the time of the arrival of the Spanish in 1539.[1] It is not surprising then that in this region of plentiful and diverse natural resources, there developed societies of highly complex sociopolitical and religious organization. The desire for both continued access to and assurance of the abundant supply of these resources led to regional political alliances, between neighboring chiefdoms, for instance, and to the development of classes of people who could efficiently exploit these resources, both by manual labor and by the appeasement of those invisible forces which controlled the growth of crops. This region can be even further subdivided, representing the present-day states of Alabama, Florida, and Georgia. The Moore collection of the Museum of the American Indian reflects this focus.

Fig. 4. Excavation crew atop a mound on the New River, Florida. Photograph by M. R. Harrington, 1908.
Museum of the American Indian–Heye Foundation

At the turn of the century, Clarence B. Moore investigated the large aboriginal earthworks found in the Southeast, particularly those on the northwest coast of Florida. Although Moore was not a professional archaeologist, much of the information we now have about Southeastern prehistory is derived from his work.[2] Aboard his steamboat, *Gopher*, he and his team of workmen followed countless rivers inland in order to solve what was then the much debated question of who had built the mounds. Moore was convinced that the mounds antedated any European contact and, therefore, were of exclusively native manufacture. Indeed, some of the pottery found in the area can now be dated to at least the second millennium B.C.

We are concerned here with the pottery of both the Woodland tradition and the Mississippian tradition that follows it. The Woodland tradition is manifest regionally in Santa Rosa–Swift Creek and Weeden Island cultures. The examples of the Santa Rosa–Swift Creek pottery tradition discussed here are somewhat arbitrarily dated between A.D. 1 and A.D. 500.[3] Weeden Island cultures can be dated between approximately A.D. 500 and A.D. 1000.[4]

The Mississippian tradition, of which the Fort Walton cultures of northern Florida were a part, covers roughly the next five hundred years, from A.D. 1000 to the time of the European invasion in the sixteenth century. Moundville in west central Alabama, the second largest Mississippian center known, spanned the period between about A.D. 1200 and A.D. 1500. Thus, when De Soto and his men landed in Florida territory in 1539 and marched through the Southeast until 1543, they encountered Mississippian societies that were near their peak. Because Mississippian societies were powerful chiefdoms with fortified towns and active warfare, De Soto was not able to take over any territory or, with his small party, to conquer any native peoples. Since gold was not discovered anywhere in the area, De Soto moved on. However, after even brief encounters, his expedition and later ones left in their wake epidemic disease, which decimated the native populations. The compound effects of disease, internal warfare, diet deficiencies, and overuse of the land vastly decreased the population of the area. Those tribes which we associate with the area today were able to move into various regions of the Southeast thus left vulnerable to invasion.

Development Of Pottery In The Southeast

Fragments of the earliest known pottery in Southeastern North America have been found in coastal Georgia and Florida and date from about 2500 to 2000 B.C.[5] The main vessel form was the undecorated bowl with palmetto fiber[6] worked into the clay before firing. The manufacture of fiber-tempered pottery spread to the Mississippi Valley and northern Alabama. It is tempting to point to South American antecedents for this early pottery, for Griffin observes that fiber-tempered pottery has been found at a coastal site in Colombia that is dated around 3500–3000 B.C.[7] But Griffin also points out that no fiber-tempered pottery has been found at intermediate sites between Colombia and the Southeast. Furthermore, there is no evidence that significant culture changes or external influences were coextensive with the appearance of this earliest pottery in Georgia and Florida. Therefore, we must also consider that it was probably a local and independent development. The people who produced this pottery were hunters and gatherers, relying mainly upon shellfish, deer, and wild foods (although there is evidence that gourds and squash were under cultivation by around 2000 B.C.).

By 700 B.C., ceramic technology was widespread in eastern North America.[8] In the Southeast at this time, however, another technological trend was developing, as evidenced by a new type of pottery.

Along the Savannah River have been found remains of innovative pottery from a culture known as Deptford. This pottery is characterized by check and linear patterns stamped on the vessels before firing.[9] Stamping is a decorative technique that persisted in various forms through the Mississippi period, usually limited to utilitarian ware. After the spread of the Deptford culture, burial mounds and ceremonial centers began to appear and population began to grow. By 300 B.C. a certain type of mound was common in the Southeast.[10] The mounds contained usually one or only a few high-status individuals buried with rich furnishings, thus pointing to some degree of social ranking.

Fig. 5. Cylindrical jar with clearly visible shell temper, Moundville, Hale Co., Alabama. Height:11.7 cm. Diameter:11.4 cm. No. 53.

The artifacts found in such mounds include rare items of copper, shell beads, dippers, and plummets, and "elaborate, often non-functional pottery vessel shapes, often combined with unusual decoration. . . . [Also found was] imported pottery."[11] Everyday cookware was seldom found in either burial mounds or ceremonial centers. At the same time that the mounds developed there was both a growth of population and a more elaborate trade network than formerly existed. There is evidence of exchange northward to Hopewellian centers in Ohio of raw material, such as Gulf Coast shell and live sharks' teeth for copper from the Midwest. Such exotic material was deposited in burial mounds apparently as validation of an individual's status and personal control of these goods. The removal from circulation by burial of such items ensured their continued rarity and high value.

Both the Midwest (the ceremonial complex known as Hopewellian) and the Southeast (in Florida, the Santa Rosa–Swift Creek cultures) participated in an exchange network that eventually included most of eastern North America. An exchange system of such proportion suggests the existence of a class of part-time specialists who produced objects for trade and transformed incoming raw material into their culture's symbolic idiom. Highly skilled potters would have been at least part-time specialists of this sort.

The Southeastern cultures had artistic influence on their northern neighbors. There is evidence that some of their stamped pottery was traded to certain Ohio Hopewellian centers. "Some of these vessels were evidently brought in as trade pieces, for they are made of micaceous clays and tempering materials from the Southeast."[12]

From A.D. 300–500, the Midwestern Hopewellian cultures gradually declined in terms of burial ceremonialism and trade of exotic goods. However, Hopewellian cultural influence (by way of Santa Rosa–Swift Creek cultures) seems to have been a major stimulus for the next phase of elaborate ceremonialism and mound building by Weeden Island cultures in the tri-state area of Alabama, Florida, and Georgia.

Weeden Island (A.D. 500–1000)

A more distinctly Southeastern expression of ceremonial activity emerges in Weeden Island cultures. The most impressive aspect of the Weeden Island-phase art is found in the ceramics of the time. Incised and punctuated designs, complicated stamping, and elaborate modeling appeared, and vessels were extremely varied in form. Stamped decoration, for instance, was more carefully executed in both its design and how it was applied to a vessel. Whereas the surface of a vessel from the previous period would have been entirely covered with stamping, only the neck or shoulders of a vessel from the Weeden Island period was decorated. Combined with a wider variety and a more graceful realization of vessel forms, a greater sense of refinement was achieved than previously discernible in the Santa Rosa–Swift Creek period. Weeden Island potters could also demonstrate a

certain amount of realism when depicting the many animal forms about them. These vessels were deposited in the east side of burial mounds. Most of the vessels placed in the mounds were exclusively non-utilitarian mortuary ware, made by skilled craftsmen for a ceremonial occasion. The everyday stamped ware is seldom found in these pottery caches.

The heightened ceremonialism and mound building and the expansion of trade networks were accompanied by an increased and more settled population. With regard to subsistence: "The Weeden Island peoples were horticulturalists. They grew maize and perhaps other cultigens to supplement the hunting, collecting and fishing of wild foods."[13] Thus deer and nuts continued to be the major resources, but there was a growing dependence on the newly developed storable food sources, such as maize.

In Weeden Island cultures, the dichotomy between the sacred and the secular is most visible in the differences between burial-mound and refuse-midden assemblages (figs. 2 and 4). In the Weeden Island middens, we find only small jars, collared bowls or jars, and simple bowls.[14] Any more elaborate forms were found in the ceremonial caches of the mounds.

Because of the high quality of the ritual vessels, Sears feels that there might have been "a complex training process which must involve social support."[15] Thus we can envision a group of specially designated artisans who were well instructed in the art of pottery making. These artisans might have been initiated in what was perhaps a sacred occupation. Thus Sears posits the potters of ceremonial ware as priests—men and/or women trained in the highly esoteric art and iconography necessary to make pottery for burial with the dead.[16] Although the quality of the work would suggest full-time practice, we do not know whether they practiced their art full time or only periodically, moving into the sphere of sacred activity when the need arose.

The religious and political organization that developed in the Weeden Island–Woodland period grew more complex in the Mississippian period that followed. The smaller communities of the Weeden Island period sought the greater solidarity and economic advantages of what are variously called chiefdoms, even states, of Mississippian societies, under the powerful rule of military-religious leaders. As the towns and ceremonial centers grew in size and social complexity, however, much of the vitality and diversity so apparent in Weeden Island ceramics were lost.

Fig. 6. *A*, wooden paddle for stamping designs on unfired vessels, Cherokee, Swain and Jackson Cos., North Carolina. Length:22..9 cm. Width:7 cm. No 1; *B*, potsherd with stamped pattern, Mound at Nacoochee, White Co., Georgia. Length:17.5 cm. Width:17 cm. No. 5; *C*, pottery trowel or smoother used as an anvil to help form and smooth the vessel walls, Moundville, Hale Co., Alabama. Length:5.7 cm. Width:6.6 cm. No. 4; *D*, stone for smoothing the surface of the vessel before firing, Mount Royal, Putnam Co., Florida. Length:8.3 cm. Width:6 cm. No. 3.

Fig. 7. Stamped vessel, Alligator Bayou, St. Andrew's Bay, Washington Co., Florida. Height: 14.3 cm. Diameter: 18.1 cm. No. 8. The zigzag lines on this vessel were made by rocking the edge of a thin instrument, possibly the edge of a shell, across the leather-hard surface of the unfired jar. The abstract design is typical of the Santa Rosa–Swift Creek period.

Mississippian (A.D. 1000–1500)

As land suitable for farming was occupied by increasing numbers of people, competition for good farming areas developed. Under cultivation at this time were maize, beans, and squash, in addition to gourd, pumpkin, and sunflower.[17] Trade with centers to the north persisted. "By about A.D. 1000, Weeden Island social organization and later economy were realigned in accordance with Mississippian models, which were beginning to circulate in the lower Southeast."[18] Mississippian traits that became evident in the Southeast included large ceremonial centers, in which could be found flat-topped temple mounds, and mounds for chiefs' houses. Also, a growing and seemingly irreversible dependence upon agriculture and an intensively productive food supply strengthened an increasing tie to a specific territory and the development of tribal boundaries.

There was a change in focus from the burial-mound ceremonialism and its specially made mortuary ceramics to activity by the living in the temple-mound areas. The large ceremonial centers indicate a growing political and religious cohesion[19] and a rise in the secular power of community leaders. Willey writes that "[the burial mound] is solely a place of burial while [the temple mound] is a means of lending prestige and impressiveness to a political or religious building and its occupants."[20] Fort Walton pottery reflects these changes in religious and political attitudes. The non-utilitarian mortuary ware is no longer found, nor are ceramics placed in large group offerings. A new trait instead was the inversion of a vessel over the dead individual's head. As Willey points out, ceramics were offered in few numbers and usually to people who had been buried singly.

Techniques Of Manufacture And Decoration

As far as it is possible to determine, vessels were most often made by coiling. Coils of clay were welded one on top of the other by pressing the bottom of the top coil into the top of, or even slightly inside, the previous ring of clay. Evidence of the coils was normally eliminated before firing by scraping and smoothing with a rib, that is, a tool such as a shell, a piece of split cane, a gourd fragment, or a corn cob. However, signs of the coils are sometimes visible in the sherds of broken vessels. Paddling clay into shape against the hand or an anvil, such as a pottery trowel (fig. 6c) or a stone, was another technique used. Whacking the plastic clay with a paddle not only helped manipulate the clay into the desired shape but also reduced any air trapped in the clay and thinned the vessel walls. Unless coiling is part of the design intrinsic to the completed vessel, however, a well-made pot will seldom give a visible clue as to its method of manufacture. In exemplary cases, the process of coiling and the paddle-and-anvil technique are virtually indistinguishable.

Various tempers might have been added to the clay in order to ease working with the sticky substance. Temper also would have aided in the firing process by controlling shrinkage, as well as the tendency for the vessel to crack or even burst when fired. Finally, tempered pottery was more resistant to thermal shock, which occurs when the vessel is used for cooking. Sonin points out that mica is a particularly useful temper in this regard.[21] It is difficult to know, however, whether tempers such as grit or fine sand were added or were already present in the potter's favorite source of clay. A knowledge of local soils would be helpful in determining this. It is obvious that during the Mississippian period shell was ground and added as temper. The appearance of shell temper is usually considered in many areas a time marker for Mississippian cultures (fig. 5).

Some vessels were fired in a smoky atmosphere, so that carbon was adsorbed onto the clay. This technique of firing is called *smudging*, and it can occur during and after the firing cycle. The result is a permanent black, or gray black, coating to the vessel. A vibrant orange color is achieved by placing the vessel with some amount of iron present in the clay in a fire with ample oxygen. When the potter did not maintain complete control over the fire, variations in color would occur. Thus, some areas of the vessel might be better fired than others, resulting in gradations of browns and oranges. A smoky ember, accidentally touching the vessel, would smudge only that small area. A draught of oxygen-rich air during firing would create an extra-hot area, resulting in a bright spot, called a *fire-cloud*. Potters sometimes took advantage of these accidental discolorations by incorporating them into a particular design. Few of the vessels from the Southeast demonstrate unusual technical skill in the control of the firing atmosphere, but the firing technique used was quite adequate.

The Southeastern potter used a multitude of decorative techniques. Stamping, incising, and punctating are elaborations commonly found on Southeastern pottery forms. The following is an enumeration derived from Willey[22] of these and other decorative techniques used by Southeastern potters.

Stamping is usually found on utilitarian vessels; therefore, pottery with stamping is rarely discovered in burial mounds. A few ceramic pieces with particularly elegant stamping, however, were chosen to serve as ceremonial vessels and were placed in mounds (fig. 10). Designs were impressed into the soft clay of unfired vessels by means of a carved wooden paddle or cylinder. Clay paddles were also used. Intricate patterns carved on a wooden surface such as a paddle reflect the presence of a rich wood-carving tradition. Because wood is so perishable, the remains of such a tradition are preserved only in the impressions on pots. However, Cushing's[23] and Sears's[24] discoveries of masterfully carved statues at Key Marco and Fort Center, Florida, indicate activity by skilled wood carvers. Earlier vessels bear the stamping all over their surfaces. The stamped designs of vessels of later periods, however, are usually confined to one region, such as the neck of a jar or shoulders of a bowl. Such stamping is smoothed over almost to the point of obscuring the pattern. Stamping is rarely combined with incising or other decorative techniques. Cylinder or paddle stamps similar to those used for pottery decoration might also have been used for applying paint designs on the body.

Fig. 8. Water bottle, Moundville, Hale Co., Alabama. Height:14 cm. Diameter:15.2 cm. No. 51. Clearly delineated finger symbols are depicted on this vessel. Moore (1907:348) suggested that their significance was that of the four cardinal points, or world-quarters.

Fig. 9. Jar with incised and punctate decoration, Kerr's Landing, Flint River, Decatur Co., Georgia. Height:20 cm. Diameter:19 cm. No. 19. Moore (1907:454) says of this vessel, "A vessel of excellent yellow ware, graceful in form, having an incised decoration..." It was found with one other vessel farther toward the center of the mound than deposits usually are.

Another type of decoration (fig. 9) is that of incised lines applied with a pointed instrument. Often, Weeden Island artisans would combine an incised line with dot or triangular punctation, made by a piece of carved bone or wood or by a hollow reed. Background is sometimes filled in with rows of parallel lines. Before the clay reaches the leather-hard state, an appropriate instrument is carefully rocked over the surface of the vessel, in order to achieve a greater degree of control and rapidity of application of parallel lines. Emphasis is added by punctation, made by a jab of the instrument at the end of incised lines. In such cases, the plain surface design delineated by the absence of incising ranges from a quite recognizable to an extremely abstract bird figure (color plate 12).

The application of pigment, usually red but sometimes white, served as a coating of color, either in zones or all over the vessel. The pigment—ground hematite, red ocher, or simply red clay—was applied before firing and could be as thin as a wash or as thick and opaque as a slip, a coating of clay paste. Elaborate painting, geometric designs, or polychrome figures such as those found in the Southwest or Mesoamerica are rarely seen. Instead, the potter's statement was made directly in the soft clay.

With the technique of rock stamping, a potter can apply thin zigzag lines to the surface of a vessel. Upon first glance, the lines appear scratched onto the surface. Actually, rocker stamping results from rocking the edge of a thin instrument back and forth on the surface of leather-hard clay without lifting the instrument from the surface. This technique is usually found on flattened globular bowls with incurved rims and is applied in areas that contrast with smooth zones. In many cases, a curvilinear figure is outlined on the vessel, and the interior space of the figure is filled in with rocker stamping (fig. 7). The reverse occurs as well when the background is filled in with rocker stamping and the figure is left plain.

Vessels with resist decoration (negative painting) have been found on the Gulf Coast and at Moundville. Although of different time periods, vessels from both locales represent the identical process of resist painting. The motifs of the design are coated with a protective substance before firing; the entire vessel is submitted to intense smudging; then the resist material is washed off, revealing the vessel's natural color, now visible as the intended figure or design, and leaving the black as background.

An unusual practice, known only in Weeden Island times, was to cut out sections of an unfired vessel, thereby creating a latticework effect (see color plate 11). This decoration is found only in mortuary ware and has no discernible function. It may be, however, an elaboration of the practice of ritually "killing" a vessel, intentionally knocking a hole in the bottom of a pot to enable the vessel's spirit to accompany its deceased owner to the next world. "Killing" a bowl may also simply prevent someone from using, and thus defiling, a deceased person's personal property.

During the Mississippian period at Moundville,

although there are new vessel shapes, the range of both vessel shapes and decorative technique is more limited than it was in the Weeden Island societies. Burial pottery most often took the form of widemouth water bottles. Popular decorative techniques were incising and indenting. Iconographic motifs were incised on pottery, often at a point when the clay was nearly dry but still retaining a little plasticity.

A careful inspection of the Moundville vessels in the Moore collection shows that the potter incised thin lines, which were applied almost as a pattern or preliminary design. The potter then retraced some of the lines, correcting lines she or he was not pleased with, enlarging and burnishing others for a bolder effect. The potter in some cases added a white pigment (fig. 22), perhaps made of calcined shell or galena (lead ore), to emphasize the incising.

After allowing the clay of the unfired vessel to dry, the potter polished it with a smooth pebble, sometimes achieving an almost lacquerlike finish. The vessel was fired and then smudged (or both could have occurred simultaneously). Contrary to what is traditionally stated in the archaeological literature,[25] few of the vessels in the Moore collection from Moundville demonstrate postfire engraving: The plasticity of the clay when the design was applied is clearly apparent, particularly where lines intersect, and this indicates that the design application occurred before firing, when the vessel was not quite dry, at the leather-hard state.[26]

Indenting was achieved by pressing an oval pebble or similarly shaped object into the leather-hard clay of an unfired vessel (fig. 8).

The Weeden Island vessel shown (color plate 11) demonstrates another method of decoration. Instead of the surface of the vessel being carved away in order to raise the comma-shaped design, a narrow band of clay was carved out around the design element so that a shadow was cast, and thus relief was achieved. Both the design element and the body of the vessel, however, are on the same plane.

Although it is quite difficult to identify the prehistoric groups as ancestral to specific historic Indian tribes, it might be helpful to look at the pottery production of the Catawba tribe of South Carolina. A comparison between the two groups might afford greater insight into the organization of the craft tradition. Although not a direct descendant of the prehistoric tradition, Catawba pottery making can suggest for testing certain values that might have operated in prehistoric Southeastern societies. To this end, we refer to Fewkes's analysis of Catawba potters.[27] Fewkes visited them intermittently between 1929 and 1941.

Fig. 10. A Weeden Island jar showing decorative stamping, Horseshoe Point, Lafayette Co., Florida. Height:17 cm. Diameter:13 cm. No. 14.

Figs. 11 through 18. The various steps followed by Catawba women when making a pottery vessel, illustrated by photographs from the collections of the Museum of the American Indian-Heye Foundation.

Fig. 11. Clay is dug from a particular clay pit by the men and is carried back home in baskets.

Fig. 12. With a wooden pestle the clay is pounded, and foreign particles are sorted from the clay.

Fig. 13. The clay is cut and rolled into coils.

Among the Catawba, pottery making is a woman's occupation. Men will do some of the heavy work, such as digging clay from the pits, but it is the women who apply their technical skill and experience to the creation of a vessel. According to Fewkes, knowledge of the process of manufacture is tribal property, known to all those on the reservation and passed along from mother to daughter or daughter-in-law. Of course, variation occurs, for some women exhibit greater skill than others. There is something of a pottery-making season from early spring to late fall. Fewkes's informants said that this is because frost would be damaging to a vessel when fired and would cause it to crack. Also, summer temperatures make drying the vessel for a few days before firing somewhat easier. The southern climate, however, does not impose great restrictions on the pottery-making season.

Good beds of clay are numerous and accessible in the area. There is no private ownership of the clay beds, but not everyone is given the knowledge of their location. A woman's favored bed of clay is a cherished item. With the aid of agricultural implements, the men dig out the clay and place it in baskets for transportation home (fig. 11).

The paste is prepared by pounding the clay with a wooden pestle, all the while turning and spreading the clay to remove any impurities (fig. 12). There is no temper added, since particles of mica are already present in the clay.

With the paste ready, the potter may then use one of three techniques of manufacture: modeling, coiling, or molding. Seated under a shady tree or on her front porch, the potter who chooses to coil places the proper amount of clay on a lapboard, cuts and rolls strips of clay with a cane knife (fig. 13), then builds up a cylindrical vessel with layers of coils (fig. 14). She uses gourd-rind or shell scrapers to obliterate the coils and to shape the vessel as she desires (figs. 15 and 16). Before firing, she smoothes the piece with a rag, then polishes it with a smooth pebble (fig. 17). Fewkes makes the interesting observation that "the polishing pebbles are regarded as somewhat of a precious possession and are retained in a family often for several generations."[28]

Prefire decoration is minimal, except for occasional incising. After a drying period of a few days the vessel is fired by placing it in a fire of wood, bark, and corncobs (fig. 18). Both a smoky atmosphere (smudging) for black and gray colors and an oxygen-rich fire for oranges and reds are used. The average temperature of the open fire is, according to Fewkes's calculations, 910°C. (1670°F.).

Pottery tools found archaeologically in the Southeast are virtually the same as those used by the Catawba—for instance, a shell scraper, a pottery trowel, a polishing pebble. Archaeological polishing pebbles have been found interred with their owners. As with the Catawba, this could be interpreted to mean that the pebble was a favorite, even valuable, tool. This could also indicate no more than that the burial was that of a potter. Similar techniques were used by both groups, with equal degrees of skill. Although perhaps more imaginative in design, the prehistoric potter was not forced to contend with the dictates of the tourist trade.

Iconography

The iconography of vessels made during the Weeden Island and Fort Walton periods is quite distinct. Particularly noticeable are the Weeden Island pots and Fort Walton adornos modeled as effigy figures. Among an incredible variety of animal forms, birds are the most common shape. Because of the realism with which these effigies are portrayed, we are able to recognize many of the species familiar to the people in this area of the Southeast a thousand years ago.

According to a list compiled by Percy (based primarily on those effigy vessels found by Moore in Florida and Alabama and by Sears at the Kolomoki site in southwest Georgia),[29] we find clear representations of: owls (color plate 11; fig. 24), specifically the great horned owl, the barred owl, and the screech owl; ducks (figs. 20 and 23), with examples of either shovelers or mallards, and a wood duck; vultures (color plate 11); wild turkeys; buzzards; hawks; parakeets (the now-extinct Carolina variety);[30] pileated woodpeckers (fig. 22); eagles, a chuck-will's-widow; a white ibis; a mourning dove; a cardinal; a quail; and a spoonbill. Percy also includes frogs, opossums, snakes, deer, bears, turtles, a puma, a canid (perhaps a dog), a rabbit, perhaps a grubworm, and a gastropod. Shells, such as clamshells, are frequently represented. Even humans are represented in both standing and kneeling positions, clothed and unclothed (fig. 25). Two plant-forms also occur modeled in pottery: acorns and gourds (fig. 19). However, there is no mention of any maize effigies.

A hypothesis tested by Brose and Percy was whether these effigy figures could be identified as clan totems.[31] They reasoned that, if such was the case, clans identifying themselves with a particular animal would be forbidden to eat that animal (although ethnographically this eating taboo is not always true). However, where effigies of particular animals occurred, Brose and Percy also found evidence in refuse deposits that these animals had been eaten. Of course, a number of clans could have resided together. Brose and Percy discovered, in addition, an interesting pattern in their sample: mammalian effigies appeared earlier than effigies of reptiles and amphibians.

On the basis of a twelve-foot-high wooden pole depicting an owl (found at Thursby's Mound, Florida), Bullen, too, suggests a correlation of the pottery animal effigies with clan totems. According to Bullen, clans were rather common among the Southeastern Indians. He says that Swanton, the great compiler of facts about Indian tribes, lists for the Timucua, a Florida tribe of the historic period, bear, bird, buzzard, fox, dog, deer, panther, rabbit, and fish clans.[32] Thus, Bullen postulates that Thursby's Mound was where the Owl Clan resided, as symbolized by the great owl pole.

Fig. 14. The coils are pressed one on top of the other.

Fig. 15. The vessel is shaped and the walls are thinned by shell scrapers (ribs), seen in the potter's lap, and with the help of a pottery trowel quite similar to that shown in fig. 6c.

Fig. 16. The vessel, now a very different shape than when it was first begun, is given the finishing touches before it is left to dry.

Fig. 17. When dry, the pot is rubbed with a smooth stone to give it a polished finish before firing.

Fig. 18. By covering the vessel with pieces of bark during firing a smoky atmosphere is created, thereby causing carbon to be adsorbed onto the clay, resulting in a black finish.

The most intriguing explanation for the effigy figure, however, is given by Sears.[33] Sears describes a ceremonial complex (A.D. 1) in southern Florida that included a charnel platform—a place where corpses and bones were treated and stored. Wood carvings of numerous varieties of birds, a life-size cat, a bear, and an otter adorned the platform. These carvings could have had possible association with totemic clans. Also, they may have been associated with the maize-agriculture–related ceremonialism developing in the Southeast at that time, for Sears writes that "the pollen grains satisfying all criteria for Zea Maize were found in some strips of white pigment adhering to, or directly adjacent to, one of the two-piece bird carvings."[34] The actual significance of the carvings is unclear, but the conclusion that they might well have acted as guardians of the charnel platform is appealing. Milanich suggests that this could also be true for the ceramic, pedestaled effigy figures (figs. 23 and 24).[35]

Sears's work (1956) at Kolomoki in southwest Georgia also supports the idea that the ceramic, pedestaled effigy figures guarded the bones of the dead. Atop the great Southeastern mounds were community temples and civic centers, as well as charnel houses—places where the bones of the dead were prepared and usually stored. According to Sears, the construction of burial mounds occurred periodically, instigated by the death of a chief. In the newly constructed burial mound were placed the remains of the chief, his retainers, and large quantities of costly grave goods, particularly pottery. At the time of the chief's death, the charnel house and community temple were ritually cleared of their contents. Pottery was ceremonially destroyed and placed with the chief. The bones of other individuals, which had been stored in the charnel house, were also deposited with those of the chief. These other bones, stored in baskets in the charnel house or even the community temple, were probably guarded by the pedestaled effigy figures, which were obviously made for a sacred, nonutilitarian purpose—that of temple furniture and charnel-house guardian.

Many of the bird effigies are of raptorial birds—bone pickers, such as the vulture or buzzard. That such a form would be found in association with the charnel house is not surprising. Also, there is a preponderance of owl effigy figures. The traditional association among numerous cultures of owls and vultures with death supports the idea that effigies of these birds guarded the bones of the dead.

Mississippian vessels bearing unusual symbolic motifs (such as the eye-hand motif [figs. 1 and 21] and the skull-long bone motif) have been found from Mississippi to Minnesota and from Oklahoma to the Atlantic Coast.[36] Such pottery indicates the extent of the Southeastern ceremonial complex known as the "Southern Cult." The many items with Southern Cult symbolism found throughout the Southeast demonstrate not so much a cult, however, as the exchange of goods to cement alliances[37] and are evidence of close cultural contacts among the different Southeastern groups. A major cult-trade center was the great site at Moundville, Alabama. This site, situated on the Black Warrior River in west central Alabama, was partially excavated by C. B. Moore in 1905. The work done since that time indicates that Moundville was a three-hundred-acre palisaded town, with an average population of approximately three thousand people.[38] There is evidence of a large central plaza flanked by mounds and a separate residential area for the elite, as well as areas for manufacture. One of these areas was for the manufacture of pottery: "On the western margin of the site large fired hearths, caches of shell, clays and fullers earth were found. The conclusion that this area was an area of pottery manufacture is inescapable."[39]

The underlying theme behind the "cult" motifs is quite warlike in nature. Certainly, warfare came to be a way of life in the late prehistoric Southeast. According to Peebles and Kus, burials were discovered at Moundville in which a pot had been placed where the head should have been.[40] Presumably the head had been taken as a trophy in war. Further, Brown also suggests that the many representations of the falcon (fig. 1) and falcon-impersonator, a human with mask, disguised as a falcon, were military symbols.[41] An individual, perhaps a military leader, who was seen as embodying the fierce and warlike aspects of a falcon was thus buried with the insignia of his rank.

Conclusion

The Weeden Island period was a time of great activity in the making of pottery. The pottery showing the most vitality and imagination was placed beyond the realm of secular use, buried in mounds. Freed from the practical considerations of utilitarian necessities, yet adhering to the tenets of a sacred tradition, the specialized mortuary ware demonstrates an exuberance on the part of the artisan that was not found in the pottery of the following periods. In Mississippian times, constraints upon the artisan were such that vessel form was more limited, and iconographic motifs reflect a society concerned with honoring its military elite.

The pottery discussed here not only reflects the aesthetic considerations of the potter, but is a sensitive marker of change as well. In the Southeast, the changes of a political, religious, and economic nature were gradual but profound. As such an indicator of change as well as reflection of the time during which it was produced, Southeastern pottery offers valuable clues to the understanding of the potter and the world in which he or she worked.

Fig. 19. A Fort Walton effigy vessel, Point Washington, Choctahatchee Bay, Washington Co., Florida. Height:8 cm. Diameter:27 cm. No.39. Gourds were often used as containers for liquids. This pottery, a gourd-shaped bowl, has a hole in the narrow end for suspension.

Fig. 20. Effigy jar, Panacea Springs, Wakulla Co., Florida. Height:22.3 cm. Diameter:25.5 cm. No. 28. Ducks are often depicted on Weeden Island vessels. This effigy vessel has a red slip and incising on the side that represents the duck's wings. Prefired holes are cut in the sides as well as the bottom (a prefired kill hole?).

Fig. 21. Jar, Hogtown Bayou, Choctawahatchee Bay, Walton Co., Florida. Height:17.1 cm. Diameter:18.7 cm. No. 36. The elaboration of this vessel is reminiscent of that on the vessel in fig. 23. The symbolism of this jar is clearly related to the Southern Cult eye-hand motif.

Fig. 22. A wide-mouth water bottle from Moundville, Hale Co., Alabama. Height:16.5 cm. Diameter:19 cm. No. 47. A pileated or ivory-billed woodpecker was incised on the leather-hard clay twice on the front and back. Downturned fingers were incised on the top of the vessel, and round elements (speech symbols?) were incised in the open bill of the bird.

Fig. 23. A large bowl from Hogtown Bayou, Choc-tawahatchee Bay, Walton Co., Florida. Height:17.7 cm. Diameter:31.1 cm. No. 33. On the rim are bird heads (called adornos) which are commonly found on Fort Walton vessels such as this. The incised decoration on the sides could be an extremely stylized skull motif.

Fig. 24. Coarse-tempered pedestalled effigy vessel representing an owl. Height:29 cm. Diameter:21 cm. No. 26. The punctate marks suggest feathers, and the wings, tail, and legs are incised on the sides and back. According to Moore, the bird's beak was knocked off prior to burial; a hole was also intentionally made in the vessel's base.

NOTES

1. Muller 1978:281.
2. See, for example, Moore 1902, 1903, 1907, 1918.
3. See Milanich 1974:41; Muller 1978:295.
4. Brose and Percy 1974.
5. Griffin 1967:180.
6. Bullen 1978:95.
7. Griffin 1967:180.
8. Muller 1978:292.
9. Sears 1971:324.
10. Muller 1978:292.
11. Sears 1971:324.
12. Griffin 1967:184.
13. Milanich 1974:32.
14. Sears 1973:34.
15. Sears 1973:39.
16. Sears 1973:39.
17. Griffin 1967:189.
18. Brose and Percy 1978:89.
19. Willey 1949:455.
20. Willey 1949:455.
21. Sonin, personal communication.

22. Willey 1949.
23. See Gilliland 1975.
24. Sears 1971.
25. McKenzie 1966.
26. See Steponaitis, n.d. for further discussion of this.
27. Fewkes 1944.
28. Fewkes 1944:87.
29. Percy 1974:72.
30. Percy 1974:72.
31. Brose and Percy 1974:8.
32. Bullen 1955:72.
33. Sears 1971.
34. Sears 1971:328.
35. Milanich, personal communication.
36. Muller 1978:317.
37. Peebles and Kus 1977:444.
38. Peebles and Kus 1977:435.
39. Peebles and Kus 1977:442-443.
40. Peebles and Kus 1977.
41. Brown 1976:127.

REFERENCES

Brose, David S., and George Percy
   1974   An Outline of Weeden Island Ceremonial Activities in N.W. Florida. Paper presented at the 39th annual meeting of the Society for American Archaeology, Washington, D.C.
   1978   Fort Walton Settlement Patterns. In Mississippian Settlement Patterns. Bruce D. Smith, ed. Pp. 81-114. New York: Academic Press.
Brown, James A.
   1976   The Southern Cult Revisited. Mid-continental Journal of Archaeology 1(2):115-135.
Bullen, Ripley P.
   1955   Carved Owl Totem, DeLand, Florida. Florida Anthropologist 8(3):61-73.
   1978   Pre-Columbia Trade in Eastern United States as Viewed from Florida. Florida Anthropologist 31(3):92-108.
Fewkes, V. J.
   1944   Catawba Pottery-Making. Proceedings of the American Philosophical Society 88(2).
Gilliland, Marion
   1975   The Material Culture of Key Marco, Florida. Gainesville: University Presses of Florida.
Griffin, James B.
   1967   Eastern North American Archaeology: A Summary. Science 156:175-191.
McKenzie, D. H.
   1966   A Summary of the Moundville Phase. Journal of Alabama Archaeology 12(1):1-58.
Milanich, Jerald T.
   1974   Life in a 9th Century Indian Household: A Weeden Island Fall-Winter Site on the Upper Apalachicola River, Florida. Bureau of Historic Sites and Properties Bulletin 4:1-44. Tallahassee, Florida.
Moore, Clarence B.
   1902   Certain Aboriginal Remains of the Northwest Florida Coast, Part 1. Journal of the Academy of Natural Sciences of Philadelphia 11:420-497.
   1903   Certain Aboriginal Mounds of the Apalachicola River. Journal of the Academy of Natural Sciences of Philadelphia 12:439-492.
   1907   Moundville Revisited. Journal of the Academy of Natural Sciences of Philadelphia 13:337-405.
   1918   The Northwestern Florida Coast Revisited. Journal of the Academy of Natural Sciences of Philadelphia 16:513-579.
Muller, Jon D.
   1978   The Southeast. In Ancient Native Americans. Jesse D. Jennings, ed. Pp. 281-325. San Francisco: W. H. Freeman & Co.
Peebles. Christopher S., and Susan M. Kus
   1977   Some Archaeological Correlates of Ranked Societies. American Antiquity 42(3):421-448.
Percy, George
   1974   A Review of Evidence for Prehistoric Indian Use of Animals in Northwest Florida. Bureau of Historic Sites and Properties Bulletin 4:65-93. Tallahassee, Florida.
Sears, William H.
   1956   Excavations at Kolomoki, Final Report. University of Georgia Series in Anthropology 5.
   1964   The Southeastern United States. In Prehistoric Man in the New World. Jesse D. Jennings and Edward Norbeck, eds. Pp. 259-287. Chicago: University of Chicago Press.
   1971   Food Production and Village Life in Prehistoric Southeastern United States. Archaeology 24:324-329.
   1973   The Sacred and the Secular in Prehistoric Ceramics. In Variations in Anthropology. D. Lathrap and J. Douglas, eds. Pp. 31-42. Urbana: Illinois Archaeological Survey.

Sonin, Robert
    1979   Personal communication.
Steponaitis, Vincas P.
    n.d.   Some Preliminary Chronological and Technological Notes on Moundville Pottery. Bulletin of the Southeastern Archaeological
            Conference No. 22. In press.
Willey, Gordon R.
    1949   Archaeology of the Florida Gulf Coast. Washington, D.C.: Smithsonian Institution.

ACKNOWLEDGMENTS

I am most grateful to Dr. James B. Griffin, who offered valuable comments and helped a great deal in the preparation of this chapter. Thanks are also due to Robert Sonin, who explained with great patience the technical aspects of pottery making and analyzed the vessels featured in the exhibit. Any errors of interpretation are, however, entirely my own responsibility.

Fig. 25. Human effigy jar, Burnt Mill Creek, St. Andrew's Bay, Washington Co., Florida. Height:20 cm. Width:11.5 cm. No. 30. Human effigy vessels have been found in addition to animal effigies. The front view of this jar shows a figure with an elaborate forelock with his hands crossed over his chest. The back view shows an equally elaborate treatment of the hair on the back of the head. Another vessel in the Moore collection shows a standing figure dressed in a loincloth with ornamental tassels.

The PAINTER:
The Sioux Of The Great Plains

1. Tipi cover (color plate 1; fig. 1)
Sioux, probably South Dakota
Muslin, paint, lead pencil, India inks
Base to apex:487.7 cm.
20/7873

2. Robe
Oglala Sioux, South Dakota
Cowhide, paint, sizing
Length:228.6 cm. Width:148.6 cm.
2/3134

3. Leggings (fig. 18)
Brûlé Sioux, South Dakota
Hide, paint, beads, cowrie shells
Length:76.2 cm.
16/2502

4. Moccasins (fig. 21)
Sioux
Hide, beadwork, paint
Length:26.7 cm.
8888

5. Moccasins
Sioux, South Dakota
Hide, glass beadwork
Length:26.7 cm.
22/9739

6. Shirt (fig. 3)
Sans Arcs Sioux
Hide, paint, human hair, glass beadwork
Length:124.5 cm. Width:157.5 cm.
1/3920

7. Shirt (fig. 11)
Oglala Sioux, South Dakota
Hide, paint
Length:83.8 Width:152.4 cm.
11/4622

8. Shirt
Sioux, probably North Dakota
Canvas, paint, hide, porcupine quillwork
Length (excluding fringe):69.9 cm. Width:157.5 cm.
12/2163

9. Shirt (color plate 2b)
Oglala Sioux, South Dakota
Hide, paint, human hair
Length:138.4 cm. Width:91.4 cm.
16/1351

10. Dress
Sioux
Muslin, paint, feathers
Length:134.6 cm. Width:141 cm.
1/741

11. Dress
Sioux
Muslin, paint
Length:121.9 cm. Width:153.7 cm.
1/3302

12. Dress (fig. 6)
Sioux, probably painted by Running Antelope, ca. 1880
Muslin, paint, India inks
Length:134.6 cm. Width:172 .7 cm.
9/9924

13. Dress (fig. 5)
Hunkpapa Sioux, South Dakota
Muslin, India inks
Length:125.7 cm. Width:127.6 cm.
21/3665

14. Shield and cover
Brûlé Sioux, probably South Dakota
Hide, paint, feathers
Diameter:41.3 cm.
16/2489

15. Shield and cover (fig. 7)
Brûlé Sioux, probably South Dakota
Hide, paint, trade cloth, feathers, horsehair
Length of trailer:100.3 cm. Diameter:48.2 cm.
16/2490

16. Shield and cover
Hunkpapa Sioux
Hide, canvas, paint, bells, feathers
Diameter:50.8 cm.
20/1422

17. Shield and cover (fig. 17)
Sioux
Hide, paint
Diameter:52.1 cm.
20/6563

18. Shield and cover
Sioux
Hide, paint, feathers, bells, bearclaws, sweetgrass
Length of trailer:99.1 cm. Diameter:49.5 cm.
20/7793

19. Shield cover (fig. 16)
Sioux
Hide, paint, sizing, trade cloth
Diameter:47 cm.
20/7794

20. Shield
Sioux
Canvas, watercolor
Diameter:36.2 cm.
1/1077

21. Shield
Sioux
Canvas, watercolor
Diameter:44.5 cm.
1/1077

22. Shield
Sioux
Canvas, watercolor
Diameter:36.2 cm.
1/1077

23. Shield (fig. 15)
Sioux
Canvas, watercolor, feathers
Diameter:45.7 cm.
1/9252

24. Shield (color plate 2a)
Sioux, Standing Rock Reservation, North Dakota
Collected by Miss Frances Densmore
Canvas, watercolor, feathers, horsehair
Diameter:51.4 cm.
6/7911

25. Shield (fig. 14)
Hunkpapa Sioux (?), North Dakota
Hide, paint
Diameter: 24.1 cm.
21/3663

26. Shield
Hunkpapa Sioux, Standing Rock Reservation, Cannon Ball, North Dakota
Canvas, watercolor, feathers
Diameter:43.8 cm.
23/2962

27. Parfleche (fig. 8)
Hunkpapa Sioux, Standing Rock Reservation, Cannon Ball, North Dakota
Hide, paint, sizing
Length:29.2 cm. Height:20.3 cm.
23/2938

28. Knife case (fig. 12)
Sioux
Hide, paint, trade cloth
Length:33.7 cm.
6/2303

29. Bag (fig. 10)
Sioux, Standing Rock Reservation, North Dakota
Collected by Miss Frances Densmore from Eagle Shield
Hide, paint, sizing
Length:39.4 cm.
6/8007

30. Bag
Sioux
Hide, paint, sizing
Length:43.2 cm. Height:29.2 cm.
4/4673

31. Bag
Sioux
Hide, paint, sizing
Length:20.3 cm. Height:14 cm.
4/5021

32. Bag
Sioux
Hide, paint, sizing
Length:19.1 cm. Height:21 cm.
6/2304

33. Bag
Oglala Sioux (?), Pine Ridge Reservation, South Dakota
Hide, paint, sizing
Length:24.1 cm. Height:20.3 cm.
16/8494

34. Bag
Hunkpapa Sioux, Fort Peck, Montana
Hide, paint, sizing
Length:68.6 cm. Width:29.2 cm.
18/819

35. Bags (pair) (fig. 19)
Sioux
Hide, paint, sizing, canvas
Length:63.5 cm. Width:27.9 cm.
12/2247

36. Boxes (pair)
Hunkpapa Sioux, Standing Rock Reservation, Cannon Ball, North Dakota
Hide, paint, sizing
Height:24.1 cm. Width:47 cm. Depth:30.5 cm.
23/2495, 23/2496

37. Drum (fig. 4)
Sioux
Wood, hide, paint
Diameter:45.7 cm.
10/5940

38. Drawing
Sioux, Standing Rock Reservation, North Dakota
Collected by Miss Frances Densmore, attributed to Jaw
Muslin, lead pencil, inks, crayon
Length:191.8 cm. Width:91.4 cm.
6/7932

39. Drawing
Sioux, Standing Rock Reservation, North Dakota
Collected by Miss Frances Densmore
Muslin, paint
Length:88.9 cm. Width:85.7 cm.
6/7933

40. Drawing
Oglala Sioux, Pine Ridge Agency, South Dakota
Collected ca. 1880, attributed to Don't Braid His Hair
Paper, lead pencil, India inks
Length:50 cm. Width:28.1 cm.
10/9627

41. Drawing (fig. 22)
Sioux, South Dakota
Lead pencil, colored pencil, crayon (?)
Length:16.5 cm. Width:26.7 cm.
23/6868

42. Drawing
Miniconjou Sioux, Cheyenne River Reservation, South Dakota
Collected ca. 1890, attributed to Pete Three Legs
Paper, India inks
Length:82.6 cm. Width:47 cm.
15/3231

43. Ledger drawing depicting Grass Dance
Sioux, probably Oglala, Pine Ridge Agency, South Dakota
Collected ca. 1898
Paper, lead pencil, crayon
Length:40.6 cm. Width:12.7 cm.
11/1708

44. Ledger drawing (fig. 9)
Portrait of Red Crow by Red Dog
Sioux, probably Oglala, Pine Ridge Reservation, South Dakota
Collected ca. 1884
Paper, lead pencil, colored pencil, inks
Length:19.1 cm. Width:12.7 cm.
20/6230

45. Seven paintbrushes
Sioux
Bone, with traces of paint and sizing
Longest:7 cm.
23/2985

46. Paint cup
Sioux
Turtle shell, hide with quillwork
Length:21 cm. Width:16 cm.
12/2250

47. Tipi ornament
Sioux
Human hair, cloth, eagle feather
Length:54 cm.
23/1160

The FEATHERWORKER:
The Karajá Of Brazil

1. *Aruaña* dance outfit, *ijaso* type (color plate 4)
Karajá, Bananal Island, Brazil
Feathers of red-and-green macaw, blue-and-yellow macaw, roseate spoonbill, *Amazona* parrot, bird of prey; palm leaf, reed, bark, cord, beeswax
Height of mask including grass fringe:125 cm. Width:49 cm. Height of skirt:69 cm.
23/2000
The feather mosaic of this mask represents an *aruaña* fish.

2. Head fan for boy (color plate 3b)
Karajá, Bananal Island, Brazil
Feathers of red-and-green macaw, scarlet macaw, harpy eagle, jabiru stork; cotton, cord, palm-leaf midrib
Diameter:130 cm.
18/9867

3. Head fan for boy
Karajá, Brazil
Feathers of hoatzin, jabiru stork, roseate spoonbill, blue-and-yellow macaw, Muscovy duck, Amazona parrot; palm wood, barkcloth, cord, cotton, palm-leaf midrib
Diameter:123 cm.
24/4058

4. Nimbus headdress for male (fig. 16)
Karajá, Araguaya River, Brazil
Feathers of red-and-green macaw, blue-and-yellow macaw, great egret, Amazona parrot, Muscovy duck; reed; cord, clay
Height:53 cm. Width:36 cm.
13/6242

5. Nimbus headdress for male (fig. 8)
Karajá, Araguaya River, Brazil
Feathers of blue-and-yellow macaw, great egret, Muscovy duck; reed, palm-leaf midrib, kaolin, cotton
Height:69 cm. Width:83 cm.
13/6243

6. Nimbus headdress for male (color plate 3a)
Karajá, Araguaya River, Brazil
Feathers of red-and-green macaw, blue-and-yellow macaw, scarlet macaw, Amazona parrot; reed, cotton, palm-leaf midrib
Height:59 cm. Width:93 cm.
13/6245

7. Nimbus headdress for male
Karajá, Araguaya River, Brazil
Feathers of red-and-green macaw, scarlet macaw; palm-leaf midrib, clay, cord, cotton, reed
Height:58 cm. Width:76 cm.
13/6247

8. Nimbus headdress for male
Karajá, Araguaya River, Brazil
Feathers of Amazona aestiva parrot, jabiru stork, scarlet macaw, Muscovy duck; palm-leaf midrib, reed, cotton
Height:37 cm. Width:39 cm.
13/6249

9. Nimbus headdress for male (fig. 26)
Karajá, Araguaya River, Brazil
Feathers of blue-and-yellow macaw, harpy eagle, jabiru stork, Muscovy duck, bird of prey; palm-leaf midrib, down, reed, tree resin
Height:53 cm. Width:70 cm.
13/6252

10. Nimbus headdress for male
Karajá, Bananal Island, Brazil
Feathers of roseate spoonbill, blue-and-yellow macaw, jabiru stork, Muscovy duck; palm-leaf midrib, cotton, palm leaf, reed
Height:51 cm. Width:54 cm.
24/4060

11. Crown headdress
Karajá, Araguaya River, Brazil
Feathers of macaw, Amazona parrot; reed, down, cotton, tree resin
Height:21 cm. Width:20 cm.
13/6254

12. Crown headdress (fig. 5)
Karajá, Araguaya River, Brazil
Feathers of blue-and-yellow macaw, macaw, Amazona parrot; reed, cotton, cord
Height:27 cm. Width:17 cm.
14/9701

13. Crown headdress
Karajá, Araguaya River, Brazil
Feathers of macaw, Amazona parrot; unspecified white feathers; cord, reed, down, resin
Height:19 cm. Width:21 cm.
14/9703

14. Crown headdress (fig. 17)
Karajá, Araguaya River, Brazil
Feathers of macaw, unspecified white feathers, reed, cotton, beeswax, resin
Height:32 cm. Width:20 cm.
14/9704

15. Cap for child (displayed as worn) (fig. 25b)
Karajá, Araguaya River, Brazil
Feathers of red-and-green macaw, Amazona parrot, macaw; palm-leaf fiber, palm-leaf midrib
Height:15 cm. Width:27 cm.
13/6255

16. Cap for child (displayed as stored) (fig. 25a)
Karajá, Goiás, Brazil
Feathers of roseate spoonbill, maguari stork; palm-leaf fiber
Height:24 cm. Width:20 cm.
18/32

17. Cap with basketry base (fig. 6)
Karajá, Brazil
Feathers of scarlet macaw, macaw, Amazona parrot, chicken; reed, liana bark, palm-leaf fiber
Height:34 cm. Width:17 cm.
18/9863

18. Head ring for boys (fig. 4)
Karajá, Brazil
Feathers of red-and-green macaw, yellow-and-blue macaw, Amazona parrot, domesticated turkey; reed, cotton, cord
Diameter:22 cm.
13/6264

19. Headband with plume
Karajá, Araguaya River, Brazil
Feathers of red-and-green macaw, blue-and-yellow macaw, razor-billed curassow; palm-leaf, cotton, wrapped quill
Height:69 cm. Width:22 cm.
18/24

20. Headband (fig. 12)
Karajá, Bananal Island, Brazil
Feathers of crested oropendula, blue-and-yellow macaw, bird of prey; cotton, cord
Height:30 cm. Width:44 cm.

21. Ear rosettes for adolescent (fig. 13)
Karajá, Araguaya River, Brazil
Feathers of macaw; palm wood, cord, shell, beeswax
Length:19 cm. Diameter:6 cm.
13/6305

22. Ear rosettes for child (fig. 13)
Karajá, Araguaya River, Brazil
Feathers of blue-and-yellow macaw; reed, capybara teeth, shell, cord
Length: 13 cm. Diameter:4 cm.
13/6308

23. Ear rosettes for child
Karajá, Araguaya River, Brazil
Feathers of macaw; palm wood, cotton, capybara teeth
Length:10 cm. Diameter:5 cm.
13/6310

24. Ear rosettes for infant
Karajá, Goiás, Brazil
Feathers of macaw; palm wood, cord, capybara teeth
Length:5 cm. Diameter:4 cm.
18/41

25. Ear rosettes for adolescent (fig. 13)
Karajá, Bananal Island, Brazil
Feathers of chicken (dyed); palm wood, cord, shell, beeswax
Length:16 cm. Diameter:7 cm.
18/9848

26. Ear rosettes for child
Karajá, Bananal Island, Brazil
Feathers of macaw, *Amazona* parrot; palm wood, cord, cotton, capybara teeth
Length:16 cm. Diameter:7 cm.
18/9850

27. Ear rosettes (fig. 13)
Karajá, Bananal Island, Brazil
Feathers of blue-and-yellow macaw, macaw; palm wood, cord, beeswax
Length:16 cm. Diameter:6 cm.
18/9851

28. Belt for wrestler
Karajá, Araguaya River, Brazil
Feathers of red-and-green macaw; cord
Length:78 cm. (including cord). Height:9 cm.
13/6256

29. Belt for wrestler (fig. 14)
Karajá, Araguaya River, Brazil
Feathers of blue-and-yellow macaw, *Amazona aestiva* parrot; cotton, reed, *Thevetia* nuts
Length:55 cm. Height:19 cm.
13/6289

30. Belt for wrestler (fig. 15)
Karajá, Bananal Island, Brazil
Feathers of blue-and-yellow macaw, *Amazona aestiva* parrot, yellow-rumped cacique, cocoi heron; palm fiber
Length:76 cm. Height:16 cm.
23/1982

31. Spool bracelets for adolescent (fig. 24)
Karajá, Araguaya River, Brazil
Feathers of macaw; cotton, urucú, pigment, cord, glass beads
Height: 16 cm. Width:11 cm.
13/6347

32. Knee bands (fig. 7)
Karajá, Goiás, Brazil
Feathers of red-and-green macaw, hawk, *Amazona* parrot, crested oropendula; cotton
Length:36 cm. (including feathers). Width:14 cm.
14/6413

33. Necklace (?)
Karajá, Bananal Island, Brazil
Feathers of red-and-green macaw, *Amazona* parrot, chicken; palm-leaf fiber, reed, shell
Length:46 cm.
24/4057

34. Comb (fig. 18)
Karajá, Bananal Island, Brazil
Feathers of macaw; palm-leaf midribs, cotton, *Thevetia* nuts
Height:15 cm. Width:24 cm.
18/9788

35. Whistle (fig. 19)
Karajá, Araguaya River, Brazil
Feathers of macaw, blue-and-yellow macaw, *Amazona* parrot, parakeet, hawk; bird bone, cotton, beeswax
Length:20 cm. Width:9 cm. (with feathers)
13/6291

36. Storage basket for feathers
Karajá, Bananal Island, Brazil
Palm leaf, cord, palm wood
Length:44 cm. Height:18 cm. Width:10 cm.
18/9784

37. Bird arrow
Karajá, Bananal Island, Brazil
Feathers of *Amazona* parrot; reed, nutshell, bark, beeswax, cord
Length:116 cm. Diameter:4 cm.
23/1893

38. Bow
Karajá, Araguaya River, Brazil
Feathers of red-and-green macaw, *Amazona* parrot; palm wood, reed, liana bark, cord, urucú pigment
Length:181 cm.
13/6410

39. Club
Karajá, Bananal Island, Brazil
Feathers of blue-and-yellow macaw; palm wood, reed, liana bark, cord
Length:89 cm.
18/9733

40. Ceremonial lances
Karajá, Araguaya River, Brazil
Feathers of various macaws, maguari stork, *Amazona* parrot, roseate spoonbill; palm wood, wax, bone, reed, bark, cord, hoof, nutshell
13/6419, 13/6421, 13/6428, 13/6430, 13/6433, 13/6436, 13/6437, 13/6439

The CARVER:
The Haida Of The Northwest Coast

1. Shaman's staff
Haida, British Columbia, Canada, and Alaska, U.S.A.
Carved wood
Crests of Eagle, Beaver, Bear, Frog, Raven, Eagle, Otter, Eagle, Eagle, Eagle
Height:140 cm. Diameter:5 cm.
5/617

2. Model of shaman
Haida (?), British Columbia, Canada, and Alaska, U.S.A.
Carved and painted wood
Height:56 cm. Diameter:15.5 cm.
1113
The shaman, or medicine man, was the important religious figure on the Northwest Coast, and he was also responsible for curing through medical arts which included a knowledge of the medicinal qualities of herbs and of setting fractures.

3. Shaman's rattle
Haida, Prince of Wales Island, Alaska, U.S.A.
Carved and painted wood
Human face
Length:26 cm. Diameter:13.5 cm.
2/431

4. Shaman's charm (fig. 19)
Haida, Queen Charlotte Islands, British Columbia, Canada
Carved stone
Zoomorphic figures
Height:9.2 cm. Length:25 cm. Width: 4 cm.
7/397

5. Shaman's "soul catcher" (fig. 11)
Haida, British Columbia, Canada, and Alaska, U.S.A.
Carved bone with haliotis shell inlay
Two Killer Whales
Height:3.8 cm. Length:15.7 cm. Width:3.2 cm.
1/8066
The soul catcher was used in war expeditions to capture the spirits of the enemy.

6. Spirits of the Canoe sculpture (fig. 20)
Haida, Queen Charlotte Islands, British Columbia, Canada
Carved argillite
Figures of Canoe Spirits in Canoe
Height:17.8 cm. Length:36.2 cm. Width:7.9 cm.
13/1875
The Canoe Spirits were supernatural beings who aided the shaman.

7. Model canoe
Haida, Queen Charlotte Islands, British Columbia, Canada
Wood, bearskin
Carved, with crew carved and painted, dressed in bearskin
Length:448 cm. Width:73 cm. Height:55 cm.
6/8874

8. Model canoe
Haida, Prince of Wales Island, Alaska, U.S.A.
Carved and painted wood
Wolf carved and painted on bow
Height:20 cm. Length:94.5 cm. Width:16.5 cm.
3/5496

9. Dance staff
Haida, Queen Charlotte Islands, British Columbia, Canada
Carved wood with copper base
Killer Whale
Length:193.7 cm. Diameter:3.5 cm.
15/4326
Dance staffs were used during the formal ceremonies of the potlatch, the ceremonies associated with accession to titles and other honors.

10. Dance staff
Haida, Queen Charlotte Islands, British Columbia, Canada
Carved and painted wood
Two salmon and a devilfish, painted in red, black, and yellow
Length:190.5 cm. Diameter:4.0 cm.
15/4324

11. Dance staff
Haida, Queen Charlotte Islands, British Columbia, Canada
Carved wood
Human (?) face
Length:187 cm. Diameter:4.2 cm.
15/4328

12. Clapper
Haida, Queen Charlotte Islands, British Columbia, Canada
Carved wood
Wolf (?)
Length:26 cm. Width:4.5 cm.
14/4348

13. Rattle
Haida, Queen Charlotte Islands, British Columbia, Canada
Carved and painted wood
Killer Whale
Height:14 cm. Length:28 cm. Width:16 cm.
12/4427

14. Rattle
Haida, Skidegate, Queen Charlotte Islands, British Columbia, Canada
Carved and painted wood
Raven
Height:12 cm. Length:40 cm. Width:18 cm.
1825

15. Chief's ceremonial helmet
Haida, Prince of Wales Island, Alaska, U.S.A.
Carved and painted wood
Bear and Killer Whale crests
Height:53 cm. Diameter:53.5 cm.
11/5400

16. Chief's ceremonial headdress
Haida, Kasaan, Prince of Wales Island, Alaska, U.S.A.
Wood, haliotis inlay, sea lion bristles, ermine, cloth
Carved, inlaid, and painted
Eagle, Eagle, and Frog head
Height:21 cm. Width:17 cm.
10/4581
Headdresses of this type were worn by clan or town chiefs on ceremonial occasions, such as potlatches, making peace, or welcoming guests. Eagle or swan's down was scattered from the headdress as the chief ceremonially danced before his guests.

17. Helmet ornaments (pair)
Haida, Prince of Wales Island, Alaska, U.S.A.
Carved and painted wood
Ravens
(1) Height:11 cm. Length:27.5 cm. Width:15 cm.
(2) Height:11 cm. Length:27.0 cm. Width:16.0 cm.
2/1452

18. Frontlet of ceremonial headdress
Haida, Skidegate, Queen Charlotte Islands, British Columbia, Canada
Wood, haliotis shell
Carved, painted, and inlaid
Face
Height:19.2 cm. Width:15.2 cm.
1/8947

19. Knife (fig. 14)
Haida, British Columbia, Canada, and Alaska, U.S.A.
Copper and wood
Killer Whale
Length:40.6 cm. Width:3.4 cm.
20/3850

20. Ceremonial ladle
Haida, Queen Charlotte Islands, British Columbia, Canada
Mountain goat horn, mountain sheep horn, copper, and haliotis shell
Horn handle decorated with Dragon Fly and Hawk; copper engraved with zoomorphic figure, with Eagle (?) below
Length:59.4 cm. Width:16 cm.
19/3542

21. Ladle (fig. 7)
Haida, British Columbia, Canada, and Alaska, U.S.A.
Carved wood
Bear, Hawk, Fish, and Hawk
Length:72.7 cm. Width:17 cm.
22/6301

22. Spoon
Haida, Queen Charlotte Islands, British Columbia, Canada
Horn, mountain goat horn handle, haliotis inlay, copper studs
Dogfish, Bear with fish, Killer Whale on underside and bowl
Length:29 cm. Width:7.6 cm.
15/4540

23. Spoon
Haida, British Columbia, Canada, and Alaska, U.S.A.
Carved cow horn or mountain sheep horn
Dragon Fly
Length:17.9 cm.
20/9761

24. Ladle (fig. 9)
Haida, Queen Charlotte Islands, British Columbia, Canada
Carved mountain sheep horn
Raven
Length:59.3 cm.
6/9695

25. Spoon (fig. 13a)
Haida, Queen Charlotte Islands, British Columbia, Canada
Carved mountain goat horn, haliotis inlay, copper studs
Dragon Fly, Beaver, and zoomorphic figure
Length:25.5 cm.
5/9076

26. Spoon (fig. 13b)
Haida, British Columbia, Canada, and Alaska, U.S.A.
Carved mountain goat horn
Dogfish, Wolf, Eagle, Bear, and Raven
Length:18 cm.
5/3211

27. Children's feast dish (fig. 10)
Haida, Queen Charlotte Islands, British Columbia, Canada
Carved wood
Dragon Fly
Height:6.1 cm. Length:35 cm. Width:12.5 cm.
9/7899

28. Feast dish
Haida, British Columbia, Canada, and Alaska, U.S.A.
Carved mountain sheep horn
Whale
Height:10.5 cm. Length:17 cm. Width:16.5 cm.
3/2260

29. Dish (fig. 15)
Haida, British Columbia, Canada, and Alaska, U.S.A.
Carved and painted wood
Killer Whale
Height:18.8 cm. Length:47 cm. Width:45 cm.
14/3616

30. Dish (fig. 18)
Haida, British Columbia, Canada, and Alaska, U.S.A.
Carved wood
Seal
Height:18.5 cm. Length:56 cm. Width:27.5 cm.
14/9621

31. Oil dish (fig. 5)
Haida, Queen Charlotte Islands, British Columbia, Canada
Carved and painted wood, inlaid with bead and bone panels
Two Bears facing one another
Height:19.5 cm. Length:48.4 cm. Width:19.5 cm.
24/8348

32. Ceremonial "slave killer" knife (fig. 8)
Haida, Queen Charlotte Islands, British Columbia, Canada
Carved and polished stone
Human face on end of handle portion
Length 37.6 cm.
7249
Slave killers were used to dispatch slaves, usually as part of the ceremonials associated with the potlatch.

33. Ceremonial copper (fig. 21)
Haida, Queen Charlotte Islands, British Columbia, Canada
Engraved and polished cast copper
Two Eagle crests, facing outward
Height:84 cm. Width:59 cm. Thickness:0.4 cm.
2134

34. Coffin head
Haida, Skidegate, Queen Charlotte Islands, British Columbia, Canada
Carved and painted wood
Killer Whale
Height:40 cm. Width:74 cm.
4663

35. Box
Haida, Queen Charlotte Islands, British Columbia, Canada
Carved and painted wood with brass tack decoration
Various totemic designs
Length:87 cm. Width:55 cm.
7/1118

36. Dice
Haida, British Columbia, Canada, and Alaska, U.S.A.
Engraved beaver incisors
Average length:4.3 cm.
1/9381

37. Adze
Haida, Prince of Wales Island, Alaska, U.S.A.
Iron blade with wooden handle
Length:29.8 cm.
1274
The adze was among the most important of the carver's tools, often doubling as an axe.

38. Plane
Haida, British Columbia, Canada, and Alaska, U.S.A.
Iron blade, wood handle, twine
Height:10.5 cm. Length:23 cm. Width:10.5 cm.
3/4798

39. Carving tool
Haida, Queen Charlotte Islands, British Columbia, Canada, and Prince of Wales Island, Alaska, U.S.A.
Iron with antler handle
Two otters
Length:20.4 cm.
2/2105

40. Maul head
Haida, Queen Charlotte Islands, British Columbia, Canada
Carved stone
Animal head
Height:10.5 cm. Length:15 cm. Width:7.5 cm.
1/8188

41. Soapberry spoon (fig. 6)
Haida, British Columbia, Canada, and Alaska, U.S.A.
Horn
Shark and human face
Length:39.3 cm.
20/2828
The flat soapberry spoon was used in eating the berries, which were whipped into a froth.

42. Halibut hook
Haida, Queen Charlotte Islands, British Columbia, Canada
Carved wood with steel barb and vegetal cordage
Halibut
Length:27 cm.
18/2293

43. Seal club (fig. 16)
Haida, Queen Charlotte Islands, British Columbia, Canada
Carved wood
Killer Whale
Height:8.5 cm. Length:56.3 cm. Width:5.5 cm.
1/9371
Seals were shot with arrows or harpooned; when they had become sufficiently tired the death blow was given with a club.

44. War club
Haida, British Columbia, Canada, and Alaska, U.S.A.
Carved wood
Killer Whale
Length:50.5 cm.
5/789
The club is of a type found in the northeastern woodlands of North America and was probably traded westward, where it was carved by the Haida.

45. Steamboat pipe (fig. 24)
Haida, British Columbia, Canada, and Alaska, U.S.A.
Carved and painted wood, ivory panels
Height:10 cm. Length:40 cm. Width:4.2 cm.
2/8685
An example of scrimshaw carving, adopted and adapted by the Haida from sailors and produced for sale as curios.

46. Miniature totem pole (fig. 23)
Haida, British Columbia, Canada, and Alaska, U.S.A.
Carved argillite
Small bear on head of shaman, above Bear and Frog
Height:15 cm.
21/8047
Miniature argillite totem poles began to be produced as curios for travelers and visitors after 1870, around the time that the true totem poles were about to end. They represent a return to tradition, and they developed as the scrimshaw art was drawing to a close.

47. Sculpture of Grizzly Bears and woman
Haida, Queen Charlotte Islands, British Columbia, Canada
Carved argillite
Grizzly Bears, woman giving birth
Height:13.9 cm. Length:13.9 cm. Width:5.7 cm.
23/6103
This carving represents the traditional legend of the woman berrypicker who was captured by and married to a Grizzly Bear. She is shown giving birth to their offspring. Characteristic of argillite carving (after 1820) was the portrayal of legendary events, myths, and creatures, in contrast to the scrimshaw, which embodied nontraditional elements.

48. Sculpture of shaman
Haida, Queen Charlotte Islands, British Columbia, Canada
Carved argillite
Shaman with traditional dress and regalia
Height:28 cm.
1/9275
Depicted on his head is the Land Otter, a source of spiritual power. His hair is worn long, as shamans never cut their hair, believing that to do so would lessen their power. Through the septum is an ivory piece; in his right hand he carries a rattle; in his left an amulet. The skirt is a Chilkat blanket.

49. Pipe (fig. 22)
Haida, Queen Charlotte Islands, British Columbia, Canada
Carved sandstone
Killer Whale, Octopus, and human head
Height:5.7 cm. Length:8.7 cm. Width:3.4 cm.
17/9796
Until the coming of the Europeans, the Haida chewed the indigenous tobacco. After the advent of the Europeans they began to smoke it and produced pipes of various materials for their own use and as curios for visitors.

50. Pipe
Haida, Queen Charlotte Islands, British Columbia, Canada
Carved and painted wood
Eagle and Sea Otter
Height:5.2 cm. Length:17.9 cm. Width:2.7 cm.
19/6660

51. Bracelet
Haida, Queen Charlotte Islands, British Columbia, Canada, and Prince of Wales Island, Alaska, U.S.A.
Engraved silver
Two ravens
Height:3.8 cm. Length:5.7 cm. Width:5.4 cm.
11/4276
Following the introduction of silver by fur traders, whalers, and others, the Haida craftsmen translated their art style into this new material.

The GOLDSMITH:
The Coclé Style Of Ancient Panama

1. Group of bead necklaces (restrung) (fig. 7)
Rio Grande, Coclé Province, Panama
Hammered, "welded," and rolled gold
Length:72 to 52 cm. Weight:.72 to .02 grams (Where possible, weights are given for the gold artifacts. It is possible that there are modal weights, arising from use of standard measures of metal.)
16/3866, 16/3869, 16/3868, 16/3867, 16/3863, 16/3861, (starting from the inside of the group)

2. Large bead
Rio Grande, Coclé Province, Panama
Hammered, "welded," and rolled gold
Diameter:2.5 cm. Weight:2.5 grams
16/3859

3. Large disc
Venado Beach, Canal Zone, Panama
Hammered and burnished gold, pierced for attachment
Diameter:14.5 cm. Weight:104 grams
24/633

4. Plaque depicting Crocodile God with antlers on his head (fig. 29)
Coclé Province, Panama
A.D. 700-1100
Embossed gold, pierced for attachment
Height:10.6 cm. Width:11 cm. Weight:37.5 grams
23/3535

5. Monkey pendant (fig.21b)
Parita, Herrera Province, Panama
A.D. 700-1100 (?)
Agate sheathed with embossed gold
Height:6 cm.
23/2349
Composite ornaments like this pendant and the following one were found in grave 11 of Mason's (1940) excavations at Sitio Conte, Coclé Province, Panama.

6. Monkey pendant (fig.21a)
Parita, Herrera Province, Panama
A.D. 700-1100 (?)
Plant resin sheathed with embossed gold (one leg missing)
Height:7 cm.
23/2352

7. Animal figurine
Parita, Herrera Province, Panama
A.D. 700-1100 (?)
Molded plant resin, probably meant to have embossed gold sheathing
Height:4.8 cm. Length:11 cm.
23/2342

8. Curly-tailed animal figurine
Veraguas Province, Panama
A.D. 700-1100 (?)
Plant resin, probably meant to have embossed gold sheathing
Height:7 cm. Length:8.5 cm.
23/3539

9. Sheaths for animal figurines
Parita, Herrera Province, Panama
A.D. 700-1100 (?)
Embossed gold
Length:0.5 cm. to 15 cm. Weight:.05 to 9.1 grams
23/2354 (13 specimens)

10. Square plaque with geometric decoration (fig. 27)
Parita, Herrera Province, Panama
A.D. 1100-1520 (?)
Embossed gold, pierced for attachment
Length:12.3 cm. Width:11.4 cm. Weight:47 grams
24/2468

11. Adjustable finger ring with geometric decoration (fig. 17)
Parita, Herrera Province, Panama
A.D. 1100–1520 (?)
Embossed gold, pierced for fastening
Diameter:1.9 cm. Width:2.1 cm. Weight:2 grams
24/2467

12. Large nose ring (fig. 3c)
Madden Lake, Canal Zone, Panama
Hammered and "welded" gold, hollow, with separate caps
Diameter:4.4 cm. Weight:7.5 grams
24/654

13. Small nose ring (fig. 3b)
Madden Lake, Canal Zone, Panama
Cast and hammered gold, with crimped caps
Diameter:2.5 cm. Weight:12.5 grams
24/649

14. Large disc with geometric decoration
Parita, Herrera Province, Panama
A.D. 1100–1520 (?)
Embossed and burnished gold, pierced for attachment
Diameter 24.9 cm. Weight:168 grams
24/2469
Possibly used as a mirror.

15. Necklace of pendants (restrung) (color plate 8a)
Parita, Herrera Province, Panama
Hammered, annealed, "welded," and embossed sheet gold
Length of pendants:5.8 cm. Weight:91 grams
24/2465
The gold pendants are made in the shape of carved shell pendants.

16. Necklace of pendants (restrung)
Venado Beach, Canal Zone, Panama
Carved shell
Length of largest pendant:5.6 cm.
23/1450

17. Helmet (fig. 18)
Parita, Herrera Province, Panama
A.D. 400–700 (?)
Embossed and burnished gold
Length:22 cm. Width:19 cm. Weight:317.4 grams
23/2339
The helmet is apparently unfinished. On the outside there are incisions and punch marks outlining a complex curvilinear design that was never embossed. The edge of the helmet is pierced, perhaps for the attachment of a fabric lining.

18. Ear rod (fig. 14a)
Temple site, El Caño, Coclé Province, Panama
A.D. 700–1100
Embossed and "welded" gold, hollow
Length:11.5 cm. Weight:12.5 grams
24/669

19. Capped ear rod (reconstructed) (fig. 14d)
Temple site, El Caño, Coclé Province, Panama
A.D. 700–1100
Embossed and incised gold cap
Length:14.6 m.
24/671

20. Capped ear rod (reconstructed) (fig. 14c)
Temple site, El Caño, Coclé Province, Panama
A.D. 700–1100
Cast pointed cap, embossed plain cap
Length:16 cm.
24/672

21. Capped ear rod (reconstructed) (fig. 14d)
Temple site, El Caño, Coclé Province, Panama
A.D. 700–1100
Embossed gold caps
Length:13.2 cm.
24/670

22. Ear spools (color plate 8b; fig. 32)
Coclé Province, Panama
Embossed and clinched sheet gold
Diameter:3.6 cm. Weight:13 grams
24/640
Each spool comes apart for easy insertion.

23. Necklace of beads and pendants in the shape of animal teeth (restrung) (fig. 38)
Parita, Herrera Province, Panama
Hammered, annealed, "welded," and embossed gold
Length:28 cm. Weight:46 grams
24/2466

24. Nose ornament (fig. 3a)
Temple site, El Caño, Coclé Province, Panama
A.D. 400–700
Excavated by A. H. Verrill
Green stone, with embossed gold caps
Diameter:3.4 cm.
13/1802
The ornament is made in the shape of a set of two concentric nose rings.

25. Nose ornament
Madden Lake, Canal Zone, Panama
A.D. 400–700
Embossed sheet gold
Diameter:4 cm. Weight: 3 grams
24/648
The nose ornament is made in the shape of a set of three concentric nose rings.

26. Tusk pendant
Parita, Herrera Province, Panama
Probably bone, with embossed gold cap
Length:10 cm.
23/2357
One of a pair, the tusk bears simple incised designs representing eyes.

27. Tusk pendant
Santiago, Veraguas Province, Panama
Carved serpentine, with embossed gold cap
Length:11 cm.
23/3892
The surface of the stone bears traces of a woven fabric.

28. Double Bat God pendant (color plate 9c; fig. 22)
Parita, Herrera Province, Panama
Cast and hammered gold
Height:4.5 cm. Width:9 cm. Weight:85.5 grams
24/2460
The pendant is decorated with six circular hammered danglers suspended from hooks. The clubs or standards in the hands of the figures were hammered after casting to obscure the remnants of the metal-pouring channels or vents. Each figure has a pair of belt streamers in the shape of profile crocodile heads.

29. Double crab pendant (fig. 37)
Panama
A.D. 700–1100 (?)
Cast gold, with hollows for insets
Length:4.9 cm. Weight:21.5 grams
23/7893
The pendant is decorated with a circular hammered dangler. A similar ornament was found in grave 5 at Sitio Conte, Coclé Province, Panama (Lothrop 1937:fig. 48b).

30. Pearl
Parita, Herrera Province, Panama
A.D. 700–1100 (?)
Diameter:1.3 cm.
24/3293
The pearl was found in a badly corroded cast tumbaga pendant, in the shape of a double insect.

31. Nose clip (fig. 24)
Panama
A.D. 400–700
Collected by Samuel K. Lothrop
Cast-gold "filagree"
Diameter:2.4 cm. Weight:8.5 grams
15/3530

32. Nose ring with decoration of four miniature frogs (fig. 26a)
Venado Beach, Canal Zone, Panama
A.D. 1100–1520 (?)
Cast gold
Diameter:2.5 cm. Weight:11.3 grams
24/650
The ornament could never have been worn, as the ends are fused together. It may have been made for burial.

33. Adjustable finger ring with decoration of three miniature frogs
Veraguas Province, Panama
A.D. 1100–1520 (?)
Cast gold
Diameter:1.9 cm. Weight:10 grams
23/3536

34. Adjustable finger ring with decoration of three miniature frogs (fig. 28b)
Parita, Herrera Province, Panama
A.D. 1100–1520 (?)
Cast gold
Diameter:2 cm. Weight:7.5 grams
24/2461

35. Frog pendant (fig. 35)
Parita, Herrera Province, Panama
Cast gold
Length:3.6 cm. Weight:7.5 grams
24/2464
Impressions on the inside of the pendant show that the model was built up of small, square sheets of wax (Sonin, personal communication).

36. Bat God pendant (fig. 1)
Costa Rica
Cast gold
Height:5.2 cm. Weight:5.2 grams
18/1589
This Coclé-style pendant was probably traded to Costa Rica from central Panama. It shows extreme attrition from wear, especially on the suspension loop, which has worn very thin. The hole at the breast of the figure was caused by the formation of an air lock during casting. The protuberances of the pouring funnels or vents can be seen on the head and heels.

37. Curly-tailed animal pendant (fig. 34)
Guapiles, Linea Vieja region, Costa Rica
Cast gold
Height:3.1 cm. Length:5 cm. Weight:13 grams
23/3876
This pendant may have been traded from central Panama to Costa Rica. The metal is very thin, the product of well-controlled casting.

38. Trophy-head bell (fig. 32)
Parita, Herrera Province, Panama
Cast gold, with copper clapper
Diameter:2.3 cm. Weight:20 grams
24/3297
The bell has faces on both sides. Remnants of two pouring channels or vents can be seen on either side of the suspension loop.

39. Double insect pendant
Parita, Herrera Province, Panama
Cast and gilded *tumbaga*
Length:2.3 cm. Weight:4 grams
24/3291
One of a pair.

40. Double curly-tailed animal pendant (fig. 19)
Las Palmas, Herrera Province, Panama
Cast and gilded *tumbaga*
Height:2.9 cm. Weight:39.5 grams
23/4975

41. Ring with geometric decoration
Panama
Cast gold
Diameter:2 cm. Weight:10 grams
23/7887

42. Bell with bird on top (fig. 36)
Parita, Herrera Province, Panama
Cast gold, with copper clapper
Height:3.6 cm. Weight:25.5 grams
24/3296

43. Crocodile pendant (fig. 30)
Veraguas Province, Panama
Carved stone sheathed with embossed gold
Length:12 cm.
23/3538
The carving is sheathed with three separate onlays. The gold sheathings show microscopic chisel marks.

44. Nose ornament in the shape of two profile crocodiles (color plate 9a)
Parita, Herrera Province, Panama
Cast gold
Length:10.5 cm. Weight:52 grams
24/3299
The remnants of a pouring channel or vent can be seen directly under the nose clip.

45. Small disc with geometric decoration
Venado Beach, Canal Zone, Panama
A.D. 400–700 (?)
Embossed gold
Height:8.8 cm. Weight:11.5 grams
22/5842
The disc was found with two others at the breast of a three-year-old child buried in the Venado Beach cemetery. The grave contained many other gold ornaments, which are now in the Robert Woods Bliss collection (Lothrop 1956; Lothrop et al. 1957:plate CVII). The zigzag or serrated border may represent the crocodile's crest.

46. Double frog pendant
Parita, Herrera Province, Panama
A.D. 700–1100 (?)
Cast and gilded *tumbaga*, with holes for inlays
Length:3.9 cm. Weight:13 grams
24/3298
The stubs of pouring channels or vents can be seen at the feet and snout.

47. Double bell with pair of crocodiles on top (fig. 31)
Panama
Cast gold
Height:2.8 cm. Weight:38 grams
23/7895

48. Disc representing the Crocodile God (color plate 9b)
Coclé Province, Panama
A.D. 700–1100 (?)
Embossed gold, pierced for attachment
Diameter:11 cm. Weight:8.5 grams
23/3534
The creature has a pair of profile crocodiles on his head.

49. Anvil stone (fig. 25k)
West bank of the Rio Grande, Coclé Province, Panama
Collected by A. H. Verrill
Ground basalt
Diameter:14 cm. Height:5.75 cm.
14/5156
The stone was probably used in the manufacture of hammered gold artifacts.

50. Cylindrical implement (fig. 25a)
Temple site, El Caño, Coclé Province, Panama
Collected by A. H. Verrill
Ground and polished stone
Length:14 cm.
14/6025
The tool may have been used as a hammer and an embossing tool.
One end is rounded, and the other is squared and shows flaking from use.

51. Burnishing stone (fig. 25b)
Coclé Province, Panama
Collected by A. H. Verrill
Agate
Length:7.5 cm.
13/1789

52. Hammer (fig. 25c)
Coclé Province, Panama
Collected by A. H. Verrill
Ground stone
Length:4.5 cm.
13/1797

53. Chipped point (fig. 25d)
Venado Beach, Canal Zone, Panama
Agate
Length:4.5 cm.
22/9407
A stone point would have been useful for scoring and cutting sheet gold.

54. Chipped point (fig. 25e)
Rio Coclé Province, Panama
Stone
Length:4.5 cm.
22/4710
The point could have been used as a drill.

55. Small celt (fig. 25f)
Venado Beach, Canal Zone, Panama
Ground stone
Length:4.6 cm.
22/9406
The celt may have been a woodworking tool and could have been used to shape wooden anvils or forms for embossing.

56. Chisel with cutting edges at both ends (fig. 25g)
Panama
Cast and hammered gold
Length:7.5 cm. Weight:3.5 grams
23/7899
The blades of the gold chisels have been hardened by cold hammering. Marks on some sheet-gold specimens suggest that gold chisels were used as cutting and incising tools. They could also have been used to shape wax models and clay molds and cores.

57. Chisel (fig. 25h)
Panama
Cast and hammered gold
Length:9.8 cm. Weight:2.75 grams
23/7898

58. Chisel (fig. 25i)
Panama
Cast and hammered gold
Length:11.6 cm. Weight:10 grams
23/7897

59. Chisel (fig. 25j)
Venado Beach, Canal Zone, Panama
Chipped and polished stone
Length:9 cm.
22/9461
A probable woodworking tool.

60. Sharpening stone (fig. 25l)
Coclé Province, Panama
Collected by A. H. Verrill
Diameter:4.6 cm.
13/1795
Possibly used to sharpen cutting tools of bone or stone.

61. Lump of pumice (fig. 25m)
Temple site, El Caño, Coclé Province, Panama
Collected by A. H. Verrill
Diameter:7.5 cm.
14/6193
Pumice might have been used for filing and polishing gold.

62. Awl (fig. 25n)
Parita, Herrera Province, Panama
Antler tine
Length:10 cm.
22/8325
Possible embossing tool.

63. Bone tool (fig. 27o)
Rancho Juan Calderon, Parita, Herrera Province, Panama
Length:14.3 cm.
22/9397
Possible embossing and burnishing tool.

64. Tweezers (fig. 6)
Coclé Province, Panama
Embossed gold
Length:4.5 cm. Weight:12 grams
24/642
It was the custom in Panama to pluck out facial hair (Wafer 1903:132, 134; Lothrop 1948b:254; Stone 1966:233).

The BASKETMAKER:
The Pomoans Of California

1. Gift basket (fig. 32d)
Made by Mary Benson, Central Pomo, Ukiah, California
Collected by Grace Nicholson 1900–1930
Sedge, dyed bulrush, willow
Coiling:three-rod
Height:9 cm. Diameter:25 cm.
24/2138
Compare the use of the design element in this basket with nos. 2, 3, and 4.

2. Mush bowl (fig. 32a)
Made by Mary Benson, Central Pomo, Ukiah, California
Collected by Grace Nicholson 1900–1930
Redbud, sedge (?), willow
Twining:full turn with alternate pairs and three-strand braiding; plain and three-strand braided finish
Height:16 cm. Diameter:25 cm.
24/2100
It is unusual to have a light design on a dark background. It is also unusual for the main part of the basket to be woven in the full turn technique.

3. Ceremonial basket (fig. 32b)
Pomoan, California, made before 1921
Sedge, dyed bulrush, willow; decorated with red woodpecker crests, black quail topknots, clamshell beads
Coiling: three-rod
Height:7 cm. Diameter:20 cm.
10/9282

4. Bowl (fig. 32c)
Probably Northern Pomo, California, made before 1927
Sedge, redbud, willow
Coiling: three-rod
Height:11 cm. Diameter:25 cm.
15/6767
The design is executed in redbud bark, which is unusual in a Pomoan coiled basket.

5. Mush cooking pot
Pomoan, California, made before 1927
Pine root (?), redbud, willow
Twining: lattice
Height:35 cm. Diameter:52 cm.
15/4598
This technique gives extra strength to the basket.

6. Storage basket
Pomoan, California, made before 1922
Pine root, dyed bracken, willow
Twining: spaced lattice; three-strand braided start; alternate pairs and three-strand braided finish; bound and reinforced rim
Height:34 cm. Diameter:56 cm.
11/3302
The openwork basketry allows air to circulate around the stored nuts.

7. Seed bin or granary
Pomoan, California, made before 1926
Sedge, redbud, willow
Twining: plain, alternate pairs; lattice reinforcing on bottom; three-strand twined finish
Height:32 cm. Diameter:48 cm.
14/5298
This type of basket was used to store various grass seeds before they were pounded into meal. Note the "dau" on the left side. This break in the design pattern has been described as a "door" through which a spirit may enter the basket to inspect the work or from which it may escape when the basket is destroyed.

8. Sifter
Pomoan, California, made before 1918
Pine root, redbud, willow
Twining: spaced lattice; plain start and finish; bound and reinforced rim
Height:13 cm. Diameter:38 cm.
8/5687
This type of basket was used as a sifter for ground nut and seed meal.

9. Winnowing or parching basket (color plate 10a)
Pomoan, California
Sedge (?), dyed bulrush, redbud, willow
Twining:plain, with full-turn design bands and lattice reinforcing; three-strand twined start
Height:17 cm. Diameter:44 cm.
21/5381

10. Dish
Northern Pomo, Eel River, California, made before 1906
Sedge, dyed bracken, willow
Coiling:one-rod
Height:9 cm. Diameter:24 cm.
8634
The overall placement of this design (sharpened arrowhead) seems to be typical for the Northern Pomo. This basket has both a start and a finish design.

11. Shallow work basket
Pomoan, California, made before 1927.
Willow
Twining: spaced plain
Height:13 cm. Diameter:55 cm.
15/6542
This basket may have been woven by a man, since the twining weft is pitched up to the right and the basket is woven with willow for both the warp and the weft. It is unusual in that there are two rows of twining in which one weft is unpeeled willow, which makes a simple design. There also appears to be a "dau" running zigzag up the side of the basket.

12. Seedbeater
Pomoan, California, made before 1909
Willow, string
Plain weft weaving; bound rim and wrapped handle
Length:53 cm. Width:31 cm.
2/4427
This implement was used for knocking seeds off the grasses into a burden basket or other collecting basket.

13. Burden basket (fig. 36b)
Pomoan, California
Pine root, redbud, willow
Twining: plain; alternate pairs start; bound and reinforced rim
Height:49 cm. Diameter:60 cm.
21/7584
This basket was carried on the back by a woven band and carrying net, which fit around both the basket and the forehead.

14. Small burden basket (fig. 36a)
Pomoan, California, made before 1906
Pine root (?), redbud, willow
Twining: alternate pairs, full turn, plain; bound and reinforced rim
Height:30 cm. Diameter:32 cm.
9495

15. Small mortar basket (fig. 12a)
Pomoan, California, made before 1926
Pine root (?), redbud, willow
Twining: plain with lattice reinforcing; bound and reinforced rim
Height:7 cm. Diameter:23 cm.
14/5299
This type of basket was placed on a stone mortar to contain the meal as it was ground. This small version may have been for a child.

16. Stone mortar (fig. 12b)
Pomoan, California
Collected by Grace Nicholson 1900–1930
Height:4 cm. Width:21 cm. Length:31 cm.
15/7092
A basketry hopper was placed on this mortar for grinding nuts and seeds into meal.

17. Miniature baby carrier (fig. 30)
Pomoan, California
Willow lashed with milkweed fiber twine; decorated with clamshell beads and abalone pendants
Height:15 cm. Width:11 cm.
24/4118
This is a miniature version of the baskets in which Pomoan infants were carried.

18. Guest platter
Pomoan, California, made before 1904
Sedge, redbud, willow; decorated with clamshell beads
Twining: alternate pairs, full turn, lattice reinforcing; plain finish
Height:13 cm. Diameter:36 cm.
2173
This type of platter was probably used for serving food to guests at feasts or other special occasions.

19. Ceremonial cup (fig. 8)
Pomoan, California
Collected by Judge Bijur about 1867
Sedge, dyed bulrush, willow; with red woodpecker crests
Coiling: three-rod
Height:7 cm. Diameter:15 cm.
20/8316

20. Ceremonial water bucket
Pomoan, California
Pine root (?), dyed bulrush, willow; decorated with quail topknots, clamshell, red glass beads
Twining: lattice; three-strand twining start; plain and three-strand twining finish
Height:16 cm. Diameter:20 cm.
24/8901
The bottom half of this basket uses wire as the rigid weft.

21. Feast bowl (color plate 10g)
Pomoan, California
Collected by Judge Bijur about 1867
Sedge, dyed bulrush, willow; red woodpecker crests; rim decorated with clamshell beads and black quail topknots
Coiling: three-rod
Height:15 cm. Diameter:25 cm.
20/8306

22. Oval ceremonial or gift basket
Central Pomo, California, made before 1923
Sedge, redbud, willow; decorated with black quail topknots, clamshell, blue glass beads
Coiling: one-rod
Height:14 cm. Length:60 cm. Width:36 cm.
12/3356
Baskets of this shape were often used for storing ritual paraphernalia.

23. Puberty or baby washing basket (fig. 17)
Central Pomo, California, made before 1919
Sedge, dyed bulrush, willow; decorated with black quail topknots and clamshell beads at rim
Coiling: three-rod
Height:19 cm. Diameter:30 cm.
4/8786
This style of basket was used for washing when a girl started her first menses. A basket such as this one was probably used for washing a newborn infant. In both cases the basket would be made especially for this purpose.

24. Ceremonial or gift basket
Eastern Pomo (?), California
Sedge, willow; fully covered with feathers—yellow, meadowlark; green, mallard duck; red, woodpecker; black, quail
Coiling: three-rod
Height:7 cm. Diameter:20 cm.
23/5715

25. Oval gift or ceremonial basket (color plate 10c)
Pomoan, California, made before 1906
Sedge, dyed bulrush, willow; decorated with red woodpecker crests and black quail topknots
Coiling: one-rod
Height:12 cm. Length:30 cm. Width:22 cm.
9486
The flared rim of this basket is unusual.

26. Ceremonial cup
Pomoan, California
Collected by Judge Bijur about 1867
Sedge, dyed bulrush, willow; with yellow and green glass beads and glass-bead pendants of many colors
Coiling: one-rod
Height:7 cm. Diameter:14 cm.
23/5732
This basket seems to have a "dau" done in yellow glass beads.

27. Beaded gift basket
Pomoan, California
Collected by Judge Bijur about 1867
Sedge, willow; covered in glass beads—light blue, dark blue, red, clear
Coiling: one-rod
Height:10 cm. Diameter:25 cm.
20/8299

28. Gift basket (color plate 10b)
Pomoan, California
Collected by Judge Bijur about 1867
Sedge, willow; fully covered with feathers—red, red-winged blackbird (?); black, brant or red-winged blackbird; yellow, meadowlark; white, meadowlark (?); red glass-bead pendants and handle
Coiling: three-rod
Height:3 cm. Diameter:4 cm.
20/8311

29. Oval gift or ceremonial basket (color plate 10i)
Pomoan, California
Collected by Judge Bijur about 1867
Sedge, dyed bulrush, willow; decorated with black quail topknots and white glass beads
Coiling: one-rod
Height:5 cm. Length:22 cm. Width:14 cm.
20/8312

30. Ceremonial or gift basket
Pomoan, California
Collected by Judge Bijur about 1867
Sedge, willow; fully covered with feathers—red, woodpecker crests; green, mallard duck; black, quail topknots; decorated with clamshell beads and pendants of clamshell beads and abalone
Coiling: three-rod
Height:8 cm. Diameter:27 cm.
23/5714
This type of basket is one of the most highly prized by all Pomoan groups. It is probably the kind of basket that Drake saw in 1579. It has often been described by collectors as a "sun basket."

31. Gift basket
Pomoan, California
Collected by Judge Bijur about 1867
Sedge, willow; fully covered in feathers—red, woodpecker crests; yellow, meadowlark (?); black, quail topknots. Decorated with clamshell beads and pendants of glass beads and abalone
Coiling: three-rod
Height:3 cm. Diameter:8 cm.
23/5722
This basket was probably meant to be hung. Note the bead start.

32. Ceremonial or gift basket
Pomoan, California, made before 1906
Sedge, willow; fully covered in feathers—green, mallard duck; red, woodpecker crests; yellow, meadowlark; decorated with clamshell beads and pendants of glass beads and abalone
Coiling: three-rod
Height:6.5 cm. Diameter:16 cm.
9488

33. Oval gift or ceremonial basket
Probably Central Pomo, California
Sedge, dyed bulrush, willow; decorated with quail topknots, clamshell, yellow glass beads.
Coiling: three-rod
Height:5 cm. Length:20 cm. Diameter:12 cm.
25/2
The dark background is unusual.

34. "Story" basket (fig. 38)
Southeastern Pomo, California
Sedge, dyed bulrush, willow; with red glass beads; rim decorated with black feathers and clamshell beads
Coiling: three-rod
Height:20 cm. Length:77 cm. Width:59 cm.
14/9639
This unusual flared oval basket with human figures is similar to several baskets known to commemorate a special event. The basket was made by Polly Holmes before 1926.

35. Awl (tip broken) (fig. 31)
Pomoan, California
Collected by Grace Nicholson before 1916
Bone: deer fibula
Length:13 cm.
5/6470
Awls of this type preceded the steel awl in basketmaking. They are generally considered to be used only for coiling; however, there is reference to an awl being used in twining to pack the weft fibers together.

36. Awl (fig. 31)
Pomoan, California, made before 1917
Steel with wooden handle
Length:8 cm.
6/8679
Awls such as this were used in coiling to pierce the foundation for the sewing fiber.

37. Wedding basket (fig. 18)
Northern Pomo (?), California
Sedge, redbud, willow; decorated with clamshell beads and black quail feathers
Twining: plain; three-strand twining start; alternate pairs and plain finish
Height:21 cm. Diameter:35 cm.
23/1146
A basket such as this would be presented by the bride's family to the groom's family when a marriage was formalized.

38. Wedding basket (fig. 16)
Central Pomo, Ukiah, California
Sedge, dyed bulrush, willow
Coiling: one-rod
Height:11 cm. Diameter:40 cm.
4/8787
This basket, made by Mary Benson in 1909, would be given to the groom's family by the bride's family.

39. Wedding basket (fig. 33)
Central Pomo, Ukiah, California
Sedge, bulrush, willow; decorated with clamshell beads
Coiling: one-rod
Height:18 cm. Diameter:34 cm.
24/2127

40. Mush pot (color plate 10h; fig. 9)
Central Pomo, Ukiah, California
Collected by Grace Nicholson 1900–1930
Sedge, redbud, willow
Twining: alternate pairs; full turn; plain finish
Height:21 cm. Diameter:36 cm.
24/2105
This is one of Mary Benson's earliest baskets. It is twined in the shape of a cooking basket, with the typical Central Pomo spiral design. Note similarity to nos. 41 and 42.

41. Mush pot (fig. 9)
Central Pomo, Ukiah, California
Collected by Grace Nicholson 1900–1930
Sedge, redbud, willow
Twining: full turn; alternate pairs and three-strand braided start; plain and three-strand braided finish
Height:11 cm. Diameter:16 cm.
24/2139
Made by Mary Benson. Note its similarity to nos. 40 and 42.

42. Small mush pot (fig. 9)
Central Pomo, Ukiah, California
Collected by Grace Nicholson 1900–1930
Sedge, redbud, willow
Twining: full turn with alternate pairs; three-strand braided start; plain and three-strand braided finish
Height:9 cm. Diameter:12 cm.
24/2104
This is one of Mary Benson's later baskets. Note its similarity to nos. 40 and 41 and how it has been woven in a smaller size.

43. Bowl-shaped basket (fig. 20)
Central Pomo, Ukiah, California
Collected by Grace Nicholson 1900–1930
Sedge, redbud, willow
Twining: three-strand braiding; plain start and finish
Height:12 cm. Diameter:18 cm.
24/2125
Made by Mary Benson using a technique she learned from her mother. It is rare for an entire basket to be woven in three-strand braiding.

44. Mush cooking pot
Central Pomo, Ukiah, California
Sedge, redbud, willow
Twining: plain; three-strand braided start and finish
Height:26 cm. Diameter:40 cm.
24/2107
Made by Mary Benson for Grace Nicholson 1900–1930. Probably Mary's largest basket. The white in the banded designs is the reverse side of the redbud bark. This basket is made in the style of the old cooking baskets.

45. Mush bowl (fig. 14)
Made by Mary Benson, Central Pomo, Ukiah, California
Collected by Grace Nicholson 1900–1930
Sedge, redbud, willow
Twining: alternate pairs, full turn; three-strand braided start; three-strand twined finish
Height:12 cm. Diameter:17 cm.
24/2102
The zigzag is mainly an Eastern Pomo design element, which was used occasionally by some Central Pomo basketmakers.

46. Gift basket (color plate 10d)
Central Pomo, Ukiah, California
Collected by Grace Nicholson 1900–1930
Sedge, dyed bulrush
Coiling: three-rod
Height:6 cm. Diameter:13 cm.
24/2140

47. Ceremonial or gift basket (color plate 10f)
Central Pomo, Ukiah, California
Collected by Grace Nicholson 1900–1930
Sedge, willow; fully covered with feathers—yellow, meadowlark; orange, oriole; green, mallard duck; red, red-winged blackbird
Coiling: three-rod
Height:7 cm. Diameter:14 cm.
24/2128
This basket took William Benson six years to weave.

48. Trinket basket
Eastern Pomo, California
Sedge, willow; with red, blue, green, and black (worn-off exterior) silk and cotton threads
Twining: alternate pairs; three-strand braided start; plain and three-strand braided finish
Height:7 cm. Diameter:11 cm.
24/2106
The basket was made in 1882 by William Benson when he was twelve years old and given by him to Grace Nicholson in 1913 in appreciation for her paying for Mary Benson's eye operation.

49. "Po" basket (fig. 6)
Central Pomo, Ukiah, California
Collected by Grace Nicholson 1900–1930
Sedge, dyed bulrush, willow; magnesite "po" start
Coiling: three-rod
Height: 6 cm. Diameter:12 cm.
24/2136
Made by William Benson, this basket took four years to complete. Note the fineness of the stitches. Magnesite is a mineral highly valued among the Pomoan people.

50. Miniature round basket (fig. 7g)
Made by Joseppa Dick, Central Pomo, California, before 1917
Sedge, dyed bulrush, willow
Coiling: one-rod
Height:0.3 cm. Diameter:0.5 cm.
7/733

51. Two miniature round baskets (figs. 7a and 7h)
Made by Mary Benson, Central Pomo, Ukiah, California
Collected by Grace Nicholson 1900–1930
Sedge, dyed bulrush, willow
Coiling: one-rod
Height:0.5 cm. Diameter:1.5 cm.
Height:0.4 cm. Diameter:1.2 cm.
24/2115

52. Two miniature oval baskets (figs. 7b and 7d)
Made by Mary Benson, Central Pomo, Ukiah, California
Collected by Grace Nicholson 1900–1930
Sedge, dyed bulrush, willow
Coiling: one-rod
Height:0.5 cm. Length:2 cm. Width:1 cm.
Height:1 cm. Length:2.5 cm. Width:1.5 cm.
24/2116

53. Miniature round basket (fig. 7j)
Central Pomo (?), California
Collected by Grace Nicholson
Sedge, dyed bulrush, willow
Coiling: three-rod
Height:1 cm. Diameter:2 cm.
24/2112

54. Miniature round basket (fig. 7c)
Made by Mary Benson, Central Pomo, Ukiah, California
Collected by Grace Nicholson 1900–1930
Dyed bulrush, sedge, willow
Coiling: three-rod
Height:1.5 cm. Diameter:3.5 cm.
24/2132

55. Miniature round basket (fig. 7i)
Pomoan, California
Sedge, dyed bulrush, willow
Coiling: three-rod
Height:2 cm. Diameter:6.5 cm.
23/6217

56. Miniature oval basket (fig. 7f)
Made by Mary Benson, Central Pomo, Ukiah, California
Collected by Grace Nicholson 1900–1930
Dyed bulrush, sedge, willow
Coiling: three-rod
Height:2 cm. Width:6 cm. Diameter:3.5 cm.
24/2119

57. Miniature feathered basket (fig. 7e)
Pomoan, California
Sedge, willow; feathered with red woodpecker crests; beaded handle of clear yellow glass beads
Coiling: three-rod
Height:1 cm. Diameter:2 cm.
16/3308

The WEAVER:
The Araucanians Of Chile

1. *Macuñ*, poncho, with *trarican* bands, ikat-dyed, and *nimin* decoration, ornamental bands (color plate 7)
Mapuche, Temuco, Cautin, Chile
Ikat-dyed and dyed wool; white cotton cord
Warp-faced plain weave ground, with warp ikat and ornamental bands of complementary-warp weave, with floats in alternating alignment
Length:134 cm. (including fringe). Width:159 cm.
17/5868

2. *Macuñ trarican*, ikat-dyed poncho (color plate 7; fig. 19)
Mapuche, Temuco, Cautin, Chile
Ikat-dyed wool
Warp-faced plain weave, with warp ikat
Length:124 cm. (including fringe). Width:143 cm.
17/5864

3. *Macuñ nimin*, poncho with ornamental bands (color plate 7)
Huilliche, Valdivia, Chile
Dyed wool
Warp-faced plain weave ground, with ornamental bands in complementary-warp weave
Length:127 cm. (including fringe). Width:129.5 cm.
17/5467

4. *Macuñ huirican*, poncho with stripes
Huilliche, Osorno, Valdivia, Chile
Dyed wool
Warp-faced plain weave
Length:156 cm. Width:122 cm.
17/5477
This textile was woven in one continuous length, cut crosswise in the center, and sewn together lengthwise.

5. *Macuñ huirican*, poncho with stripes (color plate 7)
Huilliche, Osorno, Valdivia, Chile
Dyed wool (probably natural dyes)
Warp-faced plain weave
Length:132.5 cm. Width:144 cm.
17/5485

6. *Macuñ huirican*, poncho with warp stripes
Mapuche, Chile
Dyed wool
Warp-faced plain weave
Length:139 cm. (including fringe). Width:152 cm.
17/6718

7. *Macuñ*, plain poncho (color plate 7)
Cunco, Islands of Reloncavi Sound, Llanquihue, Chile
Dyed wool; the mottled color is achieved by plying together two colors of wool
Warp-faced plain weave
Length:112 cm. (including fringe). Width:153.5 cm.
17/5494
This poncho is made of two lengths of fabric sewn up the center.

8. *Kepam*, dress
Mapuche, Truftruf, Temuco, Cautin, Chile
Dyed wool
Warp-faced plain weave, with an applied, handcrafted edge
Length:129 cm. (without tassels). Width:144.5 cm.
17/5598

9. *Kepam*, dress
Mapuche, Temuco, Cautin, Chile
Dyed wool
Warp-faced plain weave
Length:168 cm. Width:108.5 cm.
17/5870

10. *Iculla*, shawl
Chilote, La Chagra, Castro, Llanquihue, Chile
Dyed wool
Warp-faced plain weave
Length:208 cm. (including fringe). Width:82 cm.
17/5567
The surface was probably brushed with a seed pod to create the nap.

11. *Iculla*, shawl
Chilote, La Chagra, Castro, Llanquihue, Chile
Dyed wool
Warp-faced plain weave
Length:194.5 cm. (including fringe). Width:70 cm.
17/5569
The surface was probably brushed with a seed pod to create the nap.

12. *Iculla*, shawl
Araucanian, central Chile
Dyed wool
Warp-faced plain weave
Length:142 cm. Width:114 cm.
17/6669

13. *Trarihue*, belt (fig. 25)
Mapuche, Huentelulen, Canete, Arauco, Chile
Dyed wool
Warp-faced plain weave, with supplementary-warp floats on a paired-warp ground
Length:261 cm. (including fringe). Width:5 cm.
17/5579
This *trarihue* was once used by a *cacique*, a political and family leader.

14. *Trarihue*, belt
Mapuche, Carahue, Imperial, Cautin, Chile
Dyed wool; leather and metal
Complementary-warp weave, with three-span floats in alternating alignment
Length:80 cm. (excluding straps). Width:10 cm.
17/5603
This *trarihue* was noted as being for a man.

15. *Trarihue*, belt
Mapuche, Carahue, Imperial, Cautin, Chile
Dyed wool
Complementary-warp weave, with three-span floats in alternating alignment
Length:291 cm. (including fringe). Width:6.5 cm.
17/5605

16. *Trarihue*, belt (fig. 25)
Mapuche, Quepe, Temuco, Cautin, Chile
Dyed wool
Complementary-warp weave, with three-span floats in alternating alignment
Length:292 cm. (including fringe). Width:7.5 cm.
17/5628

17. *Trarihue*, belt
Mapuche, Collico (Carahue), Imperial, Cautin, Chile
Dyed wool
Complementary-warp weave, with three-span floats in alternating alignment
Length:138 cm. (including fringe). Width:6.5 cm.
17/5777

18. *Trarihue*, belt
Mapuche, Collico (Carahue), Imperial, Cautin, Chile
Dyed wool
Warp-faced double-cloth
Length:232 cm. (including fringe). Width:3.5 cm.
17/5781

19. *Trarihue*, belt
Mapuche, Collico (Carahue), Imperial, Cautin, Chile
Dyed wool
Complementary-warp weave, with three-span floats in alternating alignment
Length:206 cm. (including fringe). Width:6.5 cm.
17/5784

20. *Trarihue*, belt (fig. 25)
Mapuche, Collico (Carahue), Imperial, Cautin, Chile
Dyed wool
Complementary-warp weave, with three-span floats in alternating alignment
Length:243 cm. (including fringe). Width:6 cm.
17/5785

21. *Trarihue*, belt
Mapuche, Temuco, Cautin, Chile
Dyed wool
Warp-faced double-cloth
Length:210 cm. (including fringe). Width:8.75 cm.
17/5808

22. *Trarihue*, belt
Mapuche, Temuco, Cautin, Chile
Dyed wool
Complementary-warp weave, with three-span floats in alternating alignment
Length:221 cm. (including fringe). Width:6 cm.
17/5813

23. *Trarihue*, belt
Mapuche, Temuco, Cautin, Chile
Dyed wool
Complementary-warp weave, with three-span floats in alternating alignment
Length:296 cm. (including fringe). Width:6 cm.
17/5816

24. *Trarihue*, belt
Mapuche, Chile
Dyed wool
Warp-faced plain weave
Length:272 cm. (including fringe). Width:10 cm.
17/6733

25. *Lama*, saddle blanket used under saddle frame
Mapuche, Villarica, Cautin, Chile
Dyed wool
Complementary-warp weave, with three-span floats in alternating alignment
Length:97 cm. (including fringe). Width:63.5 cm.
17/5633

26. *Lama*, saddle blanket used under saddle frame
Mapuche, Temuco, Cautin, Chile
Dyed wool
Crossed-warp weave (a gauze weave)
Length:107 cm. (without tassels). Width:94.5 cm.
17/5842

27. *Lama*, saddle blanket used under saddle frame (fig. 21)
Mapuche, Temuco, Cautin, Chile
Dyed wool
Plain weave, with supplementary-warp floats on paired-warp ground
Length:103 cm. (including fringe). Width:54 cm. (at widest point)
17/5847

28. *Choapino* (saddle blanket) with diamond and "Greek cross" design, used over a wood-frame saddle
Araucanian, Valdivia, Chile
Dyed wool
Warp-faced plain weave, with supplementary-weft pile wrapping
Length:128 cm. (including fringe). Width:61 cm.
10/575

29. *Choapino*, saddle blanket
Araucanian, central Chile
Dyed wool
Warp-faced plain weave, with supplementary pile wraped on both warp and weft
Length:146 cm. Width:66.5 cm.
17/6671

30. *Kutama*, saddle bags
Chilote, Chonchi, Castro, Llanquihue, Chile
Dyed wool
Warp-faced simple alternating float weave, with warps of alternating colors on a background of plain weave
Length:105.5 cm. (when flat). Width:45 cm.
17/5566

31. *Kutama*, saddle bags (fig. 22)
Mapuche, Quepe, Temuco, Cautin, Chile
Dyed wool and commercial cloth
Plain weave, with supplementary-warp floats on a paired-warp ground
Length:91 cm. (when flat). Width:30.5 cm.
17/5623

32. *Kutama*, saddle bags
Mapuche, Chile
Dyed wool
Complementary-warp weave, with three-span floats in alternating alignment
Length:85.5 cm. (when flat). Width:32 cm.
17/6740

33. Spindle and whorl (fig. 5)
Mapuche, Puerto Dominquez (Laguna de Budi), Imperial, Cautin, Chile
Wood, clay, and partially spun wool yarn
Length:47.5 cm.
17/5704

34. Skein of wool (color plate 7)
Chilote, Castro, Llanquihue, Chile
17/5534
This wool was dyed black with coal mixed with the bark of *robo*, *maqui* (*Aristotelia maqui*) and *radal* trees (*Lomatia obliqua*).
(All Araucanian as well as Latin names of plants are taken from Lothrop [1930]. Latin names have not been verified and should not be considered authoritive.)

35. Skein of wool (color plate 7)
Chilote, Castro, Llanquihue, Chile
17/5535
This wool was dyed brown with the dried bark of the *radal* tree (*Lomatia obliqua*).

36. Skein of wool (color plate 7)
Chilote, Castro, Llanquihue, Chile
17/5536
This wool was dyed mustard brown with the green bark of the *radal* tree (*Lomatia obliqua*).

37. Skein of wool (color plate 7)
Chilote, Castro, Llanquihue, Chile
17/5537
This wool was dyed light mustard brown with the bark of the *muermo* tree (*Eucryphia cordifolia*).

38. Skein of wool (color plate 7)
Chilote, Castro, Llanquihue, Chile
17/5538
This wool was dyed "cocoa" brown with the bark of the *buinque* tree (*Coriaria ruscifolia*).

39. Skein of wool (color plate 7)
Chilote, Castro, Llanquihue, Chile
17/5539
This wool was dyed a "rose beige" with the bark of the *canelo* tree (*Drimys winteri*).

40. Skein of wool (color plate 7)
Chilote, Castro, Llanquihue, Chile
17/5540
This wool was dyed beige with the leaves of *cadillo* and *minamin* (Latin names not known).

41. Skein of wool (color plate 7)
Chilote, Castro, Llanquihue, Chile
17/5541
This wool was dyed a "golden" beige with the flowers of *palguin*, or *matico* (Latin name not known).

42. Skein of wool (color plate 7)
Chilote, Castro, Llanquihue, Chile
17/5542
This wool was dyed henna with the shoots of the "apple" tree (Latin name not known).

43. Skein of wool (color plate 7)
Chilote, Castro, Llanquihue, Chile
17/5543
This wool was dyed "sunburst" yellow with the flowers of the *roble* tree (*Nortofagus antarcticus*).

44. Wood-frame saddle
Tehuelche, Patagonia, Argentina
Length:42 cm. Width:29 cm.
17/7350

45. Coiled basket
Chilote, Castro, Llanquihue, Chile
Vegetal fiber
Height:23 cm. Diameter:22 cm.
17/5525

46. Wicker basket (color plate 7)
Chilote, Chonchi, Castro, Llanquihue, Chile
Vegetal fiber
Height:33 cm. Diameter:30 cm.
17/5558

47. Breast ornament
Araucanian, Chile
Hammered and engraved silver
Length:29 cm. Width:7 cm.
6/5821

48. Breast ornament
Araucanian, Chile
Hammered and engraved silver
Length:27 cm. Width:10 cm.
13/3408

49. Breast ornament
Araucanian, Temuco, Chile
Hammered and engraved silver
Length:39 cm. Width:7 cm.
13/5613

50. Headband for a woman
Araucanian, Temuco, Chile
Hammered and engraved silver
Length:57 cm. Width:5 cm.
13/5616

51. *Topo*, shawl pin
Mapuche, Nueva Imperial, Imperial, Cautin, Chile
Hammered silver
Length:39 cm. Width:17.5 cm.
17/5682

52. Pair of earrings
Mapuche, Temuco, Cautin, Chile
Hammered silver
Length:12 cm. Width:6 cm.
17/5893

53. *Topo*, shawl pin
Araucanian, Chile
Hammered silver
Length:40 cm. Width:9 cm.
19/6218

54. Pair of ear ornaments
Araucanian, Chile
Hammered silver
Length:8 cm. Width:8 cm.
19/6220

55. *Chicha* (beer) jar with handle
Mapuche, Huentelulen, Canente, Arauco, Chile
Pottery, wool yarn dyed with commercial dyes
Height:35 cm. Diameter:26 cm.
17/5574

56. Water jar with carrying apparatus
Mapuche, Puerto Dominquez (Laguna de Budi), Imperial, Cautin, Chile
Pottery, vegetal fiber, braided wool yarn
Height:44 cm. Diameter:32 cm.
17/5696

57. Pottery "duck-shaped" jar
Mapuche, Collico (Carahue), Imperial, Cautin, Chile
Pottery
Height:19 cm. Width:20 cm.
17/5736

The POTTER:
Pre-Columbian Cultures
Of The Southeastern United States

1. Wooden paddle (fig. 6a)
Cherokee, Swain and Jackson Cos., North Carolina
Collected by M. R. Harrington
Length:22.9 cm. Width:17 cm.
1/9001

2. Fragment of pottery paddle
Mound at Nacoochee, White Co., Georgia
Mississippian A.D. 1350–1500
Collected by George G. Heye
Length:7.6 cm. Width:6.6 cm.
5/184

3. Smoothing stone (fig. 6d)
Mount Royal, Putnam Co., Florida
Mississippian A.D. 1350–1500
(Unless otherwise stated, all material was excavated by Clarence B. Moore.)
Length:8.3 cm. Width:6 cm.
17/2103

4. Pottery trowel (fig. 6c)
Moundville, Hale Co., Alabama
Mississippian A.D. 1200–1500
Length:5.7 cm. Width:6.6 cm.
17/2795

5. Potsherd, rim fragment of straight cylindrical jar (fig. 6b)
Mound at Nacoochee, White Co., Georgia
Appalachian Mississippian A.D. 1350–1500
Collected by George G. Heye
Pottery with stamped decoration
Length:17.5 cm. Width:17 cm.
5/15

6. Potsherd from rim of vessel (color plate 12d)
Mound at Nacoochee, White Co., Georgia
Appalachian Mississippian A.D. 1350–1500
Collected by George G. Heye
Pottery with stamped decoration
Length:17.8 cm. Width:8.3 cm.
9/7031

7. Large jar (color plate 12a)
Ossabaw Island, Bryan Co., Georgia
Mississippian A.D. 1350–1500
Pottery with stamped decoration, "killed"
Height:42 cm. Diameter:36 cm.
17/4486

8. Jar (fig. 7)
Alligator Bayou, St. Andrews Bay, Washington Co., Florida
Santa Rosa–Swift Creek, A.D. 1–500
Pottery with rocker-stamped decoration, "killed"
Height:14.3 cm. Diameter:18.1 cm.
17/3755

9. Jar
Aspalaga, Apalachicola River, Gadsden Co., Florida
Santa Rosa–Swift Creek A.D. 1–500
Pottery with incised, punctate, painted decoration, "killed"
Height:26.5 cm. Diameter:23 cm.
17/3868

10. Vertical compound jar
Pierce Mound, Apalachicola River, Franklin Co., Florida
Santa Rosa–Swift Creek A.D. 1–500
Pottery with redware, incised and punctate decoration
Height:13 cm. Diameter:10 cm.
17/4077

11. Large globular jar
Mound near Burnt Mill Creek, Bay Co., Florida
Santa Rosa–Swift Creek A.D. 1–500
Pottery with incised decoration, "killed"
Height:20.3 cm. Diameter:23.5 cm.
8/4158

12. Jar (color plate 12b)
Hall Mound, Panacea Springs, Wakulla Co., Florida
Santa Rosa–Swift Creek/Weeden Island A.D. 400–800
Pottery with deeply incised decoration
Height:19 cm. Diameter:16.5 cm.
17/4538

13. Large jar with serrated rim
Mound Field, Apalachee Bay, Wakulla Co., Florida
Weeden Island A.D. 500–1000
Pottery with stamped decoration, "killed"
Height:20 cm. Diameter:29.3 cm.
17/4916

14. Jar (fig. 10)
Horseshoe Point, Lafayette Co., Florida
Weeden Island A.D. 500–1000
Pottery with stamped decoration, "killed"
Height:17 cm. Diameter:13 cm.
18/364

15. Jar with square base
Point Washington, Choctawahatchee Bay, Washington Co., Florida
Weeden Island A.D. 500–1000
Pottery with stamped decoration, "killed"
Height:15 cm. Diameter:15 cm.
17/4839

16. Globular jar
Mound near Hardnut Landing, Flint River, Decatur Co., Georgia
Weeden Island A.D. 500–1000
Pottery with stamped decoration, "killed"
Height:11.1 cm. Diameter:14 cm.
7/5133

17. Jar
Alligator Harbor, Franklin Co., Florida
Weeden Island A.D. 500–1000
Pottery with incised decoration, "killed"
Height:9 cm. Diameter:8.3 cm.
18/244

18. Rectangular jar
Panacea Springs, Wakulla Co., Florida
Weeden Island A.D. 500–1000
Pottery with incised decoration, reverse "s," which is partially smoothed away on the side with no incising
Height:13.7 Diameter:11.2 cm.
17/3400

19. Jar (fig. 9)
Kerr's Landing, Flint River, Decatur Co., Georgia
Weeden Island A.D. 500–1000
Pottery with incised and punctate decoration, "killed"
Height:20 cm. Diameter:19 cm.
17/4444

20. Jar with relief decoration (color plate 11a)
Warrior River, Taylor Co., Florida
Weeden Island A.D. 500–1000
Pottery with incised decoration, "killed"
Height:9 cm. Diameter:13 cm.
17/3509

21. Jar with grooved rectangular flange below rim (color plate 12c)
Fowler's Landing, Levy Co., Florida
Weeden Island A.D. 500–1000
Pottery with incised decoration, "killed"
Height:14.6 cm. Diameter:15.2 cm.
17/1459

22. Jar with incurving top
Point Washington, Choctawahatchee Bay, Washington Co., Florida
Weeden Island A.D. 500–1000
Pottery with deeply incised decoration, "killed"
Height:7.5 cm. Diameter:15 cm.
17/4517

23. Jar with eight openings
Mound near Hardnut Landing, Flint River, Decatur Co., Georgia
Weeden Island A.D. 500–1000
Pottery with incised decoration on neck, "killed"
Height:17 cm. Diameter:17 cm.
8/4152

24. Multiple-compartment tray
Fullmore's Landing, Chattahoochee River, Houston Co., Alabama
Weeden Island A.D. 500–1000
Pottery with red slip
Height:7.9 cm. Diameter:16 cm.
18/458
Moore says of this vessel, "Their form might suggest receptacles for various pigments, but never have we found a deposit of paint remaining in a vessel of this class" (1907:444).

25. Effigy jar (color plate 11b)
Bristol, Apalachicola River, Liberty Co., Florida
Weeden Island A.D. 500–1000
Pottery with latticework decoration, buzzard head on rim, prefired hole in bottom
Height:22.2 cm. Diameter:15.9 cm.
17/3955

26. Pedestaled effigy jar, representing an owl (fig. 24)
Shoemake Landing, Chattahoochee River, Early Co., Georgia
Weeden Island A.D. 500–1000
Pottery with incised and punctate decoration, "killed"
Height:29 cm. Diameter:21 cm.
17/4443

27. Pedestaled effigy jar, representing an owl
Mound Field, Apalachee Bay, Wakulla Co., Florida
Weeden Island A.D. 500–1000
Pottery with red slip, white painted decoration
Height:21 cm. Diameter:26 cm.
17/4915

28. Pedestaled effigy jar, representing a duck (fig. 20)
Panacea Springs, Wakulla Co., Florida
Weeden Island A.D. 500–1000
Pottery, red ware, prefired hole in base, incised decoration representing wings of the bird
Height:22.3 cm. Diameter:25.5 cm.
17/4902

29. Jar with head and hands in relief
Carney's Bluff, Clark Co., Alabama
Weeden Island A.D. 500–1000
Pottery with incised decoration
Height:16 cm. Diameter:11.5 cm.
17/4613

30. Effigy jar, representing a man, base missing (fig. 25)
Burnt Mill Creek, St. Andrews Bay, Washington Co., Florida
Weeden Island A.D. 500–1000
Pottery with incised and punctate decoration
Height:20 cm. Diameter:11.5 cm.
17/4876

31. "Handle" of a vessel representing an owl's head (color plate 11d)
Mound field, Apalachee Bay, Wakulla Co., Florida
Weeden Island A.D. 500–1000
Pottery with incised and punctate decoration
Height:5.5 cm. Diameter:8 cm.
17/4917

32. Four-sided jar with two birds' heads as handles
Pippens' Lake, Walton Co., Florida
Weeden Island A.D. 500–1000
Pottery with incised and punctate decoration, the incised decoration representing the birds' wings; "killed"
Height:13.7 cm. Diameter:10.5 cm.
17/3969

33. Bowl, two birds' heads and tail on notched, incurving rim (fig. 23)
Hogtown Bayou, Choctawahatchee Bay, Walton Co., Florida
Ford Walton A.D. 1000–1500
Pottery with incised and punctate decoration, "killed"
Height:17.1 cm. Diameter:31.1 cm.
6/2177

34. Bowl representing a bird with head and tail on rim
Hogtown Bayou, Choctawahatchee Bay, Walton Co., Florida
Fort Walton A.D. 1000–1500
Pottery with incised and punctate decoration
Height:15.2 cm. Diameter:28.6 cm.
6/2167

35. Jar
Hogtown Bayou, Choctawahatchee Bay, Walton Co., Florida
Fort Walton A.D. 1000–1500
Pottery with incised decoration, two small hoes on rim for suspension, Southern Cult motif around neck
Height:11.7 cm. Diameter: 12.8 cm.
6/204

36. Jar (fig. 21)
Hogtown Bayou, Choctawahatchee Bay, Walton Co., Florida
Fort Walton A.D. 1000–1500
Pottery with incised and punctate decoration, Southern Cult hand-eye motif around shoulders
Height:17.1 cm. Diameter:18.7 cm.
6/216

37. Bowl in form of six-pointed star
Hogtown Bayou, Choctawahatchee Bay, Walton Co., Florida
Fort Walton A.D. 1000–1500
Pottery with incised decoration
Height:8.3 cm. Diameter:29 cm.
6/4416

38. Large bowl
Hogtown Bayou, Choctawahatchee Bay, Walton Co., Florida
Fort Walton A.D. 1000–1500
Pottery with incised decoration over entire exterior
Height:14 cm. Diameter:34.5 cm.
6/4428

39. Bowl representing half a gourd (fig. 19)
Point Washington, Choctawahatchee Bay, Washington Co., Florida
Fort Walton A.D. 1000–1500
Pottery with incised decoration, perforation at one end
Height:8 cm. Diameter:27 cm.
17/4836

40. Jar, possibly an acorn effigy
Ossabaw Island, Bryan Co., Georgia
Mississippian A.D. 1350–1500
Pottery with obliterated-impressed decoration, horizontal around base and vertical around shoulders
Height:11 cm. Diameter:12.2 cm.
18/385

41. Acorn effigy
Thursby's Mound, Volusia Co., Florida
St. Johns II, Mississippian A.D. 1400–1600
Pottery with punctate decoration
Height:4.8 cm. Diameter:3.2 cm.
17/2221

42. Double bowl
Cartersville, Bartow Co., Georgia
Mississippian A.D. 1350–1500
Pottery with serrated ridge below rims
Height:7 cm. Diameter:23.6 cm.
19/1670

43. Large bowl
Durand's Bend, Alabama River, Dallas Co., Alabama
Fort Walton A.D. 1000–1500
Pottery with incised and punctate decoration
Height:14 cm. Diameter:31 cm.
17/4341

44. Bowl with five-pointed flaring rim (color plate 11c)
Jolly Bay, Walton Co., Florida
Fort Walton A.D. 1000–1500
Pottery with incised and punctate decoration, showing Southern Cult influence
Height:6 cm. Diameter:19 cm.
18/342

45. Large bowl
Walton's Camp, Santa Rosa Sound, Santa Rosa Co., Florida
Fort Walton A.D. 1000–1500
Pottery with incised decoration, representing stylized skulls or snakes, "killed"
Height:15 cm. Diameter:39 cm.
17/4508

46. Large bowl
Point Washington, Choctawahatchee Bay, Washington Co., Florida
Fort Walton A.D. 1000–1500
Pottery with incised decoration
Height:18 cm. Diameter:38.5 cm.
17/4830

47. Wide-mouth water bottle (fig. 22)
Moundville, Hale Co., Alabama
Mississippian A.D. 1200–1500
Pottery with incised decoration, representing a woodpecker
Height:16.5 cm. Diameter:19 cm.
17/3363

48. Wide-mouth water bottle (fig. 1)
Moundville, Hale Co., Alabama
Mississippian A.D. 1200–1500
Pottery with incised decoration, representing open hand-eye alternating with a falcon
Height:17.1 cm. Diameter:17.8 cm.
17/3342

49. Water bottle
Moundville, Hale Co., Alabama
Mississippian A.D. 1200–1500
Pottery with incised decoration, representing falcons
Height:10.1 cm. Diameter:12.7 cm.
17/1424

50. Water bottle (fig. 8)
Moundville, Hale Co., Alabama
Mississippian A.D. 1200–1500
Pottery with incised and indented decoration
Height:17.2 cm. Diameter:17.7 cm.
17/4619

51. Water bottle (fig. 8)
Moundville, Hale Co., Alabama
Mississippian A.D. 1200–1500
Pottery with incised and indented decoration
Height:14 cm. Diameter:15.2 cm.
17/3375

52. Bowl with stylized head and tail of bird on rim
Moundville, Hale Co., Alabama
Mississippian A.D. 1200–1500
Pottery with incised decoration
Height:11.5 cm. Diameter:19.5 cm.
17/4398

53. Cylindrical jar (fig. 5)
Moundville, Hale Co., Alabama
Mississippian A.D. 1200–1500
Pottery with incised decoration
Height:11.7 cm. Diameter:11.4 cm.
17/1430

54. Water bottle
Moundville, Hale Co., Alabama
Mississippian A.D. 1200–1500
Pottery with negative-painted decoration, showing hand and skull motif
Height:13.7 cm. Diameter:10.8 cm.
17/3381

The artifacts displayed in the exhibit, *The Ancestors: Native Artisans of the Americas*, are from the collections of the Museum of the American Indian–Heye Foundation. All the photographs of artifacts in the catalogue are by Carmelo Guadagno, curator of photography. The ethnographic photographs in the catalogue are from the museum's photographic archives, unless otherwise specified.